Knowledge and Freedom in Indian Philosophy

Tara Chatterjea

LEXINGTON BOOKS
Lanham • Boulder • New York • Oxford

LEXINGTON BOOKS

Published in the United States of America
by Lexington Books
An imprint of The Rowman & Littlefield Publishing Group, Inc.
4501 Forbes Boulevard, Suite 200, Lanham, Maryland 20706

PO Box 317
Oxford
OX2 9RU, UK

First paperback edition 2003

British Library Cataloguing in Publication Information Available

The hardback edition of this book was previously cataloged by the Library of Congress as follows:

Chatterjea, Tara, 1937–
Knowledge and freedom in Indian philosophy / Tara Chatterjea.
p. cm.
Includes bibliographical references.
ISBN 0-7391-0692-9 (pbk.: alk. paper) ISBN 0-7391-0456-X (alk. paper)
1. Philosophy, India. 2. Knowledge, Theory of. I. Title

B131.C518 2002
181'.4—dc21 2002009867

Printed in the United States of America

™ The paper used in this publication meets the minimum requirements of American National Standard for Information Sciences—Permanence of Paper for Printed Library Materials, ANSI/NISO Z39.48–1992.

Go back to Sanskrit texts, let them tell you what Indian thought has been like; let them stimulate your concerns and your questionings.

J. N. Mohanty, *Essays on Indian Philosophy Traditional and Modern*, ed. Purushottama Bilimoria (Oxford: Oxford University Press, 1993), 334.

Contents

Preface

My mentor and professor J. N. Mohanty advised me to assemble my philosophy articles and publish a collection. This book is the result of his advice. From my early student days at the University of Calcutta and Government Sanskrit College (Calcutta), he has guided my path. He taught me philosophy and showed me how to read original Sanskrit texts. He encouraged me to restate and reformulate, criticize and defend, the theories present in Indian philosophical systems. I owe him an incalculable debt and words are inadequate to express my gratitude.

The first drafts of many of these articles have been read in the meetings of Friday Seminar Group, Calcutta. It is a group of committed philosophers, well known for their diversity of thought and analytic minds. I have profited in their company and am grateful for their sincere criticisms and positive suggestions towards improvement of the contents and forms.

In this connection I fondly remember my professor, the late Ras Vihary Das, who in his inimitable style kindled the spirit of inquiry in a generation of young students, and I am fortunate to have come in contact with him. He instilled in me the courage to examine the problems rationally, to respect the tradition, but not to blindly accept.

I thank Bina Gupta who helped me in many ways.

I am indebted to Melaina Balbo, Kanishka Gangopadhyay, Jason Hallman, Martin Hayward, Melissa McNitt, and their colleagues at Lexington Books for taking an interest in this book and publishing it.

I am also grateful to my husband and our four children, who have helped me in various ways to carry on my research and publish this book.

Calcutta, 2002

Acknowledgments

Some articles in this anthology have been published in various journals. I thank *The Journal of Indian Philosophy*, *The Journal of Indian Council of Philosophical Research* and Jadavpur University for permitting me to reprint my articles, which were originally published in their journals.

The details are as follows:

1. "Did Prabhākara Hold the View that Knowledge Is Self-Manifesting?" published in *The Journal of Indian Philosophy*, 7:1979.
2. "The Concept of *Sākṣin*" published in *The Journal of Indian Philosophy*, 10:1982.
3. "An Attempt to Understand *Svataḥ-Prāmāṇyavāda* in Advaita Vedānta" published in *The Journal of Indian Philosophy*, 19:1991.
4. "*Mokṣa*, the *Parama Puruṣārtha*" published in *The Journal of Indian Council of Philosophical Research*, vol. IX, no.1, 1991.
5. "Krishna Chandra Bhattacharyya and *Anekāntavāda*" published in *The Journal of Indian Council of Philosophical Research*, vol. X, no. 1, 1992.
6. "The Concept of Truth in Buddhist Logic" published in *The Jadavpur Journal of Philosophy*, vol. 11, Nos.1 & 2, 1999.

Introduction

This anthology contains two groups of articles; some deal with the Indian concept of *jñāna* and the others concern the Indian concept of value.

In the first group of essays I go back to the philosophers who were thinking at a time when the differences between epistemology, logic, psychology, and ontology were yet to emerge. They looked at *jñāna* or cognition as an event in time, which is causally generated and has a logical structure of its own. They were interested in asking whether *jñāna* has an *ākāra* or form of its own or not. To call it a transparent medium is to lay the foundation for realism; to agree that it is *sākāra* is to take a step towards idealism and skepticism. They asked: how is cognition known? To say that it is known by another cognition is to treat it like any other object of the world; to say that it is self-manifesting is to assign to consciousness a special position, which might lead to a monistic ontology such as the Advaita of Śaṃkara. They were interested in the relationship between truth and cognition. Some look at these as independent of each other; truth and falsity are said to be mutually opposing properties of cognition. Such an approach encourages advancement in logic. Others look at truth as an essential constituent of cognition; cognitions are taken to be naturally true, and errors are considered to be aberrations. This might have a far-reaching effect in ontology.

This is the backdrop of my thinking in the first four articles. The first essay is on manifestation of cognition. Traditionally, the Bhāṭṭas and the Prābhākaras are supposed to maintain diametrically opposite views. The Bhāṭṭa view is called *Jñātatālingaka-anumitivāda*. They hold that cognitions manifest objects; this can be called *prākatya* or manifestedness. To explain the existence of this property we presume the existence of cognition, which produces it. The other schools describe this as an inference, where the ground is manifestedness. The Prābhākaras are supposed to hold a version of *svataḥ-prakāśavāda*, which asserts that cognitions are self-manifesting. They believe in *triputi-bhāna* or manifestation of three factors. In other words they assert that every cognition reveals its object, the knower or the self and itself. Further, as they are avowed realists,

they are criticized for missing the essential subjective nature of awareness. However, I found that the position of Prabhākara, as expressed in the *Bṛhatī Ṭīkā*, on the *Śabarabhāṣya*, is different from what has been traditionally accepted. I have shown that Prabhākara's own position is very near the Bhāṭṭa view, as he held that *jñāna* is known inferentially. But the more interesting point is that, in spite of being a staunch realist, he believes in pure subjectivity of consciousness. He starts with the diametrically opposite nature of subject and object; awareness is known as *samvit* and object as *samvedya.* This is very similar to Śaṃkara's bifurcation of reality in to *you* and *I*. Prabhākara did not develop this point, yet he cannot be blamed for missing the essential subjectivity of consciousness.

In another essay I have discussed the question of *prakāśa*. It is about *sākṣin* of Advaita Vedānta, which is said to be self-manifesting par excellence. I tried to clarify that where other systems speak of *jñāna*, the occurrent, the Advaitins are not talking about these. They do not call the cognition self-revealing. These are necessarily manifested by the continuous principle of awareness, which is treated as a backdrop of all our experience. They appear here as a participant in the debate on manifestation of cognition; but, as a matter of fact, they are showing how the highest ontological principle appears in experience.

I have written two essays on *Svataḥ-prāmāṇyavāda.* Various schools support the view that, when cognitions are known, they are known as true. The difference from the Western concept of truth deserves notice. Knowledge is called justified true belief; here, a large body of thinkers hold that justification does not add anything to the primary belief. There are interesting discussions on the nature of justification. These essays discuss the Prābhākara, the Bhāṭṭa and the Advaita views. The Prābhākaras do not accept error in the cognitive level; their point is that, to accept the reality of deviant cognitions is to question the capability of all cognitions to reveal reality and that this is skepticism. The Advaitins accept error as an event, but they do not accept it as a subclass of cognitions; they call it cognition falsely so-called. They look at truth as an integral feature of cognition. Truth as to cognition is likened to heat as to fire. Some of the Bhāṭṭas hold that cognition manifests the object with its properties and that is truth. I find their approach very interesting. Analysis of cognition on this line should have been further developed. Truth is not a property; it is the essence of cognition. A cognition asserts that the jar is black; to say that the cognition is true is not to add anything extra. It contains an appeal to revise the meaning of the concept of truth. If error can be accepted as an aberration, it would solve a number of problems.

Two other essays comprise this section. One is on Buddhist logic. Buddhist logic, although ontologically loaded, always interested me. The Buddhists develop the concept of unique particulars; they assign to the conceptual world a lower status. Truth comes back as workability. They could have treated imagination as a constitutive conceptual principle, but they did not, although the suggestions are present in the Buddhist texts. True to the idea of transitoriness of ob-

jects preached by Buddha, and momentariness of the real developed by later Buddhists, they are not interested in concepts, which would lend some sort of reality to the objects of experience.

I tried to write about K. C. Bhattacharyya's philosophy. The *Syādvāda* of Jaina thought is totally epistemological; however, it is correlated to the *anekānta*, or many-faced, reality. The Jainas hold that the judgments are essentially connected with the standpoints, so the apparently opposed statements are actually not so, being passed under different circumstances. Being strict realists they admit that all these contraries are parts of the reality. Krishna Chandra develops the idea on the conceptual level. He works out how the mutually opposed concepts constitute reality. His language is abstruse, but the ideas are fascinating. His able son Kalidas Bhattacharyya in *Anekānta Vedānta* has elaborated on this idea.

I have ventured into Indian ethics, too. It has a character of its own. Western philosophy has developed various ethical theories. A large group of thinkers are consequentialists, who judge the moral value of an action by turning to the consequences of ethical actions. The greatest happiness of the greatest number theory falls in this group. There are deontologists like Kant who speak of the mighty Categorical Imperative and for the duty for duty's sake morality. Indian theories can be described as virtue ethics. Numerous virtues and ethical rules abound. I hold that the key to understanding the value of these virtues lies in the concept of self-perfection. The ideas find culmination in the concept of *mokṣa*. Freedom has always attracted men, but freedom as *mokṣa* has its own specific nature, and it is worth inquiring how far it is practicable, and how far it is acceptable as a supreme value. In many places the concept looks like escapism and destruction of individuality. Kalidas Bhattacharyya helped me to look at it as an expansion of personality, involving transcendence of naturality. It should have been supplemented by a postscript analyzing the exact meaning of *vairāgya* or renunciation. This is the attitude which leads a person to seek *mokṣa*. Bhāmatīkāra makes it clear that true *vairāgya* is not escapism or avoidance of duties of a householder, but it is some sort of dissatisfaction with the mundane values and an urge to find out something superior.

Two essays discuss the ethics propounded in the *Gītā*. It is usual to link up the teachings of the *Gītā* with the metaphysical background present in the book. I find that, even if we sever the ties, the moral teachings themselves form a consistent whole. Attachment to the narrow self-centeredness is the root of all vice and self-expansion and transcendence of the limits of narrow personality is good. This idea of goodness invisibly constitutes the essence of the *Gītā*.

First, I turn to the concept of *svadharma*, to dismiss the idea that the caste system is traceable to the *Gītā*. Many modern thinkers have looked at it as an example of perfectionist ethics. I hold that the concept of *svadharma* does not stand by itself, without a reference to the *niṣkāma* attitude. Later on in a separate essay I turn to the concept of *niṣkāma karma* itself. The concepts of *sakāma* and *niṣkāma karma* originated in an age when the law of *karma* reigned supreme. It

constituted the foundation of retributive ethics. The law is essentially connected with the ideas of reward, punishment, rebirth, heaven, and hell. *Niṣkāma karma* was originally introduced as a tool, which helped a person to avoid retribution and escape from the cycle of death and rebirth. The concept of *niṣkāma karma* has profoundly influenced Hindu thought. Even today many people look at it as an aid to *mokṣa*. There are many thinkers who do not accept the law of *karma*, but who look at *niṣkāma karma* as valuable in itself. Whether we accept concepts such as rebirth or not, it is undeniable that self-centered desires chain up a person, so in a sense the practice of *niṣkāma karma* is freedom in itself.

The last essay deals with virtue. I find that in moral life, the basic aim has always been attainment of personal perfection. Emphasis has always been on the accompanying mental attitude. The two different spiritual values are *dharma* and *mokṣa*. Such is the importance of attitude that when some rules of conduct are practiced with desire for some end, they fall under *dharma* and yield those results. The same set of rules practiced without desire for some end leads to *mokṣa* or freedom.

In the end let me turn to a timeworn example. Some villains are chasing an innocent man. The man seeks shelter from a good person. The chasers approach the good man and ask if he has seen the other man or not. The good man lies, saying that he has not seen him. The wicked pursuers leave; the innocent fugitive is saved. We all appreciate here the moral value of the situation. But the philosopher asks: why is this act moral? Some would say that the act is good because the consequences are good. Another can rejoin that there is hierarchy in moral values, and life is a higher value and it has been saved. The ethics I am discussing would comment that an act is immoral when it is preceded by self-centered motives. This act arises out of compassion for others, so in spite of being sinful it is good and virtuous.

Mokṣa or personal perfection has always been accepted as supreme value. It stands for transcendence of narrow self-centeredness and expansion of self. Doing good to others has been accepted as a valuable moral precept, but it has only instrumental value. It makes the practitioner of this principle a better person. Perhaps only in Advaita and Mahāyāna Buddhism is there the concept of *sarvanmukti* or freedom of all. It goes to the credit of Swami Vivekananda to incorporate the good of all as a part of the goal of life. For his followers, *mokṣa* for the self and the good of the world are equally important. This idea is partly traceable to the concept of *lokasamgraha* present in the *Gītā*. However, this has not been discussed in this book.

Did Prabhākara Hold the View That Knowledge Is Self-Manifesting?

It is well known to the students of Indian philosophy that, with reference to the question of manifestation of *jñāna*, the Prābhākaras are the advocates of *svayam-prakāśa* theory. To call a cognitive awareness *svayam-prakāśa* is to say that it is self-manifesting. *Prakāśa* has also been explained as *vyavahāra-hetu*,[1] or as that which leads to verbal expression of the thing under consideration. To give a concrete example, "*ghaṭa-prakāśa*" means that experience which leads to verbal expression of *ghaṭa*. So to call a *jñāna svayam-prakāśa* is to say that the *jñāna* itself leads to its own usage in language and is not dependent for its expression on any other *jñāna* or anything other than itself. Prābhākara theory of *svayam-prakāśa* is also known as *triputi-bhāna*, which means that in every *jñāna* there is a revelation of subject, object, and *jñāna*. To quote Radhakrishnan, "Prabhākara is an advocate of *triputisamvit*, according to which the knower, the known and the knowledge are given simultaneously in every act of cognition."[2] Similarly, Hiriyanna asserts: "The word which the Prābhākaras use for knowledge of experience is *samvit* which being *svaprakāśa*, needs nothing else to make it manifest. . . . It appears and disappears; and as it does so, reveals both the object and the self, simultaneously with itself. The triple revelation is what is described as *triputi-jñāna*."[3]

Again, S. N. Dasgupta held that "cognition is not of course unknown to us, but that is of course because it is self-cognised, and reveals itself to us the moment it reveals its objects. From the illumination of objects also we can infer the presence of this self-cognising knowledge."[4] In this essay, I would like to point out that this theory has been explicitly advocated by Śālikanātha in his *Prakaraṇapañcikā* not by Prabhākara himself. Furthermore, although Śālikanātha has spoken of manifestation of all these three factors, he has assigned to *jñāna* a fundamental position, and he has shown how the manifestation of the other two are dependent on that of *jñāna*. I have not discussed Prabhākara's opinion about manifestation of self. As to cognition, he has recognized a definite distinction between two aspects, one of which he calls *samvit* and the other *jñāna*. Accord-

ing to him, *samvit* is self-revealing (*svayam-prakāśa*) and *jñāna* is inferred (*anumeya*); or, in other words, in every cognition we have an immediate awareness of *samvit* and an inferential knowledge of *jñāna*. These discussions occur in his *Bṛhatī Tīkā* on *Śabara Bhāṣya*, where he criticizes the Buddhist doctrine, which denies any independent existence to external objects.[5] It appears from these discussions that *samvit* stands for *prakāśa* or manifestation only, but what in other philosophical systems has been called *jñāna* has been termed *jñāna* by Prabhākara, too.

Let us see how Prabhākara presents his opponent's position. In immediate awareness we get only one form, the form of sound or that of color such as blue, yet we speak of three factors—the *grāhya*, the *grāhaka*, and the *samvedana* or the known object, the knowing cognition and the manifestation. What is the justification for this analysis?[6] It is useless to argue that both *samvit* and the corresponding object are manifested through one form, for we never speak of two separate entities expressing themselves through one form.

The commentary makes this even more explicit.[7] There is immediate apprehension of one form. If this form belongs either to the object or to the *jñāna*, then we are forced to the conclusion that *samvit* is formless and consequently is not perceptible. But if it is not perceptible, then *jñāna* and object cannot be established. So the form must belong to *samvit*. And if *samvit* is said to have a form, then *jñāna* and object become unnecessary and superfluous, and *samvit* becomes the only reality. This conclusion is welcomed by the Buddhists.

In answer to this position, Prabhākara gradually unfolds his own position. He advances step by step to show how, even in the absence of any specific form, we are justified in talking about both *samvit* and *jñāna*.

Prabhākara asserts that we have an immediate awareness of both object and *samvit*, of the object as object, and of the *samvit* as *samvit*.[8] That there is a distinction between the two is our basic intuition. *Samvit* is the result of our cognitive awareness, and we must posit a *jñāna*, which produces this. There is a direct apprehension of *samvit* and an inferential knowledge of *jñāna*.

When the Buddhists demand two separate forms for the immediate apprehension of object and *samvit*, they are mistaken in as much as they demand that *samvit* must also be known in the objective mode. But Prabhākara adds that *samvit* cannot be known as the accusative (*karma*), and only an accusative can be an object.[9] The commentator clarifies this. What is the implication of the apparently contradictory description of *samvit* as knowable and yet unknowable? The commentator says that *samvit* is self-manifesting, but an object is that which is manifested by *samvit*. *Samvit* can never be made an object; hence, it is unknowable as an *object*, yet it is that to which everything appears as object, it is manifestation itself, and as such it is knowable.[10]

When we assert that there is direct apprehension of *samvit*, our assertion may be misleading. *Samvit* is formless, non-objective and self-manifesting. The commentator says here that when we state that we have a perceptual knowledge of *samvit*, all that is implied is that we have an immediate awareness, and *samvit* is not meant to be an object of perception through sense organs.[11]

The *svataḥ-prakāśa* or self-manifestation theories about manifestation of *jñāna* have spoken of *jñāna* in this way. Though we analyze and talk about *jñāna*, in the way in which we look at other objects of experience, another kind of awareness of *jñāna* is possible, and this is a subjective awareness. This unreflective awareness cannot be brought in front of our eyes because by its very nature it is that which cannot be objectified. Yet we cannot deny the existence of this kind of awareness, if our basic intuition is that it is there, just because it cannot be studied objectively. This aspect of cognition has been termed *samvit* by Prabhākara. Prabhākara asserts that *samvit* is known as *samvit*, and not as *samvedya*, that is, ever as an object. Therefore, for its awareness there is no need for any separate form.

As we have already mentioned, Prabhākara has spoken of inferential knowledge of *jñāna*. He refers to his own position as that of *ānumānika-jñānavādin*, or as that of one who upholds the theory that *jñāna* is known through inference.[12] In inference, we cannot directly grasp the full nature of its object, as we grasp in perceptual awareness. Through inference, which has been called rational postulation, we can only posit the existence of the object.[13] So Prabhākara's position is safe against the Buddhists, in so far as we know about the existence of *jñāna* only through inference and so the question of form does not arise. To express this, Prabhākara describes *jñāna* as *asamvedya* but *prameya*.[14] To describe something as *asamvedya* is to call it unknowable. But *jñāna* is not unknowable in the sense in which *samvit* is unknowable; it is unknowable because we cannot have any perceptual immediate knowledge of it. But it is *prameya*, or it is an object of mediate knowledge. Prabhākara further strengthens his position by saying that *jñāna*, being transitory, can never be known perceptually, as it is destroyed when the secondary *jñāna*, which is supposed to grasp it, arises. Prabhākara characterizes this *jñāna* as *grāhaka* or as that which grasps the object, the latter being the *grāhya*.

I think that the above discussion is sufficient to show that Prabhākara did not mean the same thing by *jñāna* and *samvit*. We need not therefore accept S. N. Dasgupta's opinion expressed in the text, quoted in the first part of this essay, which ascribes to Prabhākara the view that we can infer the presence of the self-cognizing knowledge. Prabhākara definitely holds that *samvit* is self-cognizing, whereas what is inferred, namely *jñāna*, is something different from it. But here two pertinent questions may arise: first, what did Prabhākara actually mean by *samvit* and *jñāna*? and second, why did he introduce *jñāna* over and above *samvit*? Prabhākara himself raises the second question. His answer is that here he is following *lokavyavahāra* or common usage. People talk about two things—*jñāna* and object. The commentator adds that these two, that is, the object which is perceived and *jñāna* which is inferred are accepted over and above *samvit*.[15] He also adds that since common people think in terms of cause and effect, Prabhākara has posited *jñāna* to explain the existence of *samvit*, which is its effect.

Prabhākara, therefore, speaks of *jñāna* as that which produces *samvit*. *Samvit* is said to be the *phala* or result. *Samvit* is transitory, self which is always present cannot be its cause, hence we infer transitory *jñāna* as its ground.[16] Later

Prābhākaras have identified *jñāna* with the conditions which produce cognition. Here, the etymological meaning of *jñāna* is supposed to be *jñayate anena*, or that through which something is known, or in philosophical language it is the instrument of knowledge, which is termed *karaṇa*. Śālikanātha in his *Prakaraṇapañcikā* asserts that *jñāna* is the ground, which leads to the production of *samvit*, and it stands for the contact of *ātman* and *manas*.[17] But from certain observations made by Prabhākara, and from the way in which he argues, it appears that Prabhākara meant by *jñāna* not the conditions of cognition but rather cognition itself.[18]

First, let us turn to the concept of *samvit*. Prabhākara has used the term *samvit* to mean just manifestation. The commentary explicitly asserts that *samvit* means *prakāśa*, and it is child's talk to speak of any manifestation of the object other than *samvit*.[19] Prabhākara speaks of *samvit* as formless, transitory, self-manifesting, and that which cannot be made an object. But, Śālikanātha, in *Prakaraṇapañcikā*, gives a much more complicated description. It is said to be a quality of the subject, which brings about the specific verbal behavior directed towards the object.[20] Such being the nature of *samvit*, there is nothing left to be termed *jñāna*, and *jñāna* is explained as contact of self and mind (*manas*). But, Prabhākara`s *samvit* cannot even be made an object of awareness, it is not that which manifests the object, but rather it is merely the manifestation; as such the psychological occurrent which leads to this manifestation can be termed *jñāna*.

Jñāna, as already pointed out, has been termed *grāhaka*, or that which grasps the object. It has been described as *nirākāra* or formless.[21] It has been called transitory. It is said that *jñāna* cannot be made an object of perception, for being transitory it vanishes while the secondary *jñāna*, which would grasp it, comes into being.[22] Such *jñāna* is apt to be a psychological occurrent rather than the contact of self and mind, which is its ground. In view of the above, it is also difficult to understand the interpretation of *jñāna* as the instrumental cause (*karaṇa*), such as sense-object contact or knowledge of the ground and universal relation, for why should the latter be called *grāhaka* or formless or transitory. If the terminology used by other philosophical systems is permitted, then we can broadly describe Prabhākara's position by saying that he thought of *jñāna* as a *kriyā* or action, which produces a *guṇa* or attribute in the self, called *samvit*.

Had Prabhākara been a supporter of *svataḥ-prakāśa* theory of *jñāna*, he would have likened *jñāna* to a lamp that reveals its objects and also itself. Rather, he likes to compare it to a pot that does not require the help of another pot, only for the performance of its own work. *Jñāna* manifests its object, but in its own turn, its existence is to be inferred. It is not self-certifying. Prabhākara warns that this is not to be confused with the theory, which asserts that *jñāna* becomes the direct object of another *jñāna*.[23] *Jñāna* is never directly presented to another *jñāna* or to itself. We can only infer its existence from the fact that there has been manifestation of object.

Again we find that, according to Prabhākara, *samvit* cannot be the basis of memory. A critic may say that we often have a memory of the form "I remember that I knew this object." Such a piece of cognition would presuppose a previous

jñāna of *jñāna*. This point has interested many Indian philosophers. We are primarily interested in the objects surrounding us, and it is only in the reflective mood that we become aware of our cognitions. In such a mood we are not only aware of the cognition that is present but we can even recall a cognition that is past, that was present perhaps only yesterday. We can remember not only a flower that we saw yesterday but also the fact that we saw it. Indian philosophers have spoken of two types of memory; both are based on past experience.[24] But, whereas in one, the past experience is only implied, in the other the experience is also recalled in its fullness. It is easy for the upholder of the *svataḥ-prakāśa* theory to explain the second type of memory, for on this theory every cognition involves cognition of itself. Some philosophers who uphold the *parataḥ-prakāśa* theory, such as the Bhāṭṭas, have denied the existence of any such memory. They say that there is only memory of the object and never any memory of the cognition. They explain away memory of cognition as imaginary construction. Here Prabhākara's answer is that usually we recall only the object and not the experience. He, however, unlike the Bhāṭṭas, agrees that we sometimes also have the memory of the experience. He characterizes such a memory as being conditioned by perception and inference, perception of the object and inference of *jñāna*.[25] This also suggests that, through inference, we come to know knowledge proper and not the conditions which produce it.

Śālikanātha's commentary on this passage is also quite interesting. Perception is inevitable if the conditions of perception are present; so if *jñāna* were known through perception, then there would be nothing to hinder the memory of *jñāna* to arise along with the memory of the object. But Prabhākara asserts that, in memory, we usually recall the object only (where the reference to the past experience is implicit), and not as qualified by *jñāna*.[26] This is because the basis of memory is only the experience of the object and not the experience of the object plus that of the cognitive awareness. Inference is a complicated process and it is not invariably present with the *jñāna* of the object. So only in a few cases is there memory of the cognition along with that of the object. Such cases are conditioned by both perception and inference. The sum and substance of Prabhākara's argument is that if an object is remembered as previously known, that is, if the previous cognition is also recalled as qualifying the object, its basis is inferential knowledge of *jñāna*. We suggest that it is more consistent to mean by such *jñāna* cognition proper rather than contact of self and mind.

Prabhākara gives another argument to support his point. *Jñāna* always arises as *jñāna* of an object, say, that of a pot. If both cognition and object were known through perception, there would be no explanation of such a relation between the two. Color of an object and its touch are both known perceptually and one of the two does not appear as a determinant of the other. But a cognition always arises as a cognition of something and there is a necessary relation between the two. According to Prabhākara, this also implies that both object and *jñāna* are not known perceptually, but we have inferential knowledge of *jñāna*. Prabhākara sums up all that he has said by declaring that we infer the formless *jñāna* and we perceive the object in perception.[27] Here, but for the details, Pra-

bhākara's position appears to be surprisingly near that of the Bhāṭṭas, who hold that cognition is inferred from *jñatatā*.

Pārthasārathi Miśra, in his Śāstradīpikā, dwells on the problem of *jñāna* of *jñāna*.[28] He speaks of *jñāna* as an action, which produces a result in the object. Prabhākara has also spoken of *samvit* as result. Pārthasārathi, just like Prabhākara, says that to explain this result we must posit a cognition. This result is supposed to be known by *mānasa*, or inner perception, and its cause is generally called *jñāna* or *vijñāna*.

But Prabhākara and Pārthasārathi, who is a Bhāṭṭa philosopher, have spoken of this result in different ways. Pārthasārathi says that there is a difference between the known object and the unknown object, and that such a difference cannot be explained without reference to some result caused by cognition. He asserts that *jñāna*, which is an action, establishes a relation between the self, who knows, and the object, which is known. It is from this relation that we infer the existence of the cognition, which establishes the relation. Prabhākara has also said that from *samvit* we infer *jñāna*. But whereas *jnātatā* is an attribute of the object, *samvit* is an attribute of the self. It appears that this description is not to be accepted literally, for Prabhākara also asserts that *samvit* is something which cannot be grasped in the objective mode.

We have to admit that Prabhākara is often vague. Unfortunately for us, his other book, the *Laghvī*, is not extant. Many questions are therefore left unanswered. Śālikanātha in his *Prakaraṇapañcikā* is much more definite. He defends Prabhākara against other critics by using the prevalent terminology.[29] But Śālikanātha appears to drift away from Prabhākara's original position. He repeats his language, but he does not retain his spirit.

Śālikanātha declares in unambiguous language that in every cognition there is manifestation of the cognition, its object, and self. The awareness of the object may be immediate, as in perception, or mediate, as in memory or inference. But in every cognition, the subject and the *jñāna* are known directly. His argument is that the form of *jñāna* is "I know this" and never "someone knows this." Without reference to the self we cannot explain the difference between my *jñāna* and other people's cognitive experience.

About the alleged self-manifestation of *jñāna* also *Prakaraṇapañcikā* gives many justifications. As cognition is the basis of all manifestation, it can only be self-manifesting. In deep sleep we have no awareness of the object and the self, just because awareness is absent. So in experience cognition is most fundamental. It has no form of its own, but it has a nature of its own, and that is manifested in knowledge. He also gives an inferential form to his argument: that which is manifested by others cannot in its turn manifest others, like the pot, etc. So *samvit*, which manifests others must be self-manifesting. *Prakaraṇapañcikā* makes it clear that the subject and the object being dependent on knowledge for manifestation are not self-manifesting.

We have already discussed how Śālikanātha has differentiated between *samvit* and *jñāna*. Both Prabhākara and Śālikanātha agree that *jñāna* is inferred. According to Śālikanātha *jñāna* denotes the conditions, which produce cogni-

tion; but it appears that it would be more consistent to say that Prabhākara has meant by *jñāna* what other philosophers have meant by it. Śālikanātha has incorporated into *samvit* many of its functions; he means by it that which manifests the object. But Prabhākara has meant by *samvit* the mere manifestation, which is transitory, and which cannot be objectified. Hence, although both of them have called *samvit* self-manifesting, there is a gulf of difference between them. In Prabhākara's *Bṛhatī*, the content of *samvit* is so scanty that, although he calls *samvit* self-manifesting, it would be improper to describe him as one who upheld the *svataḥ-prakāśa* theory of *jñāna*.

Notes

1. Śālikanātha Miśra, *Prakaraṇapañcikā*, ed. Subrahmaniya Sastri (Varanasi, India: Benares Hindu University), editor's footnote: *prakāśa śabdena vyavahāra-hetutvam ucyate, ghaṭa-prakāśa iti ghaṭa-vyavahāra-hetur ityartha*, 171.
2. S. Radhakrishnan, *Indian Philosophy*, vol. II (London: George Allen & Unwin, 1940), 395.
3. M. Hiriyanna, *Outlines of Indian Philosophy* (London: George Allen & Unwin, 1932), 307.
4. S. N. Dasgupta, *A History of Indian Philosophy*, vol. I (Cambridge, U.K.: Cambridge University Press, 1922), 384.
5. Śabara Swāmin, *Mīmāmsā Sūtra Bhāṣya*, with Prabhākara Miśra, *Bṛhatī Tīkā*, Śāliknātha Miśra, *Ṛjuvimalāpañcikā* ed. S. K. Ramanath Sastri (MUSS 3) (Madras: University of Madras, 1934), 62.
6. Prabhākara, *Bṛhatī, Yuktam yadi grāhya-grāhaka samvedanam ākārāntareṇa syāt. Na cākārāntaram upalabhāmahe*, 59.
7. Śālikanātha, *Ṛjuvimalā*, 60.
8. Prabhākara, *Bṛhatī, Na brumaḥ samvedya samvit iti. Samvittayaiva samvit samvedy na samvedyatayā*, 64.
9. Prabhākara, *Bṛhatī, Keyam vāco yukti samvedya na samvedyeti? Yam iyam vāco yuktiḥ. Nāsya karmabhāvo vidyate ityarthaḥ*, 64.
10. Śālikanātha, *Ṛjuvimalā, Svayam prakāśarūpatvāt samvido na parādhīnoprakāśa iti na karmatā. Na ca prakāśābhāvah. Prakāśamānam cāstityucyate, na punaḥ karmataiva vivakṣitā*, 64.
11. Śālikanātha, *Ṛjuvimalā, Pratyakṣa-śabdo'pi samvidām aparokṣotayā, napunar indriya-jñāna-vedyatayaiveti mantavyam ityarthaḥ*, 64.
12. Prabhākara, *Bṛhatī, Na hi pratyakṣavādinaḥ eṣa doṣaḥ. Ānumānika-jñānavādinastu nāyam paryanuyogaḥ*, 63.
13. Śālikanātha, *Ṛjuvimalā, Manute yuktyā kalpayati. Yuktyā kalpanam mananam, grāhakaikarupam jñānam anumīyate ityarthaḥ*, 62.
14. Prabhākara, *Bṛhatī, Kim asamvedyam eva vijñānam? Bāḍham, asamvedyam, na tu aprameyam*, 65.
15. Śālikanātha, *Ṛjuvimalā, Siddham tarhi arthadvayam samvidvyātiriktam. Ekas tāvad arthaḥ jñāna-rūpaḥ, aparaśca nīlādirūpaḥ. Katham punah arthasya jñānasya ca bhedaḥ? Tatrāha . . . pratyakṣorthaḥ, anumeyam jñānam. Tena tayor bhedaḥ iti*, 65.

16. Śālikanātha, *Ṛjuvimalā, Ucyate–phalabhūtāyāḥ samvidaḥ kāryarūpatvāt, kāryasya ca kāṛaṇam antareṇa anupapatter nityakārya udayapattyā cātmanḥ sthirasya kāranatva niraste kādācitkam jñānam anumīyate*, 62.

17. Śālikanātha, *Prakaraṇapañcikā, Samvidutpattikāraṇam ātma-manaḥsannikarṣākhyam tad iti*, 190.

18. In this context it may be noted that, although traditionally Śālikanātha has been accepted as the most faithful commentator of Prabhākara, and other philosophical systems quoted Śālikanātha when they wanted to refer to any Prābhākara tenet, at the same time thinkers such as Vācaspati Miśra and Gangeśa have recognized a difference between the two. Vācaspati speaks of Śālikanātha as modern (Navīna), and Gangeśa calls him Neo-Prābhākara (Navya Prābhākara), as opposed to the old Prābhākara (Jarat Prābhākara), who is Prabhākara Miśra himself.

In fact, a modern scholar, Pt. A. Subrahmaniya Sastri, has mentioned such a difference in the context of the problem of *jñāna*. He asserts that according to the old Prābhākaras, neither cognition nor the subject are grasped in the objective mode, whereas according to the Neo-Prābhākaras such as Śālikanātha, cognition, its substrata, that is, the self, and the object are all as a matter of fact presented in the objective mode. (*Prakaraṇapañcikā*, IX and 143).

19. Śālikanātha, *Ṛjuvimalā, Tadidam bālajalpitam iva pratibhāti. Kimidam samvid vyatiriktam bhāsamānam nāma? . . . Samvideva bhāsanam, tam ca vina bhāsamānam nāstyeva*, 62.

20. Śālikanātha, *Prakaraṇapañcikā, Artha-pratibaddha–vyavahāra-viśeṣa-pravrttya nugunaḥ puruṣasya dharmaḥ samvedanam*, 190.

21. Prabhākara, *Bṛhatī, Nirākārameva hi buddhim anumīmimahe*, 68.

22. Prabhākara, *Bṛhatī, Kṣaṇikatvāccāsya pratyakṣata na sambhavati*, 65.

23. Prabhākara, *Bṛhatī*, 66 and also *Ṛjuvimalā*, 66.

24. Prabhākara, *Bṛhatī, Satyam jñātam smaranti, na tu jñātamiti*, 66.

25. Prabhākara, *Bṛhatī, Yatra hi jñāta iti smṛti, sa pramāṇadvaya-vyapāra-jātatvāt*, 67.

26. Śālikanātha, *Ṛjuvimalā, Jñātam prameyam svarupeṇa smaranti, na punar jñānaviśiṣṭam*, 67.

27. Prabhākara, *Bṛhatī, Nirākāram eva hi buddhim anumīmimahe. Sākāram cārtham pratyakṣam avagacchāmāḥ*, 68.

28. Pārthasārathi Miśra, *Śastradīpikā*, 201.

29. Śālikanātha, *Prakaraṇapañcikā*, 143.

The Concept of *Sākṣin*

I

In this essay I try to discuss some aspects of the concept of *sākṣin*, as I have found it in Advaita philosophy. *Sākṣin* is usually rendered into English as "witness"; Hiriyanna says that *sākṣī* means witness or a disinterested onlooker.[1] But witness does not necessarily mean impartial; the term has legal associations, in which a person is said to be either a witness for . . . or a witness against. . . . Thus I have preferred the Sanskrit term *sākṣin* to the corresponding English term "witness." In Advaita literature it is said that only a person who is intelligent but indifferent is fit to be *sākṣin*.[2]

In Advaita philosophy *sākṣin* means the principle of consciousness present in an individual, which sees all our experiences yet does not get involved in any. The Advaitins have spoken of self in two different senses: they have meant by self the finite empirical individual, who knows this world of name and form, who is the agent of all activities, and who enjoys and suffers the results of all the activities performed by himself. Here the self is the referent of *aham-pratyaya*; he is the knower, the enjoyer, and the doer; he has cognitive, emotive, and conative experiences. They have also meant by self, a principle of consciousness present in every individual, who knows all the changing experiences without getting involved in any. This seer self is called *sākṣin*. All these changing aspects are explained as modes of *antaḥkaraṇa*. *Sākṣin* as the passive conscious spectator constitutes the background of all these experiences. The Advaitins maintain that this seer self constitutes the essential core of an individual. I have only tried to find out what they have exactly meant by *sākṣin* at the empirical level, and how far our mundane life becomes more intelligible, if we accept such a principle.

The earliest suggestion of such a passive conscious principle as an integral part of personality occurs in the *Muṇḍaka Upaniṣada*.[3] This passage speaks of a tree on which two birds are perched. One of them tastes the fruits of a tree; the other does not eat but looks on. The obvious suggestion is that the two birds constitute two aspects of an individual, where one aspect gets involved in all

activities and the other aspect plays the role of a passive spectator. The seer aspect is called *sākṣin*; the other bird represents the active aspect of the mind.

Śaṃkara approaches the problem in a totally different way. In his masterly introduction to the commentaries on the *Brahma-sūtras*, he presents the subject and the object as the two fundamental categories of experience as much opposed to each other as light and darkness.[4] In this background he diagnoses the malady of life by saying that our experience involves a beginningless natural confusion of the two. To the discerning person our ordinary experience is unsatisfactory because we do not see the self and the not-self in their proper perspective. *Dṛk-dṛśya-viveka* or the discrimination between the knowing consciousness and its object is the basic experience upon which the whole superstructure of Advaita rests. Their fundamental claim is that things can be known either as a subject or as an object, and all our experienced contents are to be categorized under either of these two mutually exclusive heads.

Self and not-self are basically different. Śaṃkara says that we have a direct awareness of the self, the existence of the self can never be doubted, it is never questioned, for the questioner himself is the self.[5] We never say "I am not." Objects are presented to this self as an *other*, as something distinct from the self and whatever can be considered as distinct from the subject is not the self.

The difference between these two categories is best understood if we try to analyze the content of self-consciousness. Śaṃkara analyzes it thus.[6] In our everyday life our sense of ownness extends to our son, wife, etc., so that we are disturbed when they are in distress. Sometimes we feel identified with our body, so there are expressions like, "I am thin," "I am fat," and so forth. Again there are expressions such as "I am deaf," "I am blind," which show that we accept the senses as an integral part of the self. Sometimes we think that the activities of the mind are constitutive of the self. But as a matter of fact these are constituents of the individual ego. The *Bhāmatī* comments that ordinary people, as well as philosophers, refer by self to an individual active agent who enjoys and suffers.[7] But according to Śaṃkara all these aspects come to us as objective contents of experience, so they are distinct from the real self. Behind all these varied experiences there is the witness self, the manifesting principle, the unalloyed subject, who is different from, and witness of, the individual ego. Śaṃkara has spoken of this subject as the *pratyagātman*, or the inner self, as opposed to the *aham-pratyayin* or the individual referred to by *I*. Śaṃkara speaks of this inner self as *svapracāra sākṣī* or the self-manifesting witness.[8]

The Advaita position is that in all our experience we have an awareness of this self, but we can never know it as an object. It eludes our grasp if we ever try to capture it in the objective mode. The object is necessarily the *parāk*, something different from the self, and the moment we try to direct our attention to the self by making it an object, we bounce up against something artificial, the individual ego that is referred to by the *I* and the real self is there as the knowing subject.

Advaita Vedānta combines two principles in this concept of *sākṣin*. As described in the *Upaniṣads* it is absolutely passive, and as presented by Śaṃkara, it is the never-to-be-objectified principle of awareness present in every individual. Later philosophers have given this concept a more exact expression, but they have not added to the content.

So, in any discussion about *sākṣin*, it is necessary to raise two questions. First, whether there are two such mutually exclusive categories or not. Second, whether two different aspects of self are discernible or not, which are so distinct from each other that they should be classified under the above two heads. The Advaitins have answered both the questions in the affirmative. In the first place, they have assigned to consciousness a special position and have said that it is known in a special way. Second, they have said that consciousness constitutes the essence of the real self, and all other aspects of the individual belong to the realm of object. I discuss these two questions in the next two sections. In the last section I mention what other tasks have been assigned to *sākṣin*, and how far these are consistent with the real nature of *sākṣin*.

II

The first question leads to the traditional controversy in Indian philosophy about apprehension of a cognition. The Advaitins hold that all the objects of the world are manifested by consciousness, whereas consciousness alone is self-manifesting. They have the Naiyāyikas as their main opponents.

The Naiyāyikas mean by *jñāna* or cognition a transitory mental occurrent, necessarily directed towards an object other than itself. *Jñāna* is a quality of the self and is expressed by statements such as "that is a pot." The pot is said to be the object of knowledge, for the cognition of the pot is necessary and sufficient for all our dealings with the pot. The cognition manifests the object and the object only, but neither the cognizer nor the cognition itself. The Nyāya position is that for the use of the pot, the awareness of the pot is sufficient and the awareness of the self and the awareness of the cognition are redundant. Had the cognition and the self been the objects, the cognition would have led to their uses too, which is not the case. Hence, we should say that a cognition, itself unknown, reveals the object.

Nyāya asserts that the primary awareness of the *vyavasāya*, of the form "that is a pot," is revealed by the secondary introspective awareness of the form "I know the pot" or "I have knowledge of the pot." The latter is called *anuvyavasāya*. The object of this second knowledge is the primary cognition, the self that is the substratum of this cognition, and also the external object in and through the primary cognition. The structures of the primary cognition and the corresponding reflective cognition are more or less the same. Both of them manifest their objects, remaining themselves unknown. It is to be noted that according to the Naiyāyikas the primary cognitions are not necessarily followed

by the secondary cognitions. If the conditions of the *anuvyavasāya* are present and the impediments are absent, then only *anuvyavasāya* takes place.

The Advaitins have meant by *jñāna* something very different. It is a transcendental self-contained principle, which has no reference to any object. The temporal, finite mental states, which arise and perish, which have been called *jñāna* in Nyāya, are called *vṛtti-jñāna* in Advaita philosophy. These are supposed to be modifications of *antaḥkaraṇa.* At this empirical level, the Advaitins have accepted the intentional character of particular cognitions, and they have also accepted other constituent factors, such as the object, the knower, etc. But they have given a very different analysis of *vṛtti-jñāna* as far as its awareness is concerned.

The Advaitins say that when we have an awareness of an object, the object is indeed manifested, but it is not the only thing revealed; here we have an automatic awareness of the awareness, too. The two awarenesses are simultaneous, but they are not of a similar structure. When an object is known, through a mental occurrent, the occurrent is also known by the knower without the mediation of any other mental state. The mental occurrent is called *janya-jñāna*, which means that it is something that is produced or originated. Śaṃkara says that *sākṣin* and these occurrents have a different nature, and one of them is the knower, the other is known. *Sākṣin* awareness is self-intimating.[9] A modal knowledge is not complete unless it is known, and it is known because it is attached to a principle of awareness present in us, which is *sākṣin.* So a particular cognition is known not through another successive cognition. To know an object is not only to know the object but also to know that it has been known. The primary awareness is not complete without self-awareness, but particular cognitions are not literally self-aware, they are attached to a continuous principle of awareness. In Advaita literature, this is what has been meant when cognitions have been called *sākṣi-vedya.*

In *Vedānta Paribhāṣā* we find a slightly different description.[10] The author says that when the mental states are capable of being revealed only by the *sākṣin*, it is not implied that they are manifested by the *sākṣin* without the mediation of any mental state, but that they are known without any fresh inference, perception, etc. But although he holds that mental occurrents are known by the *sākṣin* through the mediation of a mental occurrent, this is not a fresh occurrent. For he says that mental occurrents are themselves their own objects. There is not much material difference between the two descriptions. It seems that the author of *Vedānta Paribhāṣā* gave such a twisted description, just in order to preserve the symmetry of his system. Some commentators of *Vedānta Paribhāṣā* have said that ordinary objects and the mental states are not objects in the same sense. As all our dealings with the object as well as the corresponding mental mode are possible through the cognition of the object, so both should be called objects. Clearly, these philosophers are speaking from the *Nyāya* platform. *Vedānta Paribhāṣā* seems to have drifted away from the original position of Śaṃkara. He spoke of the mental modes as objects, but they

were never called their own objects, rather they were called objects of the *sākṣin*.[11]

So in a sense the empirical cognitions are objectively revealed, as the primary cognitions are, according to the Naiyāyikas. There is, however, a vital difference. On the Advaita view the *vṛtti-jñānas* are revealed by the *sākṣin*, and not by another of their kind. The Advaitins hold that the basic form of all cognitions is "I know the pot." But here I feel that they should have said that expressions do not always exhaustively express the psychic occurrent, so even when we have a cognition of the form "that is a pot" an unexpressed awareness of the occurrent is present in the knower, and that is the meaning of calling them *sākṣi-vedya*.

It is to be noted that the Advaitins consider the Prābhākaras who hold that the empirical cognitions are self-manifesting as their opponents too. The Prābhākaras hold that the primary form of the cognition is "I know the pot" and the cognition manifests the object, itself, and the self as the substratum of that cognition. They are accused of *karma-kartṛ-virodha*, or of the fallacy of treating the same thing as the subject and the object. The Advaitins argue that just as even a clever clown fails to climb on his own shoulders, similarly the same cognition cannot be directed towards itself as its own object. In other words, the Prābhākaras assert that as a matter of fact these three constituents are revealed, but they do not emphasize the difference of their respective modes of revelation, so the Prābhākara position is unwelcome to them. In fact, both the Prābhākaras and the Naiyāyikas are realists, hence their treatment of awareness is criticized by the Advaitins.

When both the Prābhākaras and the Advaitins are called the supporters of *svataḥ-prakāśavāda*, their opponents mean that they both hold that the conditions, which lead to the origination of a *jñāna*, are also the conditions, which lead to its manifestation. The Advaitins and the Prābhākaras both satisfy this requirement. But as far as the Advaitins are concerned, this is not a point of importance. They want to emphasize that cognitions are qualitatively different from other objects of the world. Thus they treat the Prābhākaras as their opponents, as they do not recognize this difference. According to their theory the *sākṣin* is self-manifesting, and the cognitions are in a sense objects, being objects of the *sākṣin*; but all the same, they are very different from the objects of the world.

This attitude is also revealed through the inferences advanced by the different schools to prove their own point. The Naiyāyikas argue that *jñāna* is an object of knowledge, being a thing, like the pot. These inferences as inferences take us nowhere, as the opponents offer counter-inferences, such as: a *jñāna* is self-manifesting, being a *jñāna*, for whatever is not self-manifesting is not a *jñāna*, such as the pot. But, these inferences are interesting in as much as they reveal the attitude behind them, viz., the Naiyāyikas treat consciousness at par with other objects of the world, whereas the Advaitins assign to it a very special position.

The later Advaitins have variously tried to describe this special character of consciousness. Citsukha has examined at least eleven possible definitions. Self-manifestation could not mean manifestation of itself by itself, for that definition would extend to the Prābhākaras, it would fail to emphasize the special character of consciousness.[12] It does not mean that "to be" is "to appear," that is, the coextensiveness of absence of non-manifestation and existence.[13] This rule is no doubt true of cognitive mental states and other mental states such as joy, sorrow, etc., but it fails to emphasize the essence of consciousness.

What is then the exact significance of self-manifestation? Is it identical with the property of not being an object of knowledge?[14] Then the critic would ask: how do we talk about that which is not an object of knowledge? Or should we say that it is the property of being known immediately although not as an object?[15] Or is it the property of being that which can be expressed in language, though it is not known as an object?[16] Such a definition is unwelcome to the Advaitin, as he wants ultimately to say that in the last analysis consciousness would remain, even when the empirical expressions and the finite individuality would be transcended in the ultimate mystic realization. Through all these definitions the Advaitin tries to emphasize two points: consciousness is immediately known, yet it is not known as an object. The opponent may easily present his criticism in the form of a dilemma: if you can prove self-manifestation, then it is an object of knowledge, and if you cannot prove it, then that amounts to the admission that it has not been established. The Advaita answer to such criticism is that it is based on the dogmatic demand that a thing can be known only as an object. Citsukha accepts one of the above definitions with modification and says that self-manifestation is the property of being referred to by expressions conveying immediacy, while not being an object of knowledge.

It is customary to mention in this context certain criticisms and their answers exchanged between two schools for a long time. Śaṃkara says that we never question the existence of a certain *jñāna*; had it been sometimes unknown, it would have been an object of inquiry, just as other objects are. Citsukha elaborates this and says that if we have an experience of an object, we never have any doubt or error or absence of knowledge about the experience. So if it is inquired of a person, when he has a cognition of an object, whether he is aware of his experience or not, his answer is always in the affirmative. The Naiyāyikas have not questioned the validity of this fact, but they have shown how, even on their theory, they can account for this, and the alleged doubt is not possible. Hence this Advaita argument takes us nowhere.

It is well known how the Advaitin has accused the Naiyāyika of the fallacy of vicious infinite regress. According to the Naiyāyikas, the primary cognition is known by the secondary cognition, but the Advaitin urges that it has to be known by a third cognition and so on ad infinitum. Here the Naiyāyika defends his own position by saying that the Advaita criticism is based on a false demand that an experience has to be necessarily known, but this demand is unwarranted.

We have already said that cognition has to reveal its object, and cognition can very well do that even when it is itself unknown, hence there is no regress. As a matter of fact, the primary cognition is usually followed by a second order one, for usually the causal conditions, which produce the reflective cognition, are present. But this is not a necessary rule, exceptional cases are there, and it is unjustified to demand that cognitions must be known.

So the real controversy is about the nature and structure of cognition. When the Naiyāyika says that the cognitions of the form "that is a pot" reveal the object and the object only, he is faithful to the reports of language. But when he urges that such cognitions are usually followed by reflective cognitions of the form "I know the pot," his theory tends to become artificial. Do we, as a matter of fact, oscillate between these two attitudes? I feel that we are always engrossed in the world of objects, but at the same time all our experiences are automatically registered as integral parts of our experience, although we are not directly aware of this registration. By introducing the concept of *sākṣin* and by saying that *sākṣin*-awareness is different in structure from the cognition of the external objects, the Advaitin does justice to this situation.

The Naiyāyika should either say that the revelation of the object is sufficient, there is no need to know the experience as my experience. Then he has to explain how I am aware of my experience as *my* experience as opposed to other peoples' experience. Or he has to say that primary cognitions are necessarily accompanied by reflective cognitions, where the primary cognition is grasped as a quality of the self-substance. This he does not say, for he has spoken of cases where the *anuvyavsāya* does not take place. Had he said this, his report of the situation would have been artificial.

In our experience, we have two types of cognition, the primary cognition and the reflective cognition expressed through expressions such as "that is a pot" and "I know the pot," respectively, and any acceptable theory should be able to give satisfactory explanation of both. The Naiyāyikas believe that cognition can be both the revealer and the revealed, so they explain both the types of statements easily. The Advaita position is that cognitions are necessarily connected with the *sākṣin*, and they can never be the object of another cognition, and they find it difficult to explain these two types of experience. *Vedānta Paribhāṣā* says that in the experiences of the form "that is a pot" the *jīva* or the individual is the perceiver, whereas in the introspective perception the *sākṣin* is the perceiver, hence the difference. But this explanation utterly fails to explain how the *sākṣin* is present with all the cognitions. Citsukha also gives some strained explanations. He says that in the expressions such as "the pot is known," knownness is the adjective of the pot. Again he says that as the Advaitins speak of immediate awareness of cognitions, it is not difficult to explain expressions such as "I know the pot," for to say that the cognitions are known immediately is not to say that they are known objectively. Yet I feel that these explanations are not sufficiently clear and convincing.

The Advaitins should have acknowledged the possibility of knowing the cognitive states through other mental states, and they should have clearly

distinguished between the awareness of cognitions through the *sākṣin* and knowledge of cognitions through other cognitions. They should have stated that when cognitions are called *sākṣi-vedya*, a nonverbal, non-positional self-awareness is present with all cognitions although expressions do not report this awareness. They could have preserved the essence of their own position, by saying that these cognitions can be known as objects by other cognitions, but only here the spontaneity would be lost. Ras Vihary Das used to say that an awareness known in the objective mode is to be likened to a mirrored image, because here its originality, the living character, is lost. Unfortunately, I have not found such a distinction in Classical Vedānta.

In fact, if they accepted this distinction, it would have been easier for them to say that introspection is conditioned by inquiry, that is, we can know the mental states if we like to know them distinctly. The Naiyāyika cannot say this. The Indian philosophers hold that when we have some general idea about an object, but we do not have distinct knowledge of it, then only we take up an inquiry. Thus the Naiyāyika cannot say that we have introspection in the above way, that is, if we have a desire to know the cognition distinctly. But the Advaitins could have easily said that we always have some knowledge of mental occurrents, and if we desire to know them further we just switch to the introspective mode. In this way they could have satisfactorily explained both types of expressions. Their main point is that awareness *qua* awareness can never be objectified, but without giving up this tenet, they could have acknowledged and maintained a distinction between *vṛtti-jñāna* as an object of *sākṣin* and *vṛtti-jñāna* as an object of another *vṛtti-jñāna*. In this context sometimes *sākṣin*-awareness is explained on the analogy of modal cognitions but then its very essence is lost and the whole thing becomes a useless duplication. These complications could have been avoided with the recognition of the above distinction.

Before closing this section, I cannot resist the temptation of quoting one of our contemporary thinkers, whose analysis of the knowledge situation is strikingly similar to the Advaita analysis, although he is separated from the Advaitins by a huge gap of space and time and his ultimate conclusions are strikingly dissimilar. This is none other than Jean-Paul Sartre.

In his *The Transcendence of the Ego*, he tries to find out the content of the "I think" and he has given a clear and distinct description of consciousness.[17] He speaks of consciousness as necessarily intentional, and of object as transcendent to the consciousness that grasps it. And he says that consciousness is aware of itself insofar as it is consciousness of a transcendent object. He analyses concrete examples to find out the nature of what he calls consciousness in the first degree or unreflected consciousness. Here one is completely absorbed in the object, there is no place for the *I* or the ego. When one is reading a book there is consciousness of the book, of the heroes of the novel, but there is also a non-thetic, non-positional consciousness of the consciousness. This is said to be the very structure of consciousness.

So Sartre has spoken of two different functions of consciousness. It is a positional consciousness of the object, the object that it posits and grasps; and it is a non-positional consciousness of itself. This is strikingly similar to the Advaita position that when we have a *vṛtti-jñāna* of the object, we have a *sākṣin*-awareness of the *vṛtti-jñāna*. The Advaitin would indeed not concede that consciousness has an essential reference to the object. Yet we are speaking at the empirical level, and we are talking about the *vṛtti* and the *sākṣin* that are all empirical concepts. At the empirical level the Advaitin has accepted the object as a constituent factor.

Even the analogies Sartre uses have a vedāntic character. He likens consciousness to light, he describes it as all translucence. He says that consciousness is something very special for which "to be" is "to appear." Object is said to be something outside and external, and consciousness is spoken of as absolute inwardness. This reminds us of the favorite Advaita description of consciousness as characterized by inwardness, as opposed to the object, which is external. Sartre asserts that the object, with its characteristic opacity, is before consciousness, but consciousness is purely and simply consciousness of being conscious of that object. He is indeed looking at consciousness as essentially connected with the object, but at the same time he emphasizes that self-awareness is the essence of consciousness, and this insight is very valuable.

He repeats again and again that consciousness is known in a different way. It is not known as an object; the "subject-object dualism" or the "knower-known dyad" is not present in the realm of knowledge. And in the Advaita fashion he argues that if we accept that knowledge is known by a separate knower, we shall need a third term to know the knower and so on ad infinitum. According to him, either we accept this regress or we accept the possibility of a non-self-conscious final term, both of which are absurd. His own answer is that this regress is unnecessary "since a consciousness has no need at all of reflecting consciousness in order to be conscious of itself."[18] He maintains all along that consciousness is conscious of itself, though it never posits itself as an object. He further shows that in reflective consciousness, that consciousness which is an object loses its original character and the spontaneous living consciousness is always there as a knower. I feel this distinction is vital for understanding the nature of knowledge, but this clarification is absent in Advaita.

III

I have dwelt at length on the point that awareness is self-manifesting. But all this might lead to the conclusion that particular occurrents are self-aware, that there is nothing to show that there is continuous awareness. Śaṃkara raised this question in the second chapter of the *Brahma-Sūtra Bhāṣya*, where he was criticizing the Vijñānavādins as his opponents. The Vijñānavādins speak of a chain of cognitions as constitutive of personality. Here each occurrent is called

self-aware; each mental state is likened to a lamp, which shines by its own light. But Śaṃkara says that on the Buddhist hypothesis, these occurrents are like thousands of lighted lamps separated from each other by stony walls.[19] There must be some constant continuous principle to see their origin and destruction, to pass the judgment that there are many mental states. And this continuous consciousness is *sākṣin.* But, then, it is not a self-substance possessing consciousness as a quality; it is just a continuous process of consciousness constitutive of the essence of an individual.

Here Śaṃkara asserts that the particular cognitions and the *sākṣin* are essentially different from each other. *Sākṣin* is the continuous consciousness, which is self-aware, self-established, and always present. It always knows the occurrent cognitions, but this knowing is different in nature from the cognitions being known by secondary cognitions. Because of this special character of *sākṣin*, there is no infinite regress here. This also shows that the comparison of Sartre's analysis of consciousness and the Advaita analysis cannot be stretched too far. For, whereas Sartre speaks of each occurrent as self-conscious, the Advaitin holds that cognitions are manifested by a continuous principle of consciousness and they hold that this principle is responsible for the continuity of the personality, too.

The vast Advaita literature abounds in many technical definitions of *sākṣin*. Of them, the one given by *Vedānta Paribhāṣā*, namely, the *sākṣin* is *antaḥkaraṇopahita caitanya*, is quite illuminating.[20] *Antaḥkaraṇa* is almost identical with mind, all our changing experiences are called changing states of *antaḥkaraṇa*. *Sākṣin* is defined as consciousness that has *antaḥkaraṇa* as its limiting adjunct. *Upādhi* and *viśeṣaṇa* are two different types of differentiators. *Viśeṣaṇa* is that property which is present in an object, which helps to exclude others, and has connection with what is predicated of an object. *Upādhi* is that property which is present in an object, which excludes other properties, but is not connected with the predicates of the object. In the sentence "the colored jar is transitory," the color is a qualifying attribute or *viśeṣaṇa*, since it is connected with the transitoriness. In the sentence "the ether enclosed by the auditory passage is the ear," the auditory passage is the limiting adjunct or the *upādhi*, since it has no connection with hearing. So *viśeṣaṇa* is an essential constitutive feature, whereas *upādhi* is comparatively externally connected. At the empirical level, when one is seen as an individual or *jīva*, mind and consciousness together form a whole. Here *antaḥkaraṇa* is seen as the *viśeṣaṇa* of consciousness. But in the concept of *sākṣin*, the Advaitin is taking a step towards the ultimate monistic conclusions. So the same consciousness is viewed as a principle that stands apart, without getting involved. Here *antaḥkaraṇa* is called the limiting adjunct. So, according to Advaita, although *sākṣin* constitutes the essence of an individual, ironically its relation with all the particular aspects of an individual is only external and loose.

It is to be noted that *sākṣin* differs from individual to individual. As attached to different internal organs, they witness the private experiences of

different individuals. Some texts speak of *sākṣin* as one and common to all the individuals. Here *Vedānta Paribhāṣā* says that if *sākṣin* is one, then what Caitra has known, Maitra would recollect.[21]

In fact, *sākṣin* constitutes the groundstone of Advaita metaphysics. It is well known that the self after all distillation, when shorn of all the properties, which belong to the realm of not-self, becomes identical with the highest reality. We get a glimpse of that reality at the empirical level in *sākṣin*. *Sākṣin* is pure consciousness, yet it is not the pure consciousness that is the highest reality of the Advaitin. It is tied to an individual, although the small facts that make up a particular person belong to mind. *Sākṣin* is individuated consciousness. *Siddh-ānta-leśa Saṃgraha* quotes *Tattva-śuddhi* as saying that *sākṣin* as a matter of fact belongs to the category of Brahman, yet it appears as belonging to the category of finite individuals.[22]

Advaita philosophy entertains the concept of *ahaṃkāra* side by side with the concept of *sākṣin*. *Ahaṃkāra* refers to the concept of finite empirical ego, whereas *sākṣin* is the unalloyed subject. Both the concepts are traceable to Śam-kara. In one place he says that self is not totally a non-object, for it is referred to by *I*. Here, of course, he means by *I* the ego.[23] In other places he emphatically asserts that self can never be known as an object; it is known immediately and is the basis of all knowledge. The self is not conveyed even in the *Upaniṣads* as an object referred to by the *I* for it is even the witness of ego. It is not known through perception or inference, or even through the scriptures, for it is self-established. There are numerous other passages where Śaṃkara says that the self is not known as an object, for consciousness is its essence. Here obviously he is speaking of *sākṣin*. In other words a certain *I* can be known as an object, but the ultimate *I* is never an object.

The Naiyāyikas and the Bhāṭṭas treat knowledge of the self on par with all other knowledge. Self is known through internal perception, self is also known through inference, and self is an object like any other object. They would further hold that this position does not involve any confusion between the subject and the object, for the self, as substance is the object, whereas the self as conscious is the subject, the knower.

This conclusion is welcome to the Advaitin. He would only add that two aspects of the self are absolutely different from each other; and the self which is object is unconscious, it is called the ego, it constitutes the finite personality of an individual; whereas self as subject is pure consciousness or *sākṣin*, or the never to be objectified basis of all our experience. They assert that if we analyze the expression *I* we shall find that it is constituted of both self and not-self.[24] The not-self involves outwardness or externality, whereas self as opposed to it is marked by inwardness. The opponent may indeed ask that how is it that when both the body and the psychic self are known through cognitions, and both belong to the realm of object, people feel their distinction from the body, but also their identity with the ego? The Advaitin would say that the ordinary people identify the self with the ego, but discerning men find that the ego is a fusion of the self and not-self, and the two must be seen as distinct from each other.[25]

I think that this is the place to note how the final conclusions of the Advaitins are different from those of Sartre. Sartre has deported the *I* totally to the realm of objects. The *I* is not to be found in the primary cognition of the objects. The *I* appears in the reflective level. Sartre does not hold that in the reflective level, the formerly implicit *I* becomes explicit. He emphasizes that there is no place for the *I* in the first level consciousness, as it is an opaque object, which would disturb the translucent character of the primary cognition. He says that when we reflect upon the primary consciousness and when it is treated as an object of another cognition, its spontaneous living character is lost, and it undergoes radical modification. In and through that modification the *I*. emerges. His conclusion is that *I* is just an object like any other; it should not have any privileged position. As we have already pointed out, such a conclusion is welcome to the Advaitin. The Advaitin also holds that the referent of *I* belongs to the realm of objects. But whereas Sartre says that in the primary consciousness there is an awareness of the object and a non-positional awareness of itself, the Advaitin speaks of a principle of awareness, which is non-objectively aware of itself, and is also aware of the occurrent cognitions. Sartre has not found out any such principle.

As we have already mentioned, the concept of *sākṣin* has been used to explain the continuity of personality. Here the Advaitin likes to say that the continuity of an individual through dreamless sleep is preserved by the *sākṣin*, and the self is best manifested in the dreamless sleep. We find a clear expression of this idea in *Vivaraṇa-Prameya-Saṃgraha* put forward through the favorite analogy of the lamp.[26] *Sākṣin* is likened to the flame of a lamp, flickering because of the gusts of wind, during waking hours and dream. It is disturbed by such pieces of modal cognitions as "I am a man," etc. But in dreamless sleep such disturbing elements are absent, and the light of the *sākṣin* burns steadily. Although the analogy is very impressive, and the idea has been cherished by the Advaitins of all ages, it fails to impress me. A theory that attaches more importance to a sleeping individual rather than to a waking one has something missing in it. I think that I have dwelt at sufficient length on the point that *sākṣin* is an awareness principle different from the passing modal cognitions detectable during the waking hours. And although in many places they have spoken of the permanence and continuity of *sākṣin*, we should also be aware that in the concept of *sākṣin*, they have tried to see pure awareness, different in kind from all other objects of the world.

IV

Metaphysically, *sākṣin* is a very important concept. All the characteristics of Brahman are present in it. yet it is individuated. It is the self, which has been

described as the witness, the conscious one, the detached one, and the one who transcends all descriptions.[27]

Some philosophers stretch this too far. They assert that we experience the ultimate characteristics of Brahman in the *sākṣin*. In *Vivaranạ-Prameya-Saṃgraha* it is said that what we experience as full of sorrow, as changeable, as inert, as different from the objects and the sense organs is the mind. That which we experience as the lovable one, as intrinsic, as witness, as the consciousness present in the objects and the sense organs is the self.[28] It is very difficult to agree that these are the reports of our experience. If this were the report of our experience, then it is the experience of a philosopher, who not only is an Advaitin but also one who has accepted the basic tenets of Advaita totally and unquestionably. We can argue supporting the ultimate conclusions of Advaita that Brahman must be bliss, for the highest reality must also be the supreme value. But to demand that this is felt in experience is too much. Experience at most warrants a distinction between the subject and the object. *Sākṣin* can be discerned in experience as the detached principle of consciousness, which is the unalloyed subject, but I feel that the other descriptions are unfounded.

We have tried to show that the concept of *sākṣin* can be developed, by analyzing knowledge. Now it remains for us to comment on other tasks, which have been assigned to the *sākṣin*. Validity has been called *sākṣi-bhāṣya*, but that is a long and controversial issue and I do not want to raise it here. Happiness, sorrow, and other mental states are called *sāksi-bhāṣya*, too. These states are similar to the cognitive states and on the same logic they can be called *sāksi-bhāṣya*. These are also called *kevala-sāksi-vedya* or knowables, which are capable of being manifested only by the *sākṣin*. It is said that these states do not possess any unknown existence, or that they are necessarily manifested without the mediation of any modal knowledge, whenever they come into existence. In traditional Advaita, unknown objects are described as objects concealed by the veil of ignorance, and this veil is destroyed by the rise of knowledge. Doubt, error, etc. are possible as long as the covering is there. But objects such as *vṛtti jñāna*, pleasure, pain, and so forth do not have any unknown existence, we do not ever have any doubt about them, they are manifested directly by the *sākṣin*. Here the mediation of any modal knowledge to destroy ignorance is not required.

There are lengthy discussions about the relation between the *sākṣin* and *avidyā*. But these discussions are inessential here, for they do not throw any light on the concept of *sākṣin*. These are essential for clarifying the exact nature and status of *avidyā*. And what is the use of trying to rationalize that, which by its very nature is irrational? *Vivaraṇa-Prameya-Saṃgraha* declares that the essential nature of *avidyā*, because of which it is called *avidyā*, is that it is contrary to rationalization.[29]

I would like to conclude this discussion by mentioning another oft-quoted tenet of Advaita Vedānta, namely, all objects of the world are objects of the *sākṣin* either as known or as unknown.[30] This is the basic tenet of idealism. They want to say that all existence is thought existence; even unknown objects have

reference to consciousness through their unknownness. Though many Advaitins have quoted this I do not feel that such idealism is traceable to Śaṃkara. He does not question the givenness of the world. He has criticized the subjective idealism of *Vijñānavāda*. He developed his monism in a different way. In fact the very language of *Vivaraṇa-Prameya-Saṃgraha* shows that the Advaitins do not accept such idealism. That the known objects are related to the *sākṣin*, through their known-ness, has already been established. It is declared that although unrelated objects do not possess the property of being the object of *sākṣin*, the unknown objects, when they are known as unknown, become related to the *sākṣin*, through their unknownness.[31] This shows that they accepted the concept of unrelated objects, which has no reference to the principle of awareness and this is a mark of realism. So I do not think that this statement shows the absolute idealism of Advaita.

The concept of *sākṣin* is a fundamental concept of Advaita metaphysics. I have deliberately avoided metaphysical implications, but I feel that even on the empirical level it is an illuminating concept. I have understood by *sākṣin* a principle of awareness constituting the essence of an individual. It is expected of a theory about individual, that it should be able to explain the personal identity on the one hand, and also the difference of one individual from another on the other. The Advaita concept of *sākṣin* fulfills the first successfully, by emphasizing the essential subjectivity and the continuity of self. But difference of one individual from another must be found in the realm of objects, and thus to explain it the Advaitin employs the concept of *ahamkāra*. But the Advaita approach is also a valuational approach. They claim that the *sākṣin* is metaphysically more real than the empirical ego. How far that claim is justifiable is another question.

Notes

1. M. Hiriyanna, *Outlines of Indian Philosophy* (London: George Allen & Unwin, 1932), 342, footnotes.
2. Appaya Dīkṣit, *Siddhāntaleśa Saṃgraha*, ed. Swami Gambhirananda (Calcutta, India: Udbodhan Karyalaya, 1958), 77.
3. *Upaniṣad, Muṇḍaka*, ed. Swami Gambhirananda (Calcutta: Udbodhan Karyalaya, 1941), III/1, 245.
4. Śaṃkara, *Śārīraka Bhāṣya* on the *Brahma-Sūtra*, with *Bhāmatī* by Vācaspati Miśra, ed. Srimohan Bhattacharya (Calcutta: Sanskrit Pustak Bhandar, 1973), 44-45.
5. Śaṃkara, *Bhāṣya: Ātmanaśca pratyākhyātum aśakyatvāt. Ya eva nirākartā tasyaiva ātmatvāt*, 67.
6. Śaṃkara, *Bhāṣya*, 51.
7. Vācaspati, *Bhāmatī, Sārvajanīnaham-pratyayo-viṣayo hyātmā kartā bhoktā samsārī. Tatraiva ca laukika-parīkṣakānām ātmapada-prayogāt*, 307.
8. Śaṃkara, *Bhāṣya*, 51.

9. Śaṃkara, *Bhāṣya, Sākṣi-pratyayayośca svabhāva-vaiṣamyād upalabddhi-upalabhyabhābopapatteh, svayamsiddhasya sākṣino'pratyākheyatvāt*, 2/2/28.

10. Dharmarāja Adhvarīndra, *Vedānta Paribhāṣā*, translated and annotated by Swami Madhavananda (Howrah, India: The Ramakrishna Mission Saradapith, 1942), 31.

11. Śaṃkara, *Bhāṣya*, 2/2/28.

12. Citsukha, *Tattvapradīpikā*, ed. Swami Yogindrananda (Kasi, India: Udasina Samskrita Vidyalaya, 1956), *svasya svayameva prakāśa iti vā*, 4-5.

13. Citsukha, *Tattvapradīpikā, svasattāyām prakāsavyatireka-virahitvam vā*, 4.

14. Citsukha, *Tattvapradipīkā, Jñānaviṣayatvam vā*, 3.

15. Citsukha, *Tattvapradīpikā, Jñānāviṣayatve sati aparokṣa-viṣayatvam vā*, 4.

16. Citsukha, *Tattvapradīpikā, Vyavahārā-viṣayatve sati jñānaviṣayatvam vā*, 4.

17. Jean-Paul Sartre, *The Transcendence of the Ego*, translated and annotated by Forrest Williams and Robert Kirkpatrick (New York: The Noonday Press, 1957).

18. Sartre, *Ego*, 45.

19. Śaṃkara, *Bhāṣya*, 2/2/28.

20. Dharmarāja, *Paribhāṣā*, 39.

21. Dharmarāja, *Paribhāṣā*, 39.

22. Dīkṣit, *Siddhāntaleśa*, 79.

23. Śaṃkara, *Bhāṣya, Na tāvadekāntenāviṣayaḥ asmat-pratyayo viṣayatvāt*, 47.

24. Vidyāraṇya, *Vivaraṇa-Prameya-Saṃgraha*, Part II (Calcutta, India: Basumati, 1927), *Tasmādidamanidamātmaka aham-pratyayaḥ*, 57.

25. Vidyāraṇya, *Vivaraṇa*, 95.

26. Vidyāraṇya, *Vivaraṇa*, 80.

27. *Upaniṣad, Śvetāśvatara*: ed. Swami Gambhirananda (Calcutta, India: Udbodhan Karyalaya, 1941), *sākṣī cetā kevalo nirguṇaśca*, 6/11,450.

28. Vidyāraṇya, *Vivaraṇa*, 57.

29. Vidyāraṇya, *Vivaraṇa, Avidyayāḥ avidyātvam idamevātra lakṣaṇam yad vicā-rāsahiṣṇutvam anyathā vastu vā bhavet*, 48.

30. Vidyāraṇya, *Vivaraṇa, Sarvam vastu jñātatayā ajñātatayā vā sākṣi-caitanyasya visaya eva*, 130.

31. Vidyāraṇya, *Vivaraṇa, Kevalasya ghaṭasya sākṣivedyatv-ābhāvepi ajñātatva-dharma-viśiṣṭasya ajñānadvārā sambandhavati sākṣina pratītirupapadyate*, 130.

An Attempt to Understand *Svataḥ-Prāmāṇyavāda* in Advaita Vedānta

When we see a pot in front of us, or we have an *āmalaka* fruit in our palm, or when we know that there is fire in a distant house as smoke is coming out of its windows, or when we learn that Aśoka was a great ruler from our teacher in a history class, we naturally, automatically, and instantaneously know that these apprehensions are true, that is, there is a pot, there is an *āmalaka* and there is fire, and that there was a great king called Aśoka, and we do not wait for any verification or confirmation or justification for such knowledge. This is exactly what *svataḥ-prāmāṇyavāda*, which I want to elucidate, seeks to assert. Its main opponents, the Naiyāyikas, never question the empirical truth of these claims. But they contend that this is not what is meant by apprehension of truth. Truth in their view is a complicated property, which can be grasped only by reflective, mediate, inferential knowledge.

The *svataḥ-parataḥ* controversy about truth/*pramātva*/*prāmāṇya* is a traditional controversy in Indian philosophy, and all the major schools have participated in it. The arguments, the counter arguments, and their philosophical implications have been discussed again and again. But it is a curious fact that modern scholars have to some extent neglected the *svataḥ* theory, and even when they have turned to it, they name the Bhāṭṭas and the Prābhākaras as its main upholders, and sadly omit the Advaitins. One of the reasons for this omission is the preoccupation of the Advaitins with the absolute reality and the consequent neglect of the empirical concepts. They usually hold that the empirical concepts are logically inconsistent, hence metaphysically untenable. Their attitude is the same towards the concept of truth. After subtle dialectical criticism of the Nyāya theory, the Advaitins present their typical judgment that *pramātva* is rationally inexplicable and only the verdicts of common sense regulate our practical life. But then Madhusūdana Sarasvati, the great Advaita thinker, does something exceptional—he supplements his destructive criticism of the concept of *pramātva* by positive constructive discussion of the commonsense, naïve, practical concept.

His theory, shorn of all technicalities and in the barest outline is this: all apprehensions are known apprehensions, and they are known as true. The question of revision arises only if later circumstances suggest that the previous apprehension was false. In this essay my main aim is to find out whether this naïve approach can be retained or not. I have also tried to understand how the Advaitins have developed this theory, whether there is any scope for reconstruction of this theory on the lines suggested by them, or whether this naïve approach has to be given up in favor of other subtle philosophical considerations.

I

The *svataḥ-parataḥ* controversy centers around two questions: how is truth known, and how is truth produced? The problem is sometimes extended to related spheres, but these two are fundamental. I have tried to restrict myself mainly to the former question, and I have discussed the question of origination only in order to bring out some aspects of the former question. The questions are raised about both truth and falsehood. These problems are closely linked with another associated problem: how is an apprehension known? Here by permutation and combination of all available answers, we get numerous alternative theories, and we have considered the Advaita solution only as one such attempt. I have chosen the Naiyāyikas, the stalwart Indian logicians and epistemologists, as the main opponents. I have mainly taken the Nyāya arguments from Gaṇgeśa's *Prāmāṇyavāda* (leaving aside the technical formulations), as introduced, translated, and interpreted by J. N. Mohanty. It should be borne in mind that Gaṇgeśa directed his criticisms against the Bhāṭṭas, the Miśras, and the Prābhākaras, and never against the Advaitins. However, the Advaitins share with the Mīmāmsakas the main tenet that truth is intrinsic and falsehood is extrinsic to apprehensions. That is why I find the stage set by Gaṇgeśa most convenient for a discussion of the Advaita view. I have tried to confine myself strictly to the Advaita version of the *svataḥ-prāmāṇyavāda*, and I have made stray references to the Mīmāmsakas only in so far as that helps to bring out fully some aspects of the Advaita theory.

When the Naiyāyikas assert that truth and falsehood are extrinsic, they mean that these are certain specific properties of apprehensions, produced and determined by some factors other than those that are responsible for the production of apprehensions. They hold that the apprehensions are not self-manifesting, they are known by reflective cognition called *anuvyavasāya*. This means that an apprehension of the form "This is a pot" reveals the pot only, and the cognition itself is known by a further knowledge of the form "I have a knowledge that this is a pot." But even this reflective cognition does not grasp the truth of the first cognition. Truth is a complicated property of the cognition "This is a pot," determined by the objective situation, and it is known by mediate inferential proc-

esses based on the reflective cognition and further experience. The same is the case with falsehood.

The Mīmāmsakas and the Advaitins also agree that falsehood is extrinsic. But with truth they take an opposite stand. They hold that truth is produced by the factors which produce an apprehension, and truth is known when the apprehension itself is known. Or to borrow a description from Gaṇgeśa, according to *svataḥ-prāmāṇyavāda* cognitions are always known as possessing truth.[1]

Gaṇgeśa in his five alternate formulations has tried to express with great persuasiveness and accuracy the exact difference between the opponents.[2] He suggests that according to *svataḥ-prāmāṇyavāda* truth is known by all those apprehensions, which know the apprehension under consideration (except of course the one which knows it as untrue), whereas their opponents hold that truth is known only by some of these apprehensions (the apprehension which is the result of the truth-establishing inference). His formulations also suggest that according to *parataḥ-prāmāṇyavāda* truth is only known by a mediate knowledge, knowledge or inference based on reflective apprehension of the cognition under consideration, whereas according to *svataḥ-prāmāṇyavāda* truth is known immediately by the apprehension, which knows the initial cognition. In this context, we can quote one of J. N. Mohanty's illuminating and suggestive comments. He speaks of the *svatah-prāmāṇya* theory as asserting, "that there is no criterion of truth, though there is criteria of error."[3] This at once shows the difference of the *svataḥ* theory from the corresponding *parataḥ* theory, and the difference of the Indian controversy from the Western controversy about the criteria of truth. The Naiyāyikas assert that we need some criteria to measure truth, so knowledge of truth is always mediate—they have spoken of different criteria of truth such as coherence, correspondence, conative satisfation, etc. But according to the *svataḥ* theory truth is natural to cognition, it requires no external criterion, it is known immediately when the apprehension is known. In the Western tradition, philosophers hold that truth necessarily needs some justification and they discuss the relative merits of coherence, etc., as measures of truth, and Mohanty points out that some of them accept even self-evidence as such criterion.

The Advaitins use the term *vṛtti-jñāna* to designate the temporal mental occurrents, which are called *jñāna* in other philosophical systems. But in every individual there is said to be one continuous identical principle of awareness, always self-aware, distinct from the changing mental states called the *sākṣin*. The *sākṣin* continuously takes note of all the experiences of an individual. But this awareness is different in kind from the empirical cognitions, as it does not take place through separate mental states; the *sākṣin* is directly and automatically aware of them. When an individual knows that "This is a pot," he is aware that he has this knowledge, although there is no corresponding mental state, which explicitly formulates this knowledge. He also believes that as a matter of fact this is a pot, and it is absurd to claim that this apprehension is neutral regarding its own truth, which is to be ascertained later. Apprehensions most naturally involve the claim that objects are as they are taken to be. This is truth.

So the apprehension "This is a pot" is not complete in itself. It implies that the *sākṣin* is aware of it, and also that it is aware of its truth.

But apprehension, or rather its Indian synonym *jñāna*, has a wide scope. It covers not only all perceptual, inferential and linguistic cognitions but also such phenomenon as error and doubt. And the Advaitins, as *svataḥ-prāmāṇyavādin* has to explain how truth, which is a property that distinguishes true cognitions from erroneous ones, is cognized in both true and untrue cognitions. Is truth in the same sense present in both? How do we explain errors, which are initially accepted as true, later on rejected as lacking truth? Is truth that is initially apprehended, a real objective property or just a psychological claim to truth? Those are some of the questions which the Advaitin must answer.

The Bhāṭṭas have identified truth with the psychological claim to truth. They assert that all apprehensions are initially apprehended as true but the corrective cognition destroys that truth.[4] The corrective cognition either shows that the object is not what it has been taken to be, or the apprehension has been tarnished by some defective cause. Let the apprehension be "This is a snake." Now if subsequent experience points out that it was only a rope and not a snake, or that light had been scanty so there had been improper cognition, then the initial truth is destroyed. But the truth, which is destructible, is nothing but the initial sense of certainty, not truth proper but only a truth claim.

The Advaitins look at the problem from a different angle. They say that under normal conditions all cognitions are true to their objects. Only under abnormal circumstances, if there is something irregular in the generating factors and the presence of such irregularity is known, then doubt arises and the question of revision creeps in. The corrective cognition does not destroy truth; it only reveals that the initial apprehension being erroneous is not an apprehension at all. In other words, all apprehensions *qua* apprehensions are true, errors are similar to normal apprehensions only in appearance, actually, they are distortions. The Advaitins accept error as a phenomenon, but they do not grant it any cognitive status. Errors are produced by defects, which hinder the production of cognition proper. We see a rope as a snake only if the light is scanty; we see a yellow conch-shell only when we suffer from jaundice. So some defect or other disturbs the normal situation. The analysis is significant in as much as it implies that errors are not cognitions; they only falsely simulate *jñāna* proper, or they must not influence our analysis of *jñāna* itself.

Madhusūdana is particularly clear on this point, and he leaves no scope for misinterpretation. He speaks of error and doubt as *jñānābhāsa*, which literally means that they have semblance of *jñāna* but as a matter of fact they are not *jñāna.* He explicitly explains this by comparing error with inferential fallacy. In Indian philosophy *hetvābhāsas* stand for inferential fallacies, which hinder the inference from taking place. These literally mean those, which have the appearance of a *hetu* (or a valid middle term), but as a matter of fact they are not *hetu,* as they do not properly fulfill all the conditions necessary for being a *hetu*

proper. Madhusūdana asserts that just as *hetvābhāsas* are not *hetu* proper, similarly *jñānābhāsas* are not *jñāna* proper.[5]

This is a very important proposal, as it reveals the fundamental difference of approach of the two schools. According to Nyāya, *jñāna* includes under it both *pramā* and *apramā*, truth and falsehood. The two classes share certain common characteristics. A *jñāna* is called true if it possesses a property called truth. It is called untrue, if untruth characterizes it. Truth is said to be produced by *guṇa* or a special excellence, which is something more than the conditions, which produce *jñāna*. Similarly, untruth is said to be produced by defects in the causal conditions.

Some *svataḥ-prāmāṇyavādins* have accepted the basic Nyāya analysis, for example, the Bhāṭṭas. They share the Nyāya platform in the sense they accept truth and falsehood as subordinate classes under the wider class *jñāna.* But the Advaitins hold that *jñāna* and *pramā* are coextensive, the conditions that produce *jñāna* are those that produce truth. They consider *apramā* as an exception, a distortion, so that an analysis of distortion must not influence our analysis of cognition proper.

To sum up, the Advaitins hold that apprehensions occur, and they are known, and they are also known to be true, not by explicit, reflective, secondary judgments, but automatically and implicitly. They hold that *jñāna* has a direct natural access to reality. For them apprehensions (at the empirical level) are nothing but ascertainment of objects, and the *Vivaraṇa-Prameya-Saṃgraha* asserts that truth is as much essential to knowledge, as heat is to fire.[6] Madhusūdana says that just as when we know a particular we know the universal present in it, so also when we know an apprehension we know the truth present in it.[7]

But then the Advaita theory gives rise to a series of questions. Truth, as the Naiyāyikas have carefully defined it, is a very complicated property, and how can it be grasped so easily and automatically? If the Advaitin decides to give up the Nyāya definition, he has to come forward with alternative definitions. We have already mentioned that traditionally they have been asked, if truth is grasped initially, then how is error possible, and how is doubt possible? A modern critic may be worried that the theory blurs over the distinction between knowledge and belief. He may want to ask *svataḥ-prāmāṇyavāda* to explain the distinction on his own theory. *Pramā* is usually rendered into English as knowledge, and knowledge is explained as justified true belief. *Svataḥ-prāmāṇyavāda* treats all apprehensions as *pramā*, and describes *pramā* as true belief, holding that the question of justification does not arise, for justification is neither possible nor necessary. So *svataḥ-prāmāṇyavāda* has to explain why it rejects the commonly accepted difference between knowledge and belief. As a matter of fact we seek justification and confirmation for truth, so *svataḥ-prāmāṇyavāda* has to show in what sense these processes of validation are significant. These are some of the questions which must be discussed before finally evaluating the Advaita theory of *svataḥ-prāmāṇyavāda.*

II

Let us now turn to Madhusūdana's treatment of the concept of truth.

Madhusūdana brushes aside the different definitions of truth accepted by philosophers, including those present in the Advaita literature. *Vivaraṇa-Pram-eya-Saṃgraha* speaks of truth as the capacity of knowledge to manifest its object.[8] This is not sufficiently specific. Madhusūdana renders it as the property of being experience of the suchness of the object.[9] In the Advaita background this is not acceptable for it is well known that Advaita assigns to the object of error some existential status, so even erroneous cognitions are experience of the suchness of the object. Madhusūdana accepts that this is not to be confused with mere referential character of cognitions. At the same time it is not experience of suchness which is present in the corresponding object, for the very concepts of "existence or presence in the object" is vague. Srīharṣa, in Khandaṇa, makes another subtle point. He is afraid that this definition extends to the cases in which we accidentally come to know the suchness of the object.[10] Let us suppose a person has two coins in his hand and another person correctly guesses the number. Is it to be categorized as true?

Truth has often been called *yathārthānubhavatva*, or the property of being an accurate and exact experience of the object as it is.[11] But it does not stand scrutiny. If it stands for similarity of cognitions and object, then that is present in error, too. Nor is it *avyabhicāryanubhutatva*, or the property of being undeviating knowledge. This would unduly extend to the cases of smoke and fire.[12] Truth has sometimes been called *samyak pariccheda*, or the property of being total manifestation of the object. But what exactly does total mean? If it means awareness of all the parts, then it fails to cover even perceptual cognition, for the senses seldom grasp all the parts of a solid. It does not also stand for awareness of all the attributes, for our cognitions are usually about some attributes.

Madhusūdana next turns to the Nyāya definition of truth as *tadvati tatprakārakatva*. An apprehension is said to be true if it possesses the *tat* as a qualifier, when the *tat* as a matter of fact is present in the ontological object. J. N. Mohanty has analyzed in detail the precise meaning and significance of this definition, following the Nyāya tradition, and Gangeśa, in his introduction to *The Gangesa's Theory of Truth.* I refer to a few points that he raises which are relevant for our discussion.

J. N. Mohanty says that, according to Nyāya, "True knowledge is an experience whose qualifier is such that it belongs to the object."[13] Qualifiers are epistemic components of knowledge. In the apprehension "S is P," S-ness, P-ness, and P are qualifiers. In the apprehension "This is silver," this-ness, silver-ness, and silver are qualifiers. So to claim "This is silver" is true is to mean that this-ness, silver-ness, etc. are present in the corresponding object. Here J. N. Mohanty points out that this analysis amply shows that truth is a relational property, a hybrid entity composed of both ontological and epistemic constituents. The

first part, *tadvati*, refers to the ontological situation, where the qualifier is present in the object. The second part, *tatprakārakatva*, refers to the apprehension, which is said to involve the qualifiers. Mohanty warns us that Gangeśa did not subscribe to any copy theory; Gangeśa rejected the concept of truth as *yāthārthya* on the ground that there cannot be any similarity between cognition and object. The Nyāya concept of truth is not to be interpreted as correspondence.

When Madhusūdana says that *tadvati tatprakārakatva* is a property that is common to truth and error, he is blamed for distorting Gangeśa by misinterpreting the ontological object as the epistemological object. He is accused of twisting the *tadvati* into *tadvadviśeṣyakatve sati* and *viśeṣya* is not the ontological object, but it is the qualificandum that is relative to the apprehension. So he destroys the ontological component of truth and turns it into a fully epistemological concept. But in all fairness to Madhusūdana it must be acknowledged that he understood that the crux of the argument lies in the concept of object. First, he showed that the object in the ontological sense cannot be retained. Next, he argued that the object has to be that which appears in cognition or it has to be the epistemological object. Finally, he concludes that such definitions of truth also extend to errors.

Let us now examine the concept of truth as *tadvati tatprakarakātva* independently of Madhusūdana. The Nyāya of course does not speak of the epistemic and the ontological object. Nor does Madhusūdana mention them or state explicitly what we have suggested here. Nyāya speaks of the object and the epistemological components of an apprehension. But Nyāya is not very clear about the ontological status of these components. On the primary level they are transparent—they are not media through which the object is presented or represented. This is totally consistent with the Nyāya tenet that the apprehensions do not have any form of their own. On this level cognitions have a direct access to reality; they grasp the object and its properties and their relatedness as is expected of Nyāya realism. Nyāya further holds that the objects determine the character of apprehensions. Had this been all, Nyāya would have said that by knowing an apprehension it is possible to know the objective situation, and it would have at once automatically become a supporter of *svataḥ-prāmāṇyavāda*. But the Naiyāyikas take a different stand. He says that reflective apprehensions have no direct access to reality.[14] If the primary apprehension is of the form "this is silver," then the corresponding reflective cognition is of the form "I know this through this-ness and silver-ness" and not "I know this (and the) silver."[15] This being so, we require further investigation to determine whether all these qualifiers are present in the object or not. Although the primary apprehension has direct access to reality, the reflective apprehension is limited only to the epistemic qualifiers. Nyāya holds that we cannot judge by looking at an apprehension whether the relatedness that appears in knowledge is objective or not. So truth cannot be grasped ab initio. If this is conceded, apprehensions assume a screen like character. All the descriptive elements involved in cognition are said to be qualifiers; only the bare "this" refers to the object. Nyāya claims that the qualifiers are determined by the object, yet the relatedness of the qualifiers and the

"this" is not so determined. So the apprehension as a whole assumes a form of its own, and further investigations are needed to ascertain its truth. Thus although Nyāya rejects the concept of correspondence, it enters into it through the backdoor. Further, when Nyāya holds that apprehension comprehends two subclasses *pramā* and *apramā*, they somehow loosen the direct link of apprehension *qua* apprehension with reality. With this in mind it is easy to understand Madhusūdana's point: to say that the ontological object and the corresponding apprehension are separate from each other and there may be disparity between the two is to lose the object which can never be successfully recovered.

As we have already mentioned, Madhusūdana criticized the Nyāya definition of truth as *tadvati tatprakārakatva* by saying that it extends to error. He says this because according to him, that which appears in an apprehension is its object. In *tadvati tatprakārakatva*, the *tadvati* refers to the ontological situation. It means that the *tat* is present in the object. But what does this presence mean? When can we say that *x* is present in *y* or *y* is the substratum of *x*? Here the mere appearance of *x* in *y* does not solve the problem, for in all apprehensions the qualifiers appear in the substratum. Let us take the case of a red crystal, where the crystal appears as red because of the proximity of a red flower. The redness as well as the whiteness appears in the substratum—why do we accept whiteness as a true qualifier and reject the claim of redness? So appearance is not the sole deciding factor. If we try to account for the situation by saying that redness has no connection with the substratum as it is later on rejected, then Madhusūdana would say that we are shifting grounds, for appearance is no more the guiding factor.

In fact, existence can never be explained in terms of appearance, for appearance in its own turn has to be explained in terms of existence and the whole discussion becomes circular. For, it is asked, "where do the qualifiers exist?" It cannot be said that they exist in the object in which they appear; for the counter question "where do the qualifiers appear?" can be answered only by the circular statement that they appear in the substratum in which they exist.

Nor can the impasse be solved by introducing the concept of *viśeṣya*, by replacing the *tadvati* by *tadvadviśeṣyakatve sati*, or by substituting the ontological object by the qualificandum or the correlate of the qualifiers. Does the term "*viśeṣya*" indicate that which as a matter of fact is the object, or that which appears as the object?[16] Here Madhusūdana is aware of the difference between the ontological object and the epistemological object. The former alternative is not acceptable, for that is the very issue under discussion; we want to find out what as a matter of fact is the object. Madhusūdana criticizes the concept of the ontological object, accessible only through the bare "that." Why should that be called the real object, when it is not necessarily the substratum of the *viśeṣaṇas* appearing in an apprehension? He argues that the epistemological object or the *viśeṣya* should be accepted as the object of cognition. If we appeal to the reports of introspection, that which appears in the cognition is called the *viśeṣya*. If we look at the nature of the practical activities that arise from a cognition, then the epis-

temological object has to be called *viśeṣya*. If it is the correlate of the qualifiers, which appear in cognition, then the qualificandum is nothing but the epistemological object.[17]

Though Madhusūdana argues that it is more rational to accept that the object which appears in cognition is the real object, he does not present any revised definition of truth. As a natural corollary of all this discussion comes the cynical conclusion that truth is a concept, which is used in our everyday life but defies precise logical determination.[18]

In other words Madhusūdana suggests that truth in the sense of such a complicated property is not tenable. Later on he would argue that truth in that sense cannot be ascertained either. We shall come to that later.

Instead of splitting and analyzing the apprehension into various parts, Madhusūdana likes to speak in terms of the whole object and the whole apprehension. Truth is that property which leads to ascertainment of a hitherto unknown object; untrue apprehensions are directed towards apparent objects only.[19] True apprehensions are directed towards real objects—objects capable of possessing unknown existence. The objects of error are not preexistent; they come into existence only with the apprehensions. To give an example, a snake seen in a rope is a false snake, for it was not there before the illusion took place; so the snake as well as the corresponding experience are untrue. But the experience of a rope as a rope is correct, for the rope is there, whether anybody experiences it or not. So truth is not identical with the initial psychological sense of certainty and it does not extend to *apramā*.

Apprehensions as well as their truth are called *sākṣi-vedya*. This means that a principle of consciousness is always there which knows the apprehensions as well as their truth, without the mediation of any mental state. Or in other words when a person sees a rope, he is aware that he is seeing it, he is also aware that he is seeing a rope that independently existed even before he saw it, whether he is explicitly aware of these implications through full-fledged mental states or not. When Madhusūdana claims that truth is *svataḥ-pramā* he means exactly this. *Vivaraṇa* asserts the same point by stating that *jñāna* originates after destroying *ajñāna*. The statement "I see a snake" implies that the previous absence of knowledge or *ajñāna* of the snake has been destroyed. Illusion, does not destroy any such absence and so it lacks the claim to be called *jñāna*.[20]

When Madhusūdana states that falsehood is apprehended through extrinsic sources, he means two things. A corrective knowledge called *bādha jñāna*, or a cognition of some defect or abnormality in the generating situation called *doṣa-jñāna*, may lead to rectification of error. Perception of snake in a rope may be corrected by a proper perception of rope, or the perception of a stick bent in water may be corrected by our knowledge that the apparent bent-ness is caused by deflection of light. However, error is always caused by some defect. The most significant word in this context is that these errors are *jñānābhāsas* or only apparent cognitions. When an apprehension previously known as true is now rejected as error, the error loses not only its claim to be true but also its claim to be *jñāna*. It is a simulating process, a distortion, which should not influence our

analysis of *jñāna* proper. Or in order to accommodate error we should not think of *jñāna* as a screenlike duplicate of reality, which might give a correct picture of reality or might not. Cognitions have direct access to reality, and errors are defects to be rejected as defects. Madhusūdana explains doubt, as an *apramā*, in the same way.

III

The conclusion emerging out of all these discussions is that the Indian philosophers have spoken of knowledge and truth in two different senses. It is true that the two contending parties mean by truth a property of awareness determined by the object. But still there is a difference. In one sense truth is nothing but the naïve compelling sense of certainty of the object, which is an essential component of an apprehension; in the more sophisticated sense it stands for a complicated relational property of apprehension determined by the object. Naturally knowledge of truth also has different meanings. According to the first sense, to know an apprehension is to know that it is true, for truth is its essential component. According to the other party knowledge of truth is by definition a reflective judgment, which compares the statement and the object, confirms that the statement asserts something about the object, which as a matter of fact is present in the object.

In all fairness to Gangeśa it must be admitted that it is he who sensed the difference between these two senses of truth for the first time. He spoke of them as *arthaniścaya* and *prāmāṇya niścaya*, as ascertainment of the object and ascertainment of truth. He holds that ascertainment of object is an essential feature of an apprehension. But the ascertainment of truth takes place only if the occasion demands. Gangeśa presents this differentiation in his answer to the traditional charge of infinite regress brought against Nyāya.

The Nyāya position in a nutshell is this: the truths of all apprehensions are known through inferences. In most cases these inferences are based on familiarity, that is, similarity to clearly true and familiar apprehensions. But in the case of novel apprehensions (*anabhyāsadaśotpanna jñāna*) truth is inferred through *samvādajñāna*, or apprehension of coherence, and/or *phalajñāna* or apprehension of successful activity issuing out of the primary cognition. Here the critics urge that the Nyāya position involves a vicious infinite regress. The truth of a primary apprehension is known through an inference, but how do we know the truth of this inference, and the truth of the apprehensions involved in these inferences, such as *samvādajñāna*, *phalajñāna*, etc.? If it is known through some other inference then that inference, in its own turn needs to be justified, and so on ad infinitum.

The Naiyāyikas have answered this charge in two ways. Some of them, like Vācaspati, have said that apprehensions involved in confirmatory inference,

such as inferential processes, *samvādajñāna*, etc., are self valid, hence they need not be examined again, and thus there is no infinite regress.[21] They have of course added the explanatory note that these are *svataḥ pramā* in a very special sense. Truth in the sense of *tadvati tatprakārakatva* is not grasped immediately, but they are self valid in the sense that under no situation may their truth be doubted, and as they are beyond doubt we do not require any inference to test their validity and as such the question of regress does not arise.

Gangeśa has a slightly different answer. He says that all apprehensions involve ascertainment of object, and this is sufficient for all our practical dealings. But under special circumstances, if we doubt the claim of the initial knowledge to reveal reality, that is, if there is doubt about the certainty of the object of the primary apprehension, the normalcy of the situation is disturbed and there cannot be any unwavering activity. Now the certainty can be restored only by ascertaining the truth of the apprehension and we take recourse to inference which seeks out the truth.[22] The inference can always perform its duty without itself being justified; it has to be examined only if fresh occasions cause doubt about its validity; hence under ordinary circumstances the question of regress does not arise.

Gangeśa's answer to the charge is interesting. The *svataḥ-prāmāṇyavādin* has not denied all this, only he has given a very different interpretation of the whole situation.

We have previously said that the concept of truth as *tadvati tatprakārakatva* is untenable according to the Advaitins. They also urge that had it been tenable, because of the very nature of the concept, it would have been impossible to ascertain it. The confirmatory inferences can only confirm the initial sense of certainty, but in what way is it indicator of *tadvati tatprakārakatva*? Gangeśa himself was aware of these difficulties. Thus he poses the problem: how is truth as *tadvati tatprakārakatva* known for the first time?

The *svataḥ-prāmāṇyavāda* has criticized the superior claim of the confirmatory cognitions, to reveal reality in many places. Time and again they have pointed out that confirmation, coherence, etc., are found in wish-fulfillment dreams. These are found to be dreams when we wake up, hence why should we attach a superior sense of certainty to them? When we look at water we may doubt our perception, but when we go and touch it or taste it, we find that it is water and we confirm our previous perception. Here we are only advocating the superiority of touch over vision, but why should we propose such a differential treatment?

But then, the critic would surely ask: if confirmation is not valuable, how is it that we use so much of confirmation in our everyday life? When new grounds are trodden the scientists repeat their experiments again and again, to confirm their hypothesis. In philosophical literature philosophers have spoken highly about confirmation. These have been called the ends of cognitive situations. What is the significance of all this? How do we come out of the impasse, when there is doubt about the truth of a certain apprehension, unless we rely upon confirmatory cognitions?

In classical Advaita we get the answer in *Vivaraṇa-Prameya-Saṃgraha*. There it is said that the later apprehensions are necessary, not to find out or confirm truth, but to dispel doubt or reject error.[23] So it can be proposed that the scientists repeat their experiments to find out the mistakes if there be any, and not to confirm truth.

Both the Advaitins and Gangeśa agree that in every apprehension there is ascertainment of the object. But whereas the Advaitin further holds that here we are implicitly also aware that the apprehensions correctly ascertain the hitherto unknown object, the Nyāya speaks of no such awareness. Again both of them agree that we take up further enquiry only in cases of doubt. But, whereas Gangeśa holds that the further enquiry leads to ascertainment of truth, the Advaitin holds that ascertainment of truth in the Nyāya sense is impossible, it only leads to discovery of the defects, which led to the emergence of doubt.

Madhusūdana asserts that apprehensions are of two types, one in which defects and disturbing factors are present, another in which they are absent. In the former the natural apprehension of truth is absent and the question of revision arises.[24] In this sense even novelty and unfamiliarity, which have been called *anabhyāsa*, are defects, and we take up enquiry to get rid of these defects. To give a very simple example, if in the darkness we see something like a snake, we bring a torch and try to remove the darkness; if in the proper light we see that the apparent snake is just a rope, we give up our previous apprehension, be it doubt or error, and there it ends, we do not get involved in the analysis of proper cognition.

Ascertainments, whether true or false, are complete in themselves; it is doubt which issues in further inquiry. The doubt may be of two types. One is doubt proper, which is a very unstable state of mind. Because of some hindrances and disturbances the proper apprehension does not take place. Here we have some idea about the object, but not any definite knowledge; alternative predicates suggest themselves and we do not know which one to choose. Such uneasiness can be solved by a removal of defects. To go back to the naïve example given above, by bringing in light, we solve the doubt, "is it a snake or a rope?"

The other type of doubt is the philosophical doubt, doubt associated with academic skepticism, doubt for doubt's sake, a doubt which can never be resolved. In Indian philosophy such doubt is rare. Truth is natural, all our experiences involve a compelling sense of certainty, which does not demand any justification. All those questions arise in case of doubt. But doubt arises only in abnormal circumstances and doubt must not be universalized.

The last question, which remains to be answered, is that if truth be apprehended in true and erroneous cognitions alike, how does it serve to differentiate between the two? Here the conclusion, which seems to be most consistent with the arguments advanced by *svataḥ-prāmāṇyavāda*, is that truth is not a property at all. When the Advaitins state that *jñāna* and *pramā* are identical, he obviously denies the traditional explication that *pramā* is *jñāna* plus truth. He is trying to

take the stand that truth is the essential character of all apprehensions. Just as heat is to fire so also truth is to cognitions. It is something so natural, that we are not explicitly aware of its presence, unless and until some very special occasion makes us consciously reflective of its presence. To give a very material analogy it is something like health; we are not fully aware of its presence as long as it is there, but its absence makes us fully conscious of its previous presence.

Actually, the emphasis is totally on error. *Svataḥ-prāmāṇyavāda* has defined error, and has given different criteria of error. We can take *svataḥ-prāmāṇyavāda* as saying that to focus on and explain error, we posit a certain property called truth, but that is probably unnecessary.

In Indian philosophy error has been treated as a very important phenomenon. Even Gangeśa has not been able to deny its importance. When Gangeśa tries to find out the philosophical derivation of the concept of truth, he first lands on the concept of truth as absence of error. To quote J. N. Mohanty, "Gangeśa has said that the first apprehension truth is not of truth qua truth, but of truth taken as absence of falsity."[25] We find the same emphasis in *svataḥ-prāmāṇyavāda*. Its approach is that in order to accommodate error, we must not distort the nature of ordinary apprehension. A criterion of truth is necessary to dispel doubt, explain error, and confirm certainty. But the very concept of the "criterion of truth" is riddled with confusion. To say that the confirmatory cognition is self-justifying is to be inconsistent, for the very demand for the confirmatory cognition shows that the claim of cognition to truth is dubitable. Now, if by calling all cognitions true by their own right, and if by introducing a concept of truth we can explain error and dispel doubt, why not do it?

It is to be noted that although the importance of error has been equally acknowledged by both Nyāya and Advaita, their concept of truth vis-à-vis error is diametrically opposite. In Nyāya both truth and error are equally fundamental, so that each of them can be described as the negation of the other. Here positive and negative descriptions are interchangeable; *pramā* has been as much described as *samvādi* or coherent, as *avisamvādi* or non-incoherent. If Gangeśa has spoken of inference as grasping *pramā* as absence of error, there are many Naiyāyikas, starting from Gotama and Vātsyāyana, who hold that successful activity certifies that the cognition is true of the corresponding object.

But such negative descriptions of *pramātva* should not be welcome to the classical Vedāntin. Much has been made of *abādhitatva*, which was admitted by *Vedānta Paribhāsa* as the mark of truth. But to accept absence of falsification as the negative mark of truth, or absence of *doṣa* or defect as a factor operative in generation of truth, is to sacrifice the robust *svataḥ-prāmāṇyavāda* of Advaita. All the Advaitins agree that *bādha* or correction is the sign of error. They all agree that the absence of possibility of falsification in the past, present, and future is the essence of the highest metaphysical truth.[26] But they are divided among themselves about the tenability of *abādhitatva* as a mark of truth, with reference to empirical apprehensions. Śrīharṣa, the Vaitandika, has criticized it; Madhusūdana in his Advaitasiddhi has tried to retain it with many modifica-

tions. Citsukha in his *Tattvapradīpikā* has in unambiguous language dismissed any attempt to incorporate negative factors.

Citsukha asserts that the intrinsic nature of *prāmāṇya* means that it is produced by the factors, which produce the cognition and by nothing ab extra; these extras cover as much *guṇas* as absence of defects; to accept either/both of them is to accept too much. He goes on that it cannot be argued that as defects are conditions of errors, so by implication absence of defect is a necessary condition of truth. The mark of causality is unconditional invariability, whereas absence of defect is directly related to error, being responsible for its frustration. So it is related to truth, *via* absence of error, and it is not a necessary condition of truth. So the acceptance of absence of defect as a factor is baseless, and *pramā* originates from the conditions of cognition.[27]

In a similar way he says the corrective cognition is necessary for the detection of error, but this must not be construed to imply that the absence of awareness of falsification leads to apprehension of *prāmāṇya* The conditions responsible for the apprehension of the cognition are responsible for the apprehension of *prāmāṇya*, too. He repeats that error is known by corrective cognition or awareness of defect, yet their absence is not the cause of apprehension of truth. In fact he holds that if awareness of the absence of these two cognitions is admitted to be operative, then the *svataḥ* theory too would be subject to the fallacy of infinite regress.[28] I think that this is the most consistent explanation of the position. In Advaita truth is fundamental, error is an accidental exception[29] and to look at absence of falsification as a criterion of truth is to miss the real point of *svataḥ-prāmāṇyavāda.*

I have discussed to some extent all the questions I have raised. There remains only one charge, namely, *svataḥ-prāmāṇyavāda* glosses over the commonly accepted difference between knowledge and belief. I would like to take up the discussion in detail in some other place, but here I suggest the following explanation. According to this theory all cognitions are true unless proved otherwise, and justification does not increase the truth-value of the initial apprehension. The above accusation would be correct, if it is an accusation at all. However, in this theory apprehensions are not beliefs, if beliefs stand for the apprehensions, which we entertain, knowing full well that they may be untrue; nor are they knowledge, if knowledge stands for apprehensions which absolutely disallow any future chance of revision. The former they would perhaps categorize as an instance of doubt where due to some defect, say, lack of proper awareness of all the associated facts, the proper apprehension has not taken place, but would be resolved with further progress of knowledge.

Some critics may urge that to accept *svataḥ-prāmāṇyavāda* is to say that there can be no finality in our epistemic claims, for what is called *jñāna* today may turn out to be *jñānābhāsa* tomorrow. This, however, I feel speaks for *svataḥ-prāmāṇyavāda* for the history of science is a history of discarded certainties, in which what has been called *jñāna* by thinkers of one generation have been given up by those of the next age, when they have been found to involve

defects. It should be agreed by all concerned that finality is an ever-eluding aim, which recedes more and more with the advancement of knowledge.

Notes

1. J. N. Mohanty, *Gangeśa's Theory of Truth* (Visva-Bharati, Santiniketan, India: Centre of Advanced Study, 1966), *svataste prāmāṇyavata eva jñānasya grahāt*, 99.
2. Mohanty, *Gangeśa*, 93.
3. Mohanty, *Gangeśa*, 24.
4. Kumārila Bhaṭṭa, *Slokavārtika*, ed. S. K. R. Sastri (Madras, India: 1940), *Tasmād bodhātmakatvena prāptā buddheḥ pramāṇatā, Arthānyathātva hetutthaḥ doṣajñānād apodyate*, II/53.
5. Madhusūdana Sarasvati, *Advaitaratnarakṣaṇam* (Bombay, India: Nirnaya Sagar, 1917), *Na hi hetvābhāso hetur bhavati tāvad na jñānābhāsasya jñānatvam*, 33.
6. Vidyāraṇya, *Vivaraṇa-Prameya-Saṃgraha*, Part II, ed. Pramathanath Tarkabhusan, (Calcutta, India: Basumati Sahitya Mandir, 1927), 226.
7. Madhusūdana, *Advaitaratnarakṣaṇam*, 34.
8. Vidyāraṇya, *Vivaraṇa, Prāmāṇyam nāma jñānanasyārthapariccheda-sāmarthyam*, vol. II, 223.
9. Madhusūdana, *Advaitaratnarakṣaṇam*, 29.
10. Srīharṣa, *Khandanakhandakhādya*, ed. K. P. Sastri and G. N. Vayapurkar (Kasi, India).
11. Madhusūdana, *Advaitaratnarakṣaṇam*, 28, and Srīharṣa, *Khandana-khandakhādya*, 148.
12. Srīharṣa, *Khandanakhandakhādya*, 154.
13. Mohanty, *Gangeśa*, 37.
14. Mohanty, *Gangeśa, Maivam, idam rajatañca jānāmīti, nānuvyavasāya vahirviśesyake manaso'svātantryāt*, 154.
15. Mohanty, *Gangeśa kintvidam idantvena rajatatvena jānāmīti*, 154.
16. Madhusūdana, *Advaitaratnarakṣaṇam*, *Tathā hi kim vastu-gatyā yasmin jñāne yad viśeṣyam tatra yo dharma iti vā kim vā yasmin jñāne viśeṣyatvena yo bhāsate tasmin yo dharma iti vā.*
17. Madhusūdana, *Advaitaratnarakṣaṇam*, 30.
18. Madhusūdana, *Advaitaratnarakṣaṇam, Pramātvam anirvacanīyam lokasiddham*, 32.
19. Madhusūdana, *Advaitaratnarakṣaṇam, Kimajñātārtha-niscayātmaka-tvameva prāmāṇyam*, 32.
20. Madhusūdana, *Advaitaratnarakṣaṇam*, 33.
21. *Nyāydarśana*, ed. Taranath Nyayatarkatirtha & Amarendramohan Tarkatirtha (Calcutta, 1936), 9.
22. Mohanty, *Gangeśa*, 217.
23. Vidyāraṇya, *Vivaraṇa, Tatradvitīyādi jñānāni-prathama-jñānaprāmāṇya pratibandhaka samśāyadinirāsīni na tu tatprāmānya-niścāyakāni*, 225.
24. Madhusūdana, *Advaitaratnarakṣaṇam*, 34.
25. Mohanty, *Gangeśa*, 183.

26. Madhusūdana Sarasvati, *Advaitasiddhi*, vol. II (Mysore, 1937) *Trikālābādhyatva-rūpa tātvikaprāmāṇyam* 184; vol. I *Kasminnapi deśe kasminnapi kāle kenāpi puruṣenābādhyatvam hi pāramārthika sattvam*, 397.

27. Citsukha, *Tattvapradīpikā*, ed. Swami Yogindrananda (Kasi, India: Udasīna Samskrita Vidyālaya, 1956), *Vijñanasāmagrījanyatve sati tadatirikta-hetvajanyatvam pramāyāḥ svatastvam nāma. Vijñānasāmagrīmātrādeva prathamotpattisambhave tadatiriktasya guṇasya doṣābhāvatvasya vā karaṇatva kalpanā gaurava prasamgāt*, 215-216.

28. Citsukha, *Tattvapradīpikā, Tathā pramājñaptirapi vijñānajñāpaka sāmagrīta eva*, 218.

29. Madhusūdana, *Advaitaratnarakṣaṇam, Apramātvasya tu kācitkatvāt.*

30. Here I draw the reader's attention to an article "*Jñāna* and *Pramā*: The Logic of Knowing—A Critical Appraisal" by Purusottam Bilimoria, which appeared in the *Journal of Indian Philosophy* vol. 13, no. 1, March 1985. My position is definitely opposed to the compromise suggested by the author towards the end of that article. He tries to bring two approaches to truth (Nyāya and Advaita) a little closer. There he says that both the schools can be interpreted as saying that "a true cognition is a cognition, that is not falsified or shown to be false." My stand is that this is permissible in Nyāya but not in Advaita. In fact I have argued that the gap between the two is unbridgeable, for the views on *prāmāṇya* are necessarily linked to the respective analysis of the structure of cognition.

I have already discussed that the very concept of the criterion of truth is repugnant to the Advaitin. So I do not agree with the author when he suggests that absence of falsification, etc. are accepted as a corroborative test of what already appears to be true, or when he asserts that "In principle however Advaita does not find any difficulty in agreeing with Nyāya, on the viability of any, may be all, of the criteria proposed." I would rather agree with the comment of the same author that "Advaita does not believe in the efficacy of the empirical modes of establishing truth in contradistinction to falsity" or when he suggests that the criterial marks are used to ascertain the absence of falsity and not to ascertain truth as in the case of Nyāya.

Svataḥ-Prāmāṇyavāda in Mīmāṃsā

Svataḥ-prāmāṇyavāda asserts that *prāmāṇya* is intrinsic to cognition. The term "*prāmāṇya*" is derived from the word "*pramāṇa*" which has two meanings in Indian epistemology. In the first sense, it stands for *karaṇa*, which generates *pramā* or valid cognition. The prefix "*pra*" signifies excellence while the root "*mā*" means "to measure." So *pramāṇas* are supposed to measure well; they are as much causes as proofs. They measure the truth-value of true cognition. In the second sense, *pramāṇas* are considered to be identical with true cognition.[1] So *prāmāṇya* is truth.

Svataḥ-prāmāṇyavāda asserts that truth constitutes an integral part of cognition. All schools of Indian thought have participated in a discussion of the above view either as an exponent or as a disputant. Traditionally, the relation of truth and cognition has mainly been discussed under two heads: origination and apprehension. In other words they have discussed whether the conditions, which produce cognition, also produce truth or not. They have also discussed whether all the cognitions, which grasp the primary cognition, grasp its truth or not. In both the cases *Svataḥ-prāmāṇyavāda* accepts the affirmative clauses. I propose to discuss the views of the Mīmāṃsakas who supported this view.

Originally, the motive behind the Mīmāṃsā position was the justification of the authority of the Vedas. The Mīmāṃsakas do not accept the existence of God, so the truth of the scriptures cannot be guaranteed by appealing to the veracity of the divine author. They hold that the true cognitions are self-certifying. Later on from this position they developed an interesting concept about cognition and knowledge, *jñāna* and *pramā*, which I discuss here.

The Mīmāṃsakas are subdivided into three classes: the Prābhākaras, the Bhāṭṭas, and the Miśras. They all support *Svataḥ-prāmāṇyavāda*, and they all agree that when cognitions are known, they are known as true. But they differ from each other on the question of the nature of cognition, which grasps the primary cognition. The Prābhākaras hold that cognitions are self-manifesting. Like a lamp, cognition illuminates the object, the knower, and also itself. In

cognition there is *triputibhāna* or revelation of all three factors. The Miśras hold that a second order cognition or *anuvyavasāya* perceives the primary cognition. The Bhāṭṭas hold that this second cognition is inferential in nature. The initial cognition produces a quality called knownness or *jñātatā* in the object (or in the subject), on the basis of which the existence of the primary cognition is inferred.

To cover all these three views the "*sva*" in the "*svataḥ*" has been explained in two ways—it stands for itself and for that which is related to itself.[2] The opponents also accept this by saying that "*svataḥ*" means either from itself or from that, which is related to itself.[3] In the present context this means that truth is either apprehended by the substratum of truth or the cognition itself (as is held by the Prābhākaras) or by that which is related to the cognition (i.e., the perceptual cognition or the inferential cognition apprehending the initial cognition as is held by the Miśras and the Bhāṭṭas). We shall see that in a way the Bhāṭṭas also hold that truth is apprehended by the initial cognition. We shall come back to this later.

The Naiyāyikas are the main opponents of the above theory. Gaṇgeśa, in his *Prāmāṇyavāda*, has prefaced his defence of *parataḥ-prāmāṇyavāda*, by making his position clear through a series of *vipratipattis*. These are precise formulations of the *pūrvapakṣa* and its opposite, which makes a critical appraisal easy. Let us look at two of his formulations of the *svataḥpakṣa*. Here he is discussing the issue regarding the apprehension of truth. His first formulation is: *jñāna prāmāṇyaṃ tadaprāmāṇyāgrāhaka yāvaj jñāna-grāhaka sāmagrī-grāhya* or the truth of a cognition is apprehended by all cognitions, which are generated by the conditions, which produce a cognition of the initial cognition, excluding the cognitions, which apprehend its invalidity.[4] As here the exact nature of the cognition, which apprehends the initial cognition, has not been specified, so the description applies to all the three versions of the Mīmāṃsā School. Another one is *tajjñāna-viṣayaka jñānājanyam jñānagrāhya* or truth of cognition is grasped by a cognition, which has not been produced by a cognition, which has the initial cognition as its object.[5] This description is also common to all three. A comment coming from Gaṇgeśa is significant and it makes the issue clear. On the *parataḥ* theory truth is apprehended only after a cognition has been known, on the *svataḥ* theory a cognition is apprehend as possessing truth.[6]

We see that, in Gaṇgeśa's formulation, all the Mīmāmsaka positions have been clubbed together, for their conclusion is the same. They support the naïve view that all assertive cognitions are true, unless proved otherwise. In Indian tradition they differ from each other because they differ on the nature of the cognition, which grasps the cognition under consideration. But I find that their differences are not so superficial.

In fact, I have dwelt upon the Prābhākara and the Bhāṭṭa versions in separate sections because their treatments of the problem, their presuppositions and attitudes are all different, and their corresponding analyses of cognition are also different. Although the Miśra views are recognized as a third position, I have not discussed it at all, because no original Miśra book is available and I am not interested in reconstructing the view from references here and there.

The Indian thinkers have discussed the relation of *aprāmāṇya* with cognition too. They take five different positions in this regard:

a. *Prāmānya* is intrinsic and *aprāmānyą* is extrinsic to cognitions.
b. Both *prāmāṇya* and *aprāmāṇya* are extrinsic to cognitions.
c. Both *prāmāṇya* and *aprāmāṇya* are intrinsic to cognitions.
d. *Prāmāṇya* is extrinsic and *aprāmāṇya* is intrinsic to cognitions.
e. Both *prāmāṇya* and *aprāmāṇya* are sometimes intrinsic and sometimes extrinsic to cognitions.

The Mīmāṃsakas support position a. The second view is held by the Naiyāyikas and they are the real opponents of the Mīmāṃsakas. Both are robust realists. Both hold that cognitions are transparent mediums, which have a direct access to reality. Yet, whereas the Mīmāṃsakas staunchly support *Svataḥ-prāmāṇyavāda*, the Naiyāyikas wholeheartedly reject it. This is because their ideas about truth and cognitions are different.

The Sāṃkhyas support position c and the Buddhists adhere to position d. Both these views are metaphysically loaded. Position c is a direct corollary of the fundamental Sāṃkhya theory of *satkāryavāda*, while position d is traceable to one of the major schools of Buddhism and is implied by its general theory of momentariness. These Buddhists claim that the conceptual apparatus cannot grasp reality that is composed of momentary, unique, *svalakṣaṇa* particulars. Truth, defined in pragmatic terms or *arthakriyākāritva*, is later ascribed to cognitions through success of activities, which issue out of cognition. I do not discuss these views because it is difficult to abstract them from their strong ontology. Some other Buddhist thinkers support the last position.

Let us turn to the problem of *prāmāṇya* from the standpoint of generation. The Mīmāṃsakas consistently hold that the conditions which produce cognitions also produce its truth, while errors are produced by *doṣas* which are faults and deficiencies. They are the vitiating factors that destroy the normalcy of the cognitive situation. The Naiyāyikas accept the same analysis of *apramā*. But they hold that *pramātva* is traceable to excellences present in the generating conditions called *guṇas*, or, in other words, cognitions are neutral, as far as their truth-value is concerned.

I shall close this introductory section by briefly stating the problem which *Svataḥ-prāmāṇyavāda* faces. Commonly, truth is supposed to be a property which is present only in true cognitions as a differentia that separates true cognitions from untrue ones. In Indian thought these untrue cognitions or *apramā* include direct errors such as illusion, hallucination, dream, deviant perception, etc., and also doubt, *tarka*, and memory. The last three are not problematic because they are known to be *apramā* by their very form. Errors come disguised as true cognitions and their erroneous character is detected later. *Svataḥ-prāmāṇyavāda* has to admit that these are grasped as true initially. The burden falls on it to explain how truth is present and is known in true and erroneous cognitions alike and yet it serves to differentiate the true cognitions

from the false ones. Further, in ordinary life and in the vast tracts of philosophical literature, knowledge is called justified true belief; but if truth is grasped ab initio, then the theory has to explain the role of justification in the knowledge situation.

The Naiyāyikas hold that these justificatory cognitions lead to the ascertainment of truth. The fallacy of vicious infinite regress is hurled against them. If the truth of the initial cognition is known through the verificatory cognition, then the truth of this one has to be ascertained, in its own turn, and the series goes on ad infinitum and there is no stopping place. The search for a stopping place often leads to foundationalism, where some cognitions are marked as self-evident and very different from the bulk of our knowledge, which form the structure based on that solid foundation. We shall see that Nyāya and Mīmāṃsā are commonsense philosophers, who have not felt the need for finding some such foundation, which are beyond all doubt. The truths accepted as self-evident have been accepted as self-evident, but they have not been treated as foundations.

We shall come across all these discussions in more detail later.

I

Prabhākara's analysis of *jñāna* and *pramā* show that he believes in *Svataḥ-prāmāṇyavāda*, but he never explicitly says this. In the writings of later Mīmāṃsakas, such as Rāmānujācārya or Bhavanāth Miśra, we come across an explicit admission that they accepted this theory.

The Prābhākara position is confusing because they have introduced different synonyms of truth and each of them has distinctly different meanings. Rāmānujācārya speaks of these as *yāthārthya*, *prāmāṇya*, and *samyaktva*. *Yāthārthya* is the property of being the cognitive awareness of its own object. It is shared by all cognitions alike. It is not to be confused with mere referential character or object-directedness of cognitive awareness. It is well known that the Prābhākaras do not accept any error in the cognitive level; Rāmānujācārya declares that all cognitions are *arthāvyabhicāri* or non-deviant of their objects. This property of cognitions is called *yāthārthya.* Next in extension is *prāmāṇya*; it is the property of being cognition other than memory. This is *anubhuti* or direct experience. Traditionally, almost all the systems have banished memory from the realm of true cognition, and have variously tried to justify their stand. In the third sense, truth is *samyaktva*, which is the property of being cognition, which issues successful activity. *Tantrarahasya* claims that when there is *vyavahāra-visaṃvāda* or discrepant activity, the cognition is erroneous. *Samyaktva* is present in all cognitions, irrespective of its being memory or *anubhuti*, barring these cognitions, which issue discrepant activity.[7] To sum up, truth has three distinct meanings: the property of being non-deviant of its object, the property of not being memory, and the property of not leading to discrepant

practice. Our common belief is that the first and the third go hand in hand, and when cognition manifests its object properly, the ensuing activity is successful. However, the Prābhākaras do not accept this. All cognitions are non-deviant, they manifest objects as they are, yet some of them might fail to produce successful activity. In other words, some cognitions are *yathārtha*, yet they might lack *samyaktva*. The confusing point is that in this system truth is *yāthārthya*, but they explain untruth as absence of *samyaktva*.

It is obvious that truth in the second or the third sense cannot be self-manifesting. Some external criterion is necessary for ascertainment of the presence of such truth. According to the Prābhākaras truth in the first sense is inherent in all cognitions. Some scholars have held that they have accepted truth as both extrinsic and intrinsic. Historically, with the exclusion of Prabhākara himself, almost all his followers have labeled themselves as *svataḥ-prāmāṇya-vādins*. They held that truth in the first sense is inherent in all cognitions, and is grasped whenever the cognition is known. Let us look at the three senses in more detail.

The Prābhākaras do not accept error in the theoretical level. As they do not accept error as a cognitive phenomenon, the onus falls on them to give a plausible explanation of error. Error is split into two cognitions, and there is a non-apprehension of the non-relation between the two. Usually, of the two cognitions, one is said to be presentative and the other is memory. In the snake rope illusion, there is perception of the rope and memory of the snake, and the knower is unaware of the non-relation of the content of perception and memory. They explain it as an omission and as partial experience. They do not accept that error has a positive content, or there is a positive awareness of a nonexistent relatedness. What is positively wrong is the ensuing *vyavahāra*, and that is to be corrected. Let us follow the explanation given by *Tantrarahasya*.[8] It says that after correction of error, the object of the previous cognition is not to be discarded, for both the cognitions, the initial one and the corrective one, are equally *yathārtha*, or are equally true of their object. There is only discrepancy in behavior. A cognition is never sublated, for it is always *yathārtha*. The difficulty lies with the behavior.

Truth in the sense of *prāmāṇya* is traceable to the *sūtras*, which for very specific reasons attached great importance to it. They held that authoritative knowledge is true, because it is not dependent. The Bhāṣya explains that the truth of the scriptures is self-certifying, being dependent neither on any person nor on any previous knowledge.[9] Thus memory is here excluded from the purview of knowledge.

Traditionally, memory has been assigned lesser truth-value by the Mīmāṃsakas and the Naiyāyikas alike. Different arguments have been advanced. The *Ṛjuvimalāpañcikā* states that memory has been declared untrue on the ground that it does not manifest its object explicitly.[10] But this argument is not sufficiently persuasive, and the objection comes from within the system. Their explanation of error claims that there is confusion (in the shape of non-apprehension) between the content of memory and that of the presentative

cognition. Bhavanāth Miśra points out that if there is a qualitative difference between the two, non-apprehension of non-relation would be impossible.[11]

The denial of the claim of memory to be a species of true cognition has been very much a matter of tradition. The Bhāṭṭas and the Advaitins have accepted the property of not knowing an object as previously known as an integral constituent of truth, but they more or less hold that this property can only be known extrinsically, so it does not fall within the scope of our discussion. In fact *Vedānta Paribhāṣa* gives two definitions of *pramā*, one of them excludes memory and the other includes it.[12]

The arguments given by the Naiyāyikas are twofold. The first group admits that memory reports its object correctly, but still it is not *pramā*. For it does not issue any activity immediately, first its truth has to be inferred. It has lesser truth-value, because it borrows the same from the initial cognition. The second group claims that memory deviates from the object and is *ayathārtha*. The *Prakāśatīkā* says that it can indeed be asked, when a memory and an *anubhuti* have the same object, how is it that we call one true and the other untrue? The answer is twofold: First, during the time of *anubhuti*, the object is reported as it is by the experience, whereas memory is directed to the past object. Second, the *it* of presentative experience is turned into *that* of memory, which reduces its claim to truth.

But the Prābhākaras do not call memory *ayathārtha*. *Tantrarahasya* explicitly says that *yāthārthe'pi smṛiraprамāṇam* or in spite of being *yathārtha* or true of its object, memory is *apramāṇa*.[13] *Aprāmāṇya* is here just a synonym of recollectedness or the property of being memory and in the Prābhākara theory of *svataḥ-prāmāṇyavāda* it has no implication at all. In other words memory is *apramā* in a very technical specific sense. It is *yathārtha*—it does not deviate from its object. *Prakaraṇapañcikā* asserts that all cognitive awareness are awareness of their own objects. *Nayaviveka* says that no cognition is not proper, no cognition deviate from its object.[14] And they are here speaking about all cognitions, including memory. Further, we shall see that the Prābhākaras are not speaking about the epistemological object. Their position is that all cognitions *qua* cognitions are true and proper.

The Prābhākaras do not intend to deny *loka-vyavahāra* or common usage; they give their own explanation of irregularities called error.[15] This is shown by their acceptance of truth called *samyaktva*. But here after correction, the question of revising the cognitive status of the initial cognition does not arise; error is banished to the realm of action. There is *vyavahāra visaṃvāda* and the *vyavahāra* is to be rejected. So, although *samyaktva* is admitted as a property of cognitions, which issue successful activity, on the cognitive level it actually has no implication.

In the later Prābhākara philosophy, we come across the stereotyped discussions of the position. I think it would be more interesting to glimpse the original position held by Prabhākara, when the difference between ontology and epistemology was yet to emerge.

Prabhākara originally developed his position to counter the Buddhist theory of *Nirālambanavāda*. He is not participating in a debate in epistemology, where the stage is set by the Naiyāyikas and the focus is on the nature of knowledge. He is trying to establish the truth of judgmental cognition and he is mainly concerned with the ontological implication of the nature of knowledge. His discussions contain the seeds of arguments, which were developed by the later Prābhākaras. In doing this he takes up an extreme position that even the apparent errors are true in the cognitive level.

Let me present Prabhākara's original position under four broad arguments:

a. The *pūrvapakṣa* grants to the object of cognition *ālambanatva,* but not *paricchedyatva*; or the object produces the cognition but it is not manifested by it. Only the *nirvikalpaka* or the prejudgmental cognition has direct access to it; the judgmental cognition uses concepts and names, and so alters and adds to the given. Hence it does not faithfully depict the given. In Buddhist literature the judgmental cognition is called *samvṛti*, or that which conceals the true nature of the object.

Here the obvious assumption is that cognitions are *sākāra*. The content of cognition is immanent in it, it does not belong to the object, nor is it produced by it. This is further corroborated by their analysis of error. They claim that the silver that appears in error is a part of the cognition and it does not belong to the object, which is the shell here.

The Prabhākara answer is that it is impossible that the object involves one *ākāra* and the cognition another. An object is said to be an object, because it produces a cognition, which involves its own *ākāra*.[16] Prabhākara argues that in a cognition two contents are never detected, hence, why should we hold that the object has a different nature from the content of cognition? In error the silver is the object, only the cognition is not perception, but is memory. There is non-apprehension of the non-relation between the object of memory and perception. The Prābhākaras, as a school, have emphasized this concept of objectivity.

The object is not the bare cause of the cognition. Had that been the definition, the *karaṇas* would become the object. According to the Prābhākaras, that which produces the cognition and at the same time whose form is manifested by the cognitions is the cause. The Naiyāyikas have suggested that the presented locus towards which the activities are directed and in which the activities are realized is the object.[17] Thus in the crucial instance of silver shell illusion, the shell is the object. On the other hand, according to the Prābhākaras, the specific nature of the object, which arouses the activity, is more important in the cognitive situation. So here it is the silver and not the shell. *Nayaviveka* argues that whatever is *vyavahārānuguṇa* or favorable to activity is the object.[18] Nandīśwara is even more direct in *Prabhākaravijaya.* He rejects the above explanation, which appeals to action because preconceptual cognitions do not issue any action yet they have objects. He says that whatever is manifested in a cognition is its object—*viṣayavyavasthā bhāsamānatayā vācyā*—it is silver in the given situation.[19]

The Prābhākaras unanimously accept this analysis. Śālikanātha says that a thing which appears in cognition is to be called its object and no other criterion can decide what is an object and what is not.[20] They say that the explanation of error as an appearance of x as y is not acceptable, for we never experience it in that way, the introspective report is never of the form that the silver is essentially a shell. Even the Naiyāyikas, the opponents, have presented the Prābhākara position in this way; they mean by the object that which is manifested in cognitions, and manifestation means that by describing which a cognition is generated.

b. The second argument is more or less a continuation of the first one. It takes up the instances of dream and doubt and tries to explain how the above mentioned definition of objectivity applies to them. The explanations given by the exponent and the opponent are equally forced and one-sided and both of them deny that dream is something radically different from normal cognitions. The Buddhists analyze error and extend that explanation to ordinary cognitions, whereas the Prābhākaras do the opposite. The Buddhists are supposed to say that cognitions cannot have any real object, being cognition, the instance in point being dream. They hold that dream, as well as other cognitions, are products of *vāsanā*. The generalization is here defended by the law of parsimony. Explanation by appeal to real objects is not acceptable as it fails to explain dreams. It is said to commit the fallacy of *avyāpti*. The Prābhākara answer is that cognition is not possible without object, so even in dreams presence of objects is to be accepted. A likely rejoinder from the Buddhist is that if there is an object in dream then how can it be false? In answer to this the Prābhākara argues that if there is no object how can there be any cognition at all? These arguments are naïve for they take for granted whatever they want to establish. But a comment coming from the Prābhākaras in this discussion is valuable and suggestive.

The Prābhākara position is that if the falsity of dream is traceable to the essential nature of cognitions, then the objectlessness of dream could be extended to other cognitions, too. But the irregular nature of dream is traceable to defects such as sleep, weak sense organ, etc. So discrepancies created by accidental factors should not disturb our analysis of cognition proper. This comment contains the central truth of *Svataḥ-prāmāṇyavāda*. The theory asserts that under normal circumstances all cognitions are true, and they manifest objects. Accidental factors destroy this normalcy, and they should not affect our analysis of cognition proper. Herein lie the foundations of *parataḥ-aprāmāṇya-vāda* as regards generation. It asserts that *apramā* is produced by defects, which disturb the normal conditions producing cognitions.

c. The third argument focuses on the *ākāra* or the form of cognition. *Ākara*, more or less, stands for the content of direct cognition. According to every Indian thinker the immediate perceptual experience involves a form; the perception of a blue lotus involves the *ākāra* of blue lotus. The Buddhists hold that the cognitions are *sākāra* or have a form of their own, which comes from the object. Such a theory is apparently very accommodating to *Svataḥ-prāmāṇyavāda*, for apprehending cognition would amount to apprehending the corresponding

object. But such is not the case; the Buddhists are supposed to hold that in error the cognitions assume the form of false objects.

The Prābhākaras hold that cognitions are transparent mediums through which the reality is manifested. This is staunch uncompromising realism. The natural corollary is that to know the cognition is to know the world. The Naiyāyikas, the opponents, also hold that cognitions have a direct access to reality and they do not have a form of their own. So, why do they reject *svataḥ-prāmāṇyavāda*? It is to be remembered that they accept formlessness of cognitions on some ontological grounds. For example, they hold that a quality cannot be a seat of another quality, and cognition, being a quality inhering in the self, cannot have a form or *ākāra*, as an attribute. But then, epistemologically, they analyze cognitions into *viṣayatā, prakaratā*, etc., which are cognitional properties. Hence they claim that further cognitions are necessary to discern truth, which involves a relation of cognition and reality. In this part of the discussion, Prabhākara insists that cognitions are formless. This is essential for this version of *Svataḥ-prāmāṇyavāda*. He is accepting the naïve view that the content of cognition necessarily belongs to the object. He also accepts the corollary of this position that cognitions are never untrue, which would not be welcome to naïve viewer.

d. The last argument is rather interesting for it deals with the concept of philosophical doubt. It is usually maintained that the Indians always discuss particular doubts conditioned by specific factors, and they try to find out how these can be resolved. Here it is said that if we accept error in the cognitive level, and if we admit that cognitions occasionally fail to manifest its object then we land into complete skepticism. Rāmānuja asserts that if in some cases the object, which is manifested, is not the true object, then we are likely to suspect that the same is true of all cognitions, so that there would be no faith in cognitions anywhere in the world. The same skeptical consequence is feared by Śālikanātha, who says that if cognition ever deflects from its object and goes astray then we know that it may deviate from its object, and then one would lose all faith in it. Nandīśwara repeats the same argument.[21]

So by exiling error to the realm of conation, the Prābhākaras have tried to preserve *Svataḥ-prāmāṇyavāda*. Error is nothing but true cognition, there is no readjustment in the cognitive level after correction, there is only an omission—there is non-apprehension of non-relation. But can they really avoid the problem? It is usually held that a positive awareness of relatedness of the object and the qualifier is necessary for cognition. To explain error as non-apprehension is to admit that this positive factor is not essential for the constitution of cognition. These, in its own turn, gives rise to many other questions such as can action arise out of the negative state of non-apprehension?

Here the most pertinent question is what exactly is irregular in this untrue cognition? The obvious Prābhākara answer is that it is the *vyavahāra* that is irregular and it is *vyavāhara* that is corrected. *Prakaraṇapañcikā* asserts that we call cognition erroneous when there is contradiction in *vyavahāra* and the corrective cognition is so called because it corrects the *vyavahāra* aroused by the

cognition of silver. Or again let us turn to *Tantrarahasya*: it holds that cognitions are never sublated, for all cognitions are true of their objects or are *yathārtha*; but it is *vyavahāra,* which is sublated.[22]

The term *vyavahāra* has at least two meanings that are worth consideration. It may stand for the verbal expression used to articulate cognitions. If we accept this meaning then the Prābhākara position is that cognitions are always correct but expressions misrepresent them. The expression is that silver is actually present whereas the experience is explained as a memory of silver with the past reference omitted. Hence the expression is to be rejected. But this only shifts the problem from the realm of cognition to that of expression. It involves the very dubious assumption that the expression expresses an experience, which as a matter of fact is not there.

The other alternative is to take the term *vyavahāra* in its most ordinary sense, as meaning action, behavior, and conduct and say that the action, which ensues from cognition, is irregular. Monier Williams describes *vyavahāra* as "doing, performing action, practice, conduct, behavior," "activity, action, or practice of."[23] This meaning is more reasonable in the present context. The Prābhākaras draw a definite distinction between theory and practice. They assert that all cognitions are *yathārtha* and banish error to the realm of practice. At the cognitive level, they speak of non-apprehension. But this much concession is not sufficient; they totally ignore the unitary character of cognition and herein lies the basic weakness of their analysis of cognition.

Some specialists have said that in the Prābhākara explanation of error, one of the constituents of the error is *smṛti.* And as memory is *apramā* so the cognition has been called *apramā.* This explanation is not acceptable. We have already shown that memory is *apramā* in one sense and error is so in another. *Prakaraṇapañcikā* says that the cognition of shell as silver is a case, which is at once *pramā* and *apramā*, the two constituents being of two categories. Further, all errors are not explained by bringing in memory, as for example, the perception of conch as yellow. Such cases are described as error, but they are categorized as *pramā* and *yathārtha.* In fact the very concept of *smṛti-pramoṣa*, or memory with its past reference destroyed, is unsatisfactory. It is the reference to the past that makes a cognition *smṛti*, yet if that reference were there, then the fusion of the presentative and the representative contents would be impossible. All this suggests that the cognitive explanation of error in Prābhākara thought is weak, and as such their theory of *Svataḥ-prāmāṇyavāda* does not stand.

II

The Bhāṭṭas were the supporters of intrinsic truth and extrinsic untruth. All cognitions are apprehended as true and generated as true. Vitiating factors present in the causes produce untruth. Through corrective cognitions, which expose the real nature of the object or which point to the presence of *doṣas*, untruth is

revealed. But then they were aware of the dilemma of *Svataḥ-prāmāṇyavāda*. If they assert that truth is intrinsic to true cognitions only, then they are asserting something which is irrefutable but trivial. If it is intrinsic to all cognitions, then how can it be a meaningful adjective, which serves to exclude error? The critics would claim that if truth were manifested automatically, error should also be known by exclusion or *pariśeṣa*. Then what is the use of this elaborate apparatus of corrective cognition, or the knowledge of vitiating factor, etc.?

The Bhāṭṭas were aware of all this. Pārthasārathi Miśra claims that in erroneous cognitions truth is absent, yet it appears to be present, so the method of exclusion does not work.[24] He asserts that the "*sva*" stands for cognitions as such and truth is manifested in all cognitions. Truth is described as "suchness of the object." Doubt involves an attitude of alternation, where mutually opposed descriptions are directed towards an object, so it does not assert something definitely about it. Memory is not self-sufficient to assert any content. So barring these, all cognitions that assert something are intrinsically true.

However, this interpretation is not acceptable to all the Bhāṭṭas. Pārthasārathi Miśra is a controversial thinker. Some Mīmāmsā scholars have praised him for understanding the real essence of the Bhāṭṭa philosophy, while others have accused him of distorting it. In fact, Kumārila's writings itself have contradictory suggestions. He proposes that his enquiry is about all cognitions—*Sarva vijñāna viṣayam*; but then he asserts that *svataḥ sarva pramāṇānām prāmāṇyam* or the truth of all true cognitions is intrinsic.[25] Commentators like Pārthasārathi have selectively chosen from these alternate views and emphasized whichever they liked.

Let me quote some relevant couplets from the *Ślokavārttika*. One asserts that all cognitions possess truth because of their cognitive nature and this is destroyed by the awareness of the different nature of the object or by the awareness of the presence of defective causes.[26] Here two commentators, Sucarita and Pārthasārathi, definitely support a straightforward explanation.[27] They hold that all cognitions possess truth by virtue of their nature of being cognitive awareness, which is destroyed under special circumstances. Here obviously all cognitions exclude doubt and memory and we are talking about cognitions, which have assertive nature; but the moment they admit that the truth under consideration is a truth that can be destroyed, we ask that are they talking about the psychological claim to truth?

Another couplet asserts that there are three different types of *apramā,* which are error, absence of truth and doubt.[28] This shows that they have accepted error as a type of cognition. Their definition of true cognitions also supports this. Ślokavārttika holds that a true cognition is certain, which means that doubt is to be excluded; it is something produced which means that the purely negative category of absence of cognitions is to be excluded and it is the one which has not been contradicted by other cognitions, which means that error is to be excluded. To accept *apramā* as a specific type of cognition implies that they accept truth as a specific property of true cognitions.

The later Bhāṭṭa thinkers form two distinct groups who emphasize these two sides of Kumārila's position. Sucarita, Mandaṇa, etc. call truth a generic property and, though this is quite consistent with the theory of *svataḥ-prāmāṇya*, it is difficult to understand why they call it truth at all? Gāgā Bhaṭṭa, Umbeka, etc. look at truth as a specific property present only in true cognitions. This, of course, is nearer to the popular use of the term. But it remains for us to find out why and in what sense this is called *svataḥ-pramā*. It is needless to repeat that the vagueness of Kumārila's statements on this matter has encouraged this conflict of opinion among his commentators.

Kumārila's attitude is ontological. His argument is that truth is intrinsic to cognitions. Truth is nothing but the property of cognition to reveal the respective object, and unless it is naturally present in an object, it cannot be generated by extrinsic factors. Objects are produced by their causes but once they come into being they do not depend on any thing for the performance of their own duty.[29] Kāśikā clarifies that here the performance of its own work is nothing but the ascertainment of its object. The commentators explain Kumārila in their own way. Kāśikā holds that this means that cognitions manifest objects themselves and do not depend on external excellence, etc. for the performance of this. Umbeka says that cognitions are not dependent upon their apprehension for the performance of their own work; they naturally manifest the objects.[30]

To sum up, thus far we have seen that truth is said to be common to all cognitions including error; error is accepted as a cognitive phenomenon; and perhaps to reconcile these two contradictory statements it is said that in error truth is destroyed. Let us now look at these two groups of thinkers.

a. The first group consists of philosophers who have called truth a generic property; they call it *bodhakatva* or the property of being awareness. As we have already noted Sucarita asserts that cognitions naturally possess truth because of their conscious cognitive character. Maṇḍaṇa states that the conditions responsible for the production of awareness are the same as the conditions, which produce true cognitions. Again, he repeats that the Mīmāmsaka tradition is to say that truth is generated by conscious cognitive character.[31] Vācaspati asserts that cognitions naturally manifest objective facts and this is known by inference or perception, which grasps the cognition and this is what is meant by calling it intrinsic. Truth as related to cognitions is compared to burning capacity as related to fire.[32]

Sucarita tries to explain the position. He says that the so-called validating processes such as awareness of coherence, or presence of *guṇa*, etc. only confirm the already existent truth and we cannot say that before the origination of these processes truth was not there. We cannot say that originally an apprehension is *apramā* and these processes generate truth. Cognitions originate as assertive judgments and what else is truth? The processes of justification do not in any way alter the truth-value of initial judgment; they do not affect it qualitatively; hence these processes are superfluous. The initial judgmental cognition gives rise to *vyavahāra* and *pravṛtti*, or expression and activity and

truth does not mean anything else.[33] We get a more specific description of truth in the works of Pārthasārathi Miśra and Gāgābhaṭṭa.

We find a refined statement of this argument in the writings of Pārthasārathi Miśra. He anticipates a *pūrvapakṣa*, namely, if cognition does not manifest itself but reveals only the object, then how does it grasp truth, which is related to it? Pārthasārathi Miśra asserts that that which makes cognition true and determine the nature of true cognition is grasped by the cognition itself. This is said to be the suchness of the object.[34] A cognition grasps the object as such and such, that is, under a specific description and that property of the object is called suchness of the object or *arthatathātva*. This is truth itself and does not require the help of cognition of *guṇa* or of coherence or of successful activity.[35]

In his commentary on Ślokavārttika, Pārthasārathi says that truth is not grasped as related to cognition but is grasped as suchness of the object. Because it grasps the object so we ascribe truth to cognitions. It is grasped by the cognitions even when it is itself unknown. Hence, the demand for second order cognitions is useless. Rāmānuja confirms that truth is here conceived as an attribute of the object.[36]

Pārthasārathi says that three constituents combine to form truth. The first one is the property of being not known as previously apprehended by another cognition; this has been inserted to leave out memory from the purview of true cognitions for various reasons which we have discussed before. The second one is the suchness of the object. The third one is the property of cognitions to produce the ascertainment of such objects.[37] For Pārthasārathi, this second factor is really important and he is clearly polishing up the tradition of Kumārila.

Cognitions manifest objects without any mediation; hence, there is no question of comparison of object and cognitions for the apprehension of truth. But the difficulties arise when we face error. The Bhāṭṭas accept error as a species of cognition and the critics ask: what do they manifest? The Bhāṭṭas do not accept any false object or apparent truth, yet Pārthasārathi's language betrays a tendency towards it. He asserts that truth is manifested in all cognitions; even in erroneous cognitions truth is said to be manifested although it is not there.[38] Falsity is not manifested through exclusion, but it is manifested later through sublation of apparent truth. But this is not acceptable. Either he should have said that truth is not manifested in error before correction, or he should have said that what is manifested is not truth. How can something be absent and at the same time be manifested? The problem of error is only shifted from the realm of object to that of cognition. Pārthasārathi does not say anything and this is the weakness of his position.

b. The second group consists of Bhāṭṭas thinkers, who have tried to develop the concept of truth as a specific property. The foremost among these is Gāgābhaṭṭa. He has shared the Nyāya platform, as he has discussed both the questions of origination and apprehension of truth and has defined truth in the Nyāya fashion. He speaks of truth as *yathārthānubhavatva* or the property of being cognition other than memory, which does not deviate from its object. He paraphrases the definition as *tadvad-viśeṣyakatve sati tatprakāraka jñānatva* or

the property of being a cognition which has *x* as a qualifier where the *x* resides in the substantive.[39] Here Mohanty has pointed out that in the Nyāya definition the corresponding term is *tadvati*, which means that the qualifier *x* is said to be present in the ontological object. By replacing it with *viśeṣya*, which is the epistemological object, the Mīmāmsakas destroy the heterogeneous character of truth. But in all fairness, it has to be acknowledged that Mohanty's comment does not apply to Gāgā. If the term *viśeṣya* meant the epistemological object then the definition would apply as much to error as to truth. Silverness belongs to the epistemological "this" as much in error as in truth. But Gāgā uses the term "*viśeṣya*" in the ontological sense and it is inserted to differentiate truth from error. Gāgā is here accepting the Nyāya definition of truth. He makes it clear that if an erroneous cognition takes a shining paper and a silver as a silver and a silver paper, respectively, it is not to be taken as an instance of truth. Rather, the definition of truth is to be made more precise by saying that *yāthārthya* is the property of being a cognition which has *x* as its qualifier, limited by the *x* residing in the *viśeṣya*, the object.

Gāgā's arguments for *svataḥ-prāmāṇyavāda* are twofold. First, he proves that truth is not generated by *guṇa* or special excellences in the originating conditions, or *doṣābhāva* or absence of defects, therefore apprehension of truth is not dependent upon awareness of these conditions. His second argument is critical; he criticizes the Nyāya position, taking for granted that the falsity of the opponent's position proves the truth of the exponent's.

His other discussions are unfoldment of the Bhāṭṭa tradition. He gives an analysis of cognition using Nyāya terminology, which brings forward the radical difference of Bhāṭṭa approach. Cognition generates a property called *jñātatā*, or knownness in the object, say a pot; then we infer the existence of the cognition. The form of the inference is: I have cognition in the pot, because there is *jñātatā* in it. He analyses the cognition by using the technical terms of Nyāya. Each ontological object is supposed to have at least two faces, one as a substantive and the other is the qualifying adjective, which determines the substantival character. The corresponding cognitional components are *viśeṣyatā*, or the property of being a substantive, and *prakāratā*, or the property of being a qualifier. Gāgā says that in the known object there is *viśeṣyatā* as determined by *prakāratā*. Here *viśeṣyatā* present in the pot is determined by *prakaratā* present in potness. These are cognitional in nature, and are seen as constituting a relation, which leads to the inference of the cognition of the pot. Truth is nothing more than that. By saying that the cognition of pot is true, we are only asserting that there is this *viśeṣyatā* as determined by this *prakaratā*. That is why truth is called *svataḥpramā*. Here the emphasis is totally on the object; a quality created in the object certifies the presence of cognition as well as of truth. It cannot be argued that knownness is not coextensive with truth, for they are not saying that we infer truth by linking it with knownness. They are looking at truth as a property of the object of cognition, that it is known by the cognition, which infers the existence of the initial cognition.[40]

Yet that is exactly the criticism urged against Gāgā. In error also we infer cognition. Critics have pondered where knownness resides. Here too we are aware of something like truth and what is the status of this truth.

The other Bhāṭṭa, who has spoken of truth as a specific property, is Umbeka. The property of being awareness cannot be truth for it is present in erroneous awareness, too. The property of being awareness, which does not deviate from its object, is truth. He does not try to answer the question as to how such a property is apprehended intrinsically. True to the Bhāṭṭa tradition he holds that cognition does not depend on anything for the performance of its own function, which is manifestation of the object. And this is what is meant by intrinsic nature of truth.

III

In this final section, let us first make an appraisal of the Mīmāmsaka criticism of *parataḥ-prāmāṇyavāda.*

The Mīmāmsā attack on Nyāya is basically two-pronged. It is claimed that a. Nyāya fails to explain the status of the initial cognition vis-à-vis the ensuing activity, and b. their dependence on inference for the ascertainment of truth is unsatisfactory. These arguments run as follows:

a. The Mīmāmsakas hold that all cognitions give rise to unwavering activity, which means we accept them as true. The Naiyāyikas hold that cognition causes unwavering activity if it is not known to be false. Here they are asked that if unwavering activity does not require ascertainment of truth, then what is the need of finding out truth at all? We shall come back to this question later. The Mīmāmsakas say that if the initial cognition is neither true nor false, then what is its status? Modern logicians speak of three attitudes—that of acceptance or assertion, that of disbelief or rejection, and that of suspended belief, in which the assertive attitude is missing and is withheld for the time being. This third attitude is missing in most Indian philosophical systems, in which it is not accepted as a natural state. The state of suspended belief is doubt. The Naiyāyikas elaborate the complicated features of doubt, which the initial cognition under consideration does not satisfy. Doubt involves an attitude of alternation, which cannot issue any activity. Nor can it be just a neutral state. Cognition is logically analyzable because of the distinct proposition embedded in it. It is a proposition plus the attitude. The cognition asserts something by virtue of which it is called true.

The Buddhists have tried to establish that even doubt issues activity and even encourages activity. The activity of the farmer is said to be an instance in point. The farmer is not sure of a successful harvest and yet he works. Here it is said that the farmer does not act out of doubt, but he works in spite of doubt. Śrīharṣa, the Advaitin, has said that the state of mind of the farmer is not doubt

but *utprekṣā* or conditional certainty. He works with the hope that if things go well, he will be successful.

In some cases doubt leads to activity. To find out the real nature of the presented object we go near it. Here the explanation is that what prompts us to activity is not doubt, but the belief that if we act in spite of doubt, we shall come to know the exact situation and our doubt would be resolved. So the initial cognition, which issues activity, cannot be mere doubt.

As we have pointed out before, the Naiyāyikas say that the Mīmāmsā criticism is based upon the unfounded assumption that activity requires awareness of the truth of the initial cognition. This they do not accept. Cognitions are said to be in the nature of ascertainments; they state something about the object. And this is sufficient to give rise to unwavering activity.

b. The second group of criticisms is directed against processes of justification. Nyāya maintains that the initial cognition is the seat of truth, and that truth is ascertained inferentially. Such inference can have as its *hetu* either *tajjātiyatva*, which literally means the property of belonging to the same class, or *samvāda jñāna* or cognition of coherence which is the awareness that the later experience is consistent with the initial cognition or *guṇajñāna* or awareness of presence of some excellences in the generating conditions which are responsible for the production of truth, or *arthakriyājñāna* or awareness of fulfillment of the practical expectations aroused by the initial cognition. The Mīmāmsakas have examined and rejected the last three marks. We find that though the Naiyāyikas themselves have frequently appealed to the first mark, they were not very comfortable about a logical explanation of it. The Mīmāmsakas have also criticized the basic idea of knowing truth inferentially. The normal criticism is that the truth of the inference must in its turn be established, and the process goes on, and there is no stopping place or there is *anavasthā*.

The Naiyayikas hold that in unfamiliar, novel situations we employ one of the last three marks, but in familiar instances we are aware of the truth-value of the initial cognition without the help of any such inference. The concept of *tajjātiyatva* may be practically useful, but it evades precise logical formulation. It is the property of belonging to the same class, but what exactly does "same class" mean? It cannot be the property of belonging to the class of cognitions, which issue successful activity, for it is supposed to work before the emergence of any activity. An object is said to be familiar when it has been experienced many times, but what does *many* mean? Ultimately it reduces to the "class of true cognitions," which is precisely that which we are trying to define. In fact it is asked that in familiar cases is truth known automatically, or is it known *svataḥ*? This, the Naiyāyikas would not accept. But if it is a mark, like any other mark, then an appeal to it does not repel the charge of infinite regress.

We have spoken of three other types of mark, in unfamiliar cases. One is about the generation of true cognitions, in which the generating conditions involve *guṇas*. This one need not be discussed here for we have not discussed the question of origination here.

Another mark is coherence or consistency. What does *samvāda* mean? It is the property of having the same object as the cognition under consideration. Pārthasārathi says that it is another cognition having the same object.[41] Here the supporters demand that coherence proves correspondence; the Bhāṭṭa attitude is that truth is either present in the initial cognition or it is not; if it is not present, then no amount of coherence can create it and if it is there then coherence is superfluous. *Ślokavārttika* says that if we depend upon *samgati* or coherence, then there would always be dependence on further cognitions, which ends in infinite regress.[42] Again they say that here all the cognitions are directed towards the same object and as such they become optional alternatives, in which one of them really manifest the object the others are superfluous.[43] All the cognitions possess the same object, so if the initial one does not possess the inherent capacity to reveal the object then the others cannot add or introduce it. The commentators unanimously agree that truth is not determined by *samvāda*. Pārthasārathi says that truth is manifestation of the object; and that is equally present in all cognitions; their united effort does not in any way increase it.[44] Sucarita explains that if all cognitions have the same object and nothing extra, then one of them and preferably the first one is true cognition, the others only translate it.[45]

The only other mark that remains to be discussed is *phalajñāna*, or confirmatory cognition in form of successful termination of activity. The standard Nyāya inference is: The cognition under consideration is true, as it issues successful activity. Udayana explains that "success" here means connection with the result, hence, the critics have naturally asked: how do we apprehend the truth of this *phalajñāna*?

The Buddhists have called this cognition *arthakriyājñāna*. *Arthakriyā* means fulfillment of our requirement or our expectation, and the knowledge of this fulfillment is vital to any inference of truth. If we have cognition of fire and that fire burns our hands when it is touched, or when it enables us to cook, the latter is called *phalajñāna* and it proves the truth of the initial cognition. Similarly, the truth of cognition of water is confirmed, when it quenches our thirst.

Those who have presented these inferences have variously tried to show that there is no need of any further inference to find out the truth of these cognitions. Udayana says that truth is here inferred through familiarity. But the point is that once we speak of inference, the question of infinite regress remains unanswered. Vācaspati claimed some sort of intrinsic truth for the process of inference and also for *phalajñāna*. Udayana argues that these are ends of cognitive situations so there is no need of examining their truth.[46] The Naiyāyikas speak of two classes of cognition, those which issue activity and those which are the results of that activity. They tacitly take for granted that the ends need not be examined, as they do not issue any activity. The Buddhist logicians have spoken in the same way. The initial cognition starts a purposeful action as they direct us to an object possessing the capacity to satisfy our need; but the others are in the form of attainment, hence, they are intrinsically true.

They are said to be naturally clear and distinct. As if here we are in direct touch with reality. This difference is not advocated purely on a cognitive basis. They are presented in the background of practice and the cognitions, which lead to action and those which are ends of action are allotted different status. The cognition of fire may be directed towards a bunch of red flowers, but the sensation of being burnt can never follow from touching red flowers. They say that in the case of visual perception of fire, we appeal to verification by touch; so it is asked: are they advocating the supremacy of one sensation over another, that of touch over vision? Here the contrary cases are also available, where we touch a piece of velvet, and to confirm our perceptual cognition we turn to the reports of eye. Here the real issue is: is there a difference in kind between ordinary cognitions and confirmatory cognitions?

It is to be noted that the Naiyāyikas are not looking for foundations of knowledge. These cognitions, which are beyond doubt, are not contingent personal experiences such as "this looks like a red pot to me." Such experiences are accepted as beyond all doubt. The Naiyāyikas would accept this, but these are merely considered as examples of internal perception as opposed to external perception and they are not considered to have any active role in explaining knowledge. Perceptual knowledge coming from the five external senses, and that coming from internal sense or *manas*, has the same cognitive status. Rather, they think that the ends of action are experiences, which touch reality.

The Bhāṭṭas have repeatedly criticized such differential treatment. First, they have asked, what happens if a person not desirous of drinking water sees water? Mere fulfillment of desire is always questionable. In dreams our thirsts are quenched yet we wake up to find that our fulfillment was wrong. The proponents of the *parataḥ* theory often argue that the sense of well-being cannot be there if it is not there; but the Bhāṭṭas assert that the sense of well-being proves only the existence of well-being and nothing else. In the *Ślokavārttika* it is said that if we ultimately assign intrinsic truth to some cognitions then why do we hesitate to grant it to the initial cognitions?[47]

Their basic charge against inference is that this would lead to vicious infinite regress. Here Kumārila has been unfair to Nyāya and has misrepresented their view. The Bhāṭṭas read the Nyāya position as asserting that cognition would not manifest its object as long as it has not been established that the generating conditions involve excellences or *guṇa*. Then, they continue, that this inference showing the perfection of the cause would need certification from another inference and the process would go on ad infinitum. Now, the Naiyāyikas do not say this. The accepted interpretation is that the truth of the initial cognition is known through inference; but the truth of this inference has to be ascertained through a second inference and this process would go on ad infinitum. One of the Nyāya ways of answering this charge is to differentiate between *arthaniścaya* and *prāmāṇyaniścaya* or certainty about object and certainty about truth. All assertive cognitions involve certainty about object, and this is sufficient to issue unwavering activity. If under special circumstances, there arises doubt about this primary certainty present in the initial cognition, we

depend upon inference, which apprehends the truth of the initial cognition and dispels doubt. So ascertainment of truth is necessary only under very special circumstances. Unless there arises doubt about the truth of the inference, there is no need of a second inference to find out its truth.

The Bhāṭṭa description of such a situation is almost identical with the one given by Nyāya. Gaṇgeśa asserts that the ascertainment of the truth of an assertion is not required for the ascertainment of the object of that knowledge. Umbeka's comment occurring in the commentary on *Ślokavārttika* is exactly the same. He says that true cognition does not await its own apprehension for the performance of its own duty; it manifests its own object even when its truth has not been ascertained.[48] The Bhāṭṭas have always insisted that doubt is necessarily conditioned by some defect. Kumārila says in the *Ślokavārttika* that we must not suspect the presence of untruth as long as our awareness of some defect does not come into being.[49] It is wrong to indulge in unwarranted doubt; such doubt questions the claim of cognition to reveal its object, and leads to total skepticism and destruction of all activity.[50] The supporters of *Svataḥ-prāmāṇyavāda* should explain the situation in a different way. The doubt, which questions *arthaniścaya* or ascertainment of the object, should be dispelled by an inquiry into the nature and existence of the object and not in the roundabout way by ascertaining the truth of the corresponding judgment. A very clear explanation comes here from *Vivaraṇa-prameya-samgraha*, the Advaita text. It says that these second cognitions, that is, the inferences are meant to dispel doubt, which hinders the truth of the initial cognition from shining forth, these are not meant to ascertain truth.[51]

So both the Mīmāmsaka and the Naiyāyika agree with each other that *arthaniścaya* or the ascertainment of the object gives rise to unwavering activity. But then the difference between the two is not merely verbal; they entertain very different idea about the nature of truth. The Bhāṭṭas mean by truth *arthatathātva*, or suchness of the object, and this is grasped by cognitions. They have insisted that truth is a property of the object of cognition. It is grasped by cognitions even when they are themselves unknown. Pārthasārathi Miśra draws a distinction between truth as pertaining to object and truth as pertaining to cognitions. But he adds that the former is most important and truth is extended to cognitions only as an afterthought. *Nāyakaratna* clarifies that truth is here an attribute of the object.

The Naiyāyika looks at the situation from the metalevel. To call a cognition true is to say that it has grasped reality correctly. Truth is a property of cognition. Mohanty says that this is not a copy theory; there is no gap between cognition and reality. This is traceable to Gaṇgeśa, who refuses to call truth *yāthārthya*. Mohanty claims that truth is a hybrid entity, involving both cognition and reality, both epistemological and ontological components. Truth is here defined as *tadvati tatprakārakatva*, or the property of a cognition, which possess the *tat* as a *prakāra,* when as a matter of fact the *tat* is present in the object. But then it can be asked: how can the *tat* present in the object and the *tat* present in the cognition, as a qualifier be one and the same?

The Bhāṭṭas hold that cognition has a direct access to reality, it grasps the reality, and that is truth. The Nyāya would agree with the Bhāṭṭa that cognition grasps reality. But it looks at truth as a property of cognition, and the cognition is known in reflective perception, and mind has no independence in the case of outer objects, so it can never judge whether the cognition has grasped reality correctly or not. According to *svataḥ-prāmānyavāda* the form of the cognition of cognition should be "I have a knowledge of this silver"; but the Nyāya analysis is that the form of *anuvyavasāya* is "I know this as qualified by thisness and silverness." Gaṇgeśa says in most unambiguous language that the relatedness of thisness and silverness with the presented object is not grasped by the *anuvyavasāya*; hence, truth is not apprehended intrinsically. According to the Bhāṭṭas, the substance, qualifier, and their relatedness have the same status, and hence all three of them are grasped by cognitions.

Here the Bhāṭṭa, as also the Prābhākara, attitude is that, by conceding that cognitions sometimes fail to grasp reality, one lands into skepticism. Even if it is said that cognitions fail to apprehend reality under very special circumstances, still this means that the claim of cognitions to manifest reality is questioned, and this can be extended to all cognitions.

But, then, the Bhāṭṭas too fail to give a satisfactory explanation of error. They accept error as a species of cognition. Error is explained as *samsarga-graha* or apprehension of a relation between the presentative and the representative contents, which is not there. They should give a uniform explanation of cognition, which applies equally to true and erroneous ones. They cannot say that the relatedness grasped in cognitions is sometimes real and sometimes ideal. We are reminded of Pārthasārathi Miśra's comment that truth is manifested in cognitions even when it is not there. Such a truth can be nothing but the psychological claim to truth, which is present in all cognitions.

Notes

1. Udayana, *Nyāyavārttika Tātparyapariśuddhi*, ed. V. P. Dvivedi (Calcutta, 1911), *Iha dvividha pramāṇaśabdasya arthaḥ pramīyate'neneti pramāṇam pramitiḥ pramāṇam*, 43.
2. Pārthasārathi Miśra, *Nyāyaratnamālā* with Rāmānujāchāryya, *Nāyakaratna*, ed. B. Bhattacharya (GOS LXXV) (Baroda, India: 1937), *Sva śabdaḥ kim ātmavacana atmīyo-vacano vā*, 48.
3. Gangeśopadhyaya, *Tattvacintamaṇi*, with Raghunātha Siromaṇi, *Dīdhiti*, and Gadādhara Bhattāchārya, *Prāmāṇyavāda*, ed. P. B. Ananthachariar (Conjeevaram, India: 1901), *Svataḥ svasmāt svakīyāt*, 15.
4. J. N. Mohanty, *Gangeśa's Theory of Truth* (Visva-Bharati, Santiniketan, India: Centre of Advanced Study, 1966), 93.
5. Mohanty, *Gangeśa*, 97.
6. Mohanty, *Gangeśa*, 99.

7. Rāmānujacārya, *Tantrarahasya*, ed. R. S. Sastri (GOS XXIV) (Baroda, India: 1956), *Katham yāthārthyam sādhāraṇam? Sarvasyāpi jñānasy-ārthāvyabhicāritvena tanniyamāt, Smṛti vyatiriktā ca samvit anubhuti, Yatravyavahāra visamvādaḥ tatra pūrva-jñānasya bhrāntatvam yatra tu na tatra samyaktvam*, 2-3.

8. Rāmānuja, *Tantrarahasya, Sa ca na pūrvajñāna-viṣayāpahārah tayor yāthārthyatvāt kim tu vyavahāra visamvāda eva. Na hi jñānam bādhyam. Tasya yāthārthyatvāt. Kim tu vyavahārah*, 3.

9. Śabara Swāmin, *Mīmāmsā Sūtra Bhāṣya*, with Prabhākara Miśra, *Bṛhatī*, Śālikanātha Miśra, *Ṛjuvimalāpañcikā* ed. S. K. Ramaanath Sastri (MUSS 3) (Madras: University of Madras, 1934), *Tasmāt tat pramāṇam anapekṣatvāt. Na hyevam sati pratyayāntaram apekṣitavyam puruṣāntaram vāpi; svayam pratyayo hi asau*, 46.

10. Śālikanātha, *Ṛjuvimalā, Yathā smṛti-jñānam vāhyam vastu na gṛhṇāti asphutāvabhāsitvāt*, 53.

11. Bhavanātha Miśra, *Nayaviveka*, ed. S. K. R. Sastri (MUSS 12) (Madras: 1937), *Aviśadatve hi viśadāvabhāsena saha bhedāgraho na syāt*, 78.

12. Dharmarājādvarīndra, *Vedānta Paribhāsā*, ed. Srimohan Tarka-Vedantatirtha (Calcutta: 1970), 5.

13. Rāmānuja, *Tantrarahasya*, 4.

14. Śālikanātha Miśra, *Prakaraṇapañcikā*, ed. M. Sastri (Kasi, India: Chowkhamba, 1904) *Yathārtham sarvameveha vijñanam*, iv/i, 32.

Bhavanātha, *Nayaviveka, Na hi asamīcīnam kiñcij jñānam*, 87; also, *Na hi jñānam vyabhicarati vedyam*, 50.

15. Bhavanatha, *Nayaviveka, Lokasiddha pratyakṣādi vyabhicāra darśana*, 84.

16. Prabhākara, *Bṛhatī, Idam eva hi ālambanasya ālambanatvam yad utātmākāram eva jñānam utpādayati*, 61.

17. Vācaspati Miśra, *Nyāya-Vārttika-Tātparyatīkā*, ed. Taranath Nyāyatarkatīrtha (Calcutta: 1936), *Yad yadarthinām niyamena yatra pravartayati tad vijñānam tad viṣayam*, 75.

18. Bhavanātha, *Nayaviveka, Yadartha vyavahārānuguṇam hi yad bhānam tat tadartha bhānam ityucyate*, 88.

19. Nandīśwara, *Prabhākara Vijaya*, ed. A. K. Sastri & R. N. Sastri (Calcutta: 1926) *Viṣaya-vyavasthā bhāsamānatayā vācyā*, 17.

20. Rāmānuja, *Tantrarahasya, Yasyām samvidi yo'rtho'vabhāsate sa tasya viṣayaḥ. Nānyaḥ. Tasya tatrānavabhāsāt*, 2.

21. Rāmanuja, *Tantrarahasya, Kim ca kasyacid bhānasya artha vyabhicāre sarvasyāpi tathātva śamkāyām jagati viśvāso na syāt*, 4.

Nandīśwara, *Prabhākara Vijaya, Kim ca ayathārthe sarvatrānaśvāsah syāt*, 22.

22. Śālikanātha, *Ṛjuvimalā, Tad grahaṇa-vyavahāra hetutām pratipadyamānam vyavahāre visamvādakatvātvyavahāreviparyayam āvahati*, 67.

Rāmānuja, *Tantrarahasya, Na hi jñānam bādhyam, tasya yathārthatvāt, kim tu vyavahārah*, 3.

23. Monier Williams, *Sanskrit-English Dictionary* (Oxford: Clarendon Press, 1963), 1034.

24. Pārthasārathi, *Nyāyaratna-mālā, Tataścāpramāṇa-jñānādapi prāmāṇyam evātmano-'sadapi bodhyata iti nāpramāṇasyapariśeṣa siddhiḥ. Na ca pramāṇa-jñānānyadhikrtya cinteyam pramāṇanam prāmāṇyam svataḥ parato veti. Kintarhi, Yāni tāvat sthāṇurvā puruṣo veti parasparopamardaka aneka-koti-samsparśī-jñānebhya smṛti-jñānebhyas cāt-iriktāni ghato'yam pato'yam ityevam rūpāni jñānāni tāni sarvānyadhikrtya cinteyam*, 54.

25. Kumārila Bhaṭṭa, *Ślokavārttika*, Bhaṭṭombeka, *Tātparyatīkā*, ed. by S. K. R. Sastri, (MUSS 13) (Madras, India: 1940), II/3, II/47.

26. Kumārila Bhaṭṭa, *Ślokavārttika, Tasmād bodhātmakatvena prāptā buddheḥ pramāṇatā. Arthānyathātva-hetuttha doṣa-jñānād apodyate*, II/53.

27. Kumārila Bhaṭṭa, *Ślokavārttika*, with Pārthasārsathi Miśra, *Nyāya-ratnākara*, ed. M. R. Sastri (Kasi, India: 1896), II/53.

Kumārila Bhaṭṭa, *Ślokavārttika*, With Sucarita Miśra, *Kaśikā*, ed. K. S. Sastri (TSS XC) (Trivandrum, India: 1926), *Tasmād bodha-svabhāvānubandhiḥ jñānānām autsargikam prāmāṇyam karaṇa doṣārthanyathātva-jñānābhyām apodyata iti upasamharati*, II/53.

28. Kumārila, *Ślokavārttika, Aprāmāṇyam tridhā bhinnam mithyātvājñāna-samśayaih*, II/54.

29. Kumārila, *Ślokavārttika*,

Svataḥ sarva-pramāṇānām prāmāṇyam iti gṛhyatām.
Na hi svato'sati śaktiḥ kartum anyena śakyate. II/47.
Ātmalābhe ca bhāvānām kāraṇāpekṣitā bhavet.
Labdhātmanām sva-kāryeṣu pravṛttiḥ svayameva tu. II/48.

30. Sucarita, *Kāśikā, Ātmalābhamātra eva hi bhāvāh kāraṇam apekṣante, na kārya-niṣpattau*, II/48.

Bhaṭṭombeka, *Tātparyatīkā, Naiva hi pramāṇam svakārye svagrahaṇam apekṣate*, II/48.

31. Maṇḍaṇa Miśra, *Vibhrama Viveka*, ed. S. K. Sastri (Madras, India: 1933), *Bodhād eva pramāṇatvam iti mīmāmsaka sthitim*, 83.

32. Vācaspati Miśra, *Nyāyakaṇikā*, ed. T. R. Sastri (Kashi, India:1907), *Yat punar tattvāvavodha rupatvam vijñānasya tadapi tad grāhiṇaḥ pratyayāntarān mānasād ānumānikād vāvagamyamānam svata ityucyate*, 166-167; also *Tad yathā bahner dāhana-sāmarthyam iti*, 167.

33. Sucarita, *Kāśikā* II/47.

34. Pārthasārathi, *Nyāyaratnamālā, Yad vastuto jñānasya prāmāṇyam yad vaśāj jñānam pramāṇam bhavati tat pramāṇa-buddhi-śabdayor bhāvakatayā labdha-prāmāṇya-padābhidhānīyakam ātmanaiva jñānena gṛhyata iti ucyate. Kim punas tat arthatathātvam?* 52.

35. Pārthasārathi, *Nyāyaratna-mālā, Tena svata eva jñānād artha-tathātva-rūpam ātmīyam prāmāṇyam niścīyate. Na tu guna-jñānad samvāda-jñānād arthakriyā-jñānād vā*, 52.

36. Rāmānuja, *Tantrarahasya, Kim tu viṣaya dharmāḥ kaścit prāmāṇyam nāma*, 53.

37. Pārthasārathi, *Nyāyaratnamālā, Pramāṇāntaradhigatatayā-nānusandhiya-mānatvam tathābhāvas cārthasya jñānasya tanniścayajanakateti tritayam militam pramāṇa-buddhi-śabdayor vācakam*, 55.

38. Pārthasārathi, *Nyāyaratnamālā, catas cāpramāṇajñānādapi prāmāṇyam evātmano'sadapi bodhyata iti nāprāmāṇyasya pariśeṣa-siddhiḥ. Aprāmāṇyantu pratīta-prāmāṇyāpavāda-rūpeṇa paścād bodhyate*, 54.

39. Gāgābhaṭṭa, *Bhāṭṭacintāmaṇi* ed. S. N. Sukla (CSS 25 & 27) (Benaras, India: 1933), 10.

40. Gāgābhaṭṭa, *Bhāṭṭacintāmaṇi, Tatra ghaṭatvaniṣṭha-prakāratā-nirūpita-viśeṣyatā-sambandhena jñānānumitau tādṛśa prakāratā-nirūpita viśeṣyatā-rūpa-prāmāṇya-graha*, 13; also *Na ca jñātatayā pramātva-vyāpyatayā tad anumāpakatvā-sambhava iti vācyam. Pramātvasyānanumeyatvāt jñānānumāne samāna-samvit-samvedyatayā pramātvasya svatastva sambhavāt*, 13.

41. Pārthasārathi, *Nyāyaratnamālā, Samvādo nāma tadviṣayam jñānāntaram*, 37.

42. Kumārila, *Ślokavārttika*,
Samgatyā yadi ceṣyeta pūrvapūrva-pramāṇatā
Pramāṇāntaram icchanto na vyavasthām labhāmahe. II/75.
43. Kumārila, *Ślokavārttika*, *Tulyārthānām vikalpyatvāt ekam tatra hi bodhakam*, II/73.
44. Pārthasārsathi, *Nyāya-ratnākara*, *Artha-pariccheda-hetutvena tulyānām eva sāmarthyam na samuccitānām*, II/74.
45. Sucarita, *Kāśikā*, *Ayam abhiprāyah—yadi tāvad anadhika-viṣayānyeva tāni sārvāṇi, tat ekam eva tatrādya pramāṇam. Itarāṇi tvanuvāda-bhūtāni*, II/74.
46. Udayana, *Nyāya Pariśuddhi*, *Phalajñānam hi phalasya siddhāvasthasya sādhanārhatayā niṣprayojanibhūtatvād vā na parikṣyate*, 108.
47. Kumārila, *Ślokavārttika*,
Kasyacit tu yadiṣyeta svata eva pramāṇatā.
Prathamasya tathābhāve pradveṣa kim nivandhana. II/76.
48. Bhaṭṭọmbeka, *Tātparyatīkā*, *Naiva hi pramāṇam svakārye svagrahaṇam apekṣate*, II/48.
49. Kumārila, *Ślokavārttika*, *Doṣa-jñāne tvanutpanne naśamkā niṣpramā-ṇikā*, II/60, 89.
50. Sucarita, *Kāśikā*, *Śamkā tu notprekṣā-mātreṇa kartum ucitā sarva-vyavaharoccheda prasamgāt*, II/60.
51. Vidyāraṇya, *Vivaraṇa-prameya-samgraha*, Part II, ed. Pramathanath Tarkabhusan (Calcutta: Basumati Sahitya Mandir, 1927), *Tatra dvitīyādi jñānāni prathama-jñānaprāmāṇya-pratibandhaka samśāyādi nirāsīni, na tu tat prāmāṇya-niścāyakāni*, 225.

The Concept of Truth in Buddhist Logic

I

In Buddhist logic and epistemology we notice an attitude of indecision about the truth-value of inference. In *Nyāyavindu*, Dharmakīrti classifies true cogni-tions into two classes: perception and inference.[1] The commentary makes it clear that both are equally true and true in the same sense. But the commentary on the very next *sūtra* remarks that inference is erroneous.[2] This means that inference is true and erroneous at once. Such an apparently inconsistent conclusion calls for further in-depth investigation.

We find that the Buddhist logicians like Diṇnāga, Dharmakīrti, and others were interested in the two faces of the cognitive experience, which, for the time being, I call the strictly theoretical and the practical aspects of cognition. In the first *sūtra* of *Nyāyavindu*, Dharmakīrti says that the satisfaction of all human needs is preceded by true cognition and that is why he wants to examine its nature. The practical tilt is always discernible in the Buddhist treatment of cognition. The property of cognition that determines the practical success of activities ensuing from cognition is called *prāmāṇya.* It is essentially connected with all our practical dealings. But side by side with this the Buddhist thinkers have also tried to determine how far cognition can grasp reality or whether all cognitions have access to reality or not. We might say that they are also interested in the *yāthārthya* or the nondeviating character of cognition. These two I call the practical and the theoretical aspects of cognition. In Western thought, we see that the two different approaches to knowledge have developed in two different directions with different philosophical commitments. One is pragmatic, where the knower and the practical success of all activities ensuing from cognition are important; the other is foundationalistic, where there is a constant search for an incorrigible irrevisable base for knowledge. In our pre-critical understanding of knowledge the two are seen as essentially connected with each other, where practical success confirms the truth of the initial cognition, that is, it certifies that the cognition has correctly mirrored the object. Certain Indian philosophical systems such as Nyāya develop this belief, taking some sort of correspondence

as the essence of truth and practical success among others as the criterion. But the Buddhist wavers between these two attitudes. In some texts they clearly introduce the dual concepts of truth—the *pāramārthika* or the ultimate truth and the *vyavahārika* or the practical truth. The ultimate reality has been described as of non-artificial, unconcealed form.[3] They think of it as composed of extremely particularized point instants. The basic question is how much access do we have to this raw unadulterated reality? They ask: what do we grasp? (This being the Buddhist way of saying: what is the given?) But side by side with this there is the *vyavahārika*, or the practical, which is entwined with all our practical dealings. In fact, in their discussions about knowledge, they are more interested in this second concept. And if *vyavahāra* is taken to mean linguistic usage, then the *vyavahārika* becomes the linguistic real. So they are interested both in the nature of pure cognition and in the linguistic cognition, which is practically convenient. Hence we may ask: are they really dealing with two separate concepts of truth and, if so, are they consistently able to reconcile the two?

II

The Buddhists subscribe to another peculiar theory called *pramāṇa-vyavasthā*. J. N. Mohanty says: "the theory of *pramāṇa-vyavasthā*, i.e., a settled order of *pramāṇa*, according to which each *pramāṇa* has its own object type, so that no entity of a certain type can be a possible object of two or more *pramāṇas*."[4] This means that each *pramāṇa* has its own exclusive domain, which never intersect. What is perceivable is only perceivable, and what is inferred can never be perceived. As opposed to this, the general opinion of the other schools is that, in many cases, the self same object can be known by alternative *pramāṇas*. This dichotomy is traceable to a dichotomy in reality, in which all possible objects of cognition are split into two mutually exclusive realms. These are the unique particulars on the one hand and the conceptual constructs on the other. We shall see that the former are considered to be true reals, whereas the latter are the products of imagination imposed on the bare real for the sake of practical convenience. In this section I give a summary of their ontological position. I neither support nor oppose their position. But as their ideas about truth are directly based on their views about reality, I try to elucidate it as a necessary background.

Buddhists hold that the only existents are momentary reals called *svalakṣaṇa*, which literally means the self-definable, or self-characterized. These reals are extreme particulars, whose nature and essence belong to them. They are totally structureless and have no sharable property. Thus each of them is unique and has no similarity with anything else in the world. Their uncommon nature is only grasped by perception. The *svalakṣaṇa* is considered to be the *grāhya*, or that which is grasped and only prejudgmental perception, untarnished by judgment, has access to it. The particular has no duration in time and no position in space. According to the Buddhists, even the minimum concept, which we would

require to talk or think about reality, belongs to the realm of *sāmānya* or universal and as such, are not applicable to these. All universal properties and relations come under *sāmānya*. The Vṛttikāra mentions the prevalent concepts such as those of substance, quality, action, relation, number, and conjunction-disjunction as instances of *sāmānya*.[5]

Perception grasps the momentary real, but it cannot express the content in language. To turn it into a simple judgment, one has to depend upon imagination. Diṇnāga says that in perception one can know the blue, but not as blue, that is, not as "this is blue."[6] The ascription of the name "blue" is a function of imagination. Although perception itself is dumb, we can identify its content in the report of the corresponding judgment. There is a part of the cognitive judgment which directly varies with the position of the perceiver vis-à-vis the object of perception. The content, which is clear and distinct when the knower is near and becomes vague and indistinct when the knower moves away, comes from the *svalakṣaṇa*.[7] When a person looks at a hill, his image is clear when he is near it and fades away as he moves away. This content is called the *ākāra* produced by the *svalakṣaṇa*, and we have spoken of it as "form." In the *Pramāṇavārttika* and the *Vṛtti*, it is said that when a real is known it lends its *ākāra* to the cognition. The cognition of blue floats the blue form. This is the sign of its reality.[8]

The Buddhists have differentiated between the particular and the conceptual at least in three different ways. First, the *svalakṣaṇa* is unique; the form, which floats in *jñāna*, excludes all similarities with other particulars. The epithet *lakṣaṇa* is especially significant here. The *svalakṣaṇa* is essentially self-differentiating. Second, it cannot be described in language; it can be referred only through suchness (*tattva*) and otherness (*anyatva*) from everything else.[9] Here we directly encounter reality and the experience does not lead to any recollection of any linguistic term (literally, recall any sign), nor is the experience impregnated with any concept. It is ineffable. The direct apprehension of the strictly particularized reality is possible, but the awareness is neither conceptual nor linguistic. Finally, the particular is causally efficient, and as causal efficiency or *arthakriyākāritva* is the mark of ultimate reality, so it is the real. We come across at least two explanations of causal efficiency in Buddhist logic. The term *artha* literally means that which we desire. This desire might present itself in two ways: either as a desire to attain the object or as a desire to avoid it. If the object has the power to satisfy the expectations aroused by its cognition, then it is said to be real. This explanation comes from Dharmottara.[10]

As against this, the concept is common to many. We need it to explain the apparent sharable property of the particulars. We know that in Buddhist epistemology the concept does not refer to anything positive, and it is understood only in terms of exclusion. With *svalakṣaṇa*, the positive content excludes everything else in the world, but the universal does not have any positive content at all. Moreover, not only is the universal referred to by words but also its very existence is said to be linguistic. And it lacks causal efficiency, and so, in the ultimate analysis, it is unreal.

Perhaps the Buddhist account of the *sāmānya* requires a little more elucidation. Our sense organs grasp the unique particular, but they do not encounter any property, which the particular shares with others. The particular is strictly self-contained. It is momentary and shares nothing with other moments and other contemporaneous particulars. It excludes universality and continuity. They say that the *rūpa* or the visual form, which belongs to one particular, cannot be present in another particular and if it is not common to many, then it does not stand for any common property. Again, they argue that had *sāmānya* been present in the object, two forms or *ākāras* would constitute the content of perception, which is not the case. In perception we grasp only one form, and that is the form of the unique particular. The *sāmānya* is the function of *kalpanā*, and as such is said to be unreal. Every judgment is said to be a product of *kalpanā*.[11] We see that the Buddhist is giving a particular analysis of experience. The opponent, the Naiyāyika for instance, would look at it differently, saying, as he does, that we see the given "this" as well as the color blue, and even the universal blueness. But the Buddhist consistently focuses the extreme particularity and the uniqueness of the given and that only is said to be the content of perception.

Their arguments are no doubt naïve, but the philosophical insight contained in them is to be appreciated. The Buddhist is aware that in thinking, the mode of awareness is different from that which only accepts the particular presentations. But the next step is unwarranted. Because, from this, they conclude that the concepts are not a part of reality. Instead of accommodating them in a different way, they exile them altogether. They attach special importance to perception, and just because the concepts are not directly presented, they are said to be ontologically inferior.

However, the essential point in Buddhist ontology is the equation of reality and particularity. But in thought, language, and practical dealings, we cannot avoid the universal. The extreme particulars are unrelated and what relates them is the *sāmānya*. The self-defined point instant is momentary and whatever assigns to the object continued existence is the *sāmānya*. According to the Buddhist analysis whatever floats in perception is the form of the object, but whatever transposes the content into a judgment is *kalpanā*, which works with the help of *sāmānya*. So to understand clearly the ontological difference between the particular and the universal, we have to dwell upon the nature of *kalpanā*.

Diṇnāga says that we get the object of ordinary experience through *nāma-jātyādi-yojanā* or application and addition of name, universal, etc. to the perceived content. He means by *nāma* proper names like Devadatta; the others include universals like cowhood, actions such as movement, qualities such as white, substantive qualifiers such as stick in the case of a person with a stick. We have already said that the *Vṛtti* gives more details like number, conjunction, disjunction, etc. But mere prescription that these adjuncts are to be added, does not rule out the possibility of these adjuncts being real. Their general position is that whatever makes the content of perception amenable to thought and language is the product of *kalpanā*.

Dharmakīrti gives a more complicated definition which is rather difficult to decipher. It is *abhilāpa-samsarga-yogya-pratibhāsa-pratīti.*[12] Here *pratibhāsa* is the content floated in cognition and *pratīti* is its awareness. *Abhilāpa* means words, so *abhilāpa-samsarga* amounts to being related to words. Thus the definition of *kalpanā* amounts to awareness of content, which is suitable for expression in language. Dharmottara comments that in *kalpanā*, the form of the object and the word coalesce with each other to form the content of cognition. Stcherbatsky translates the definition as "the denoted aspect and its verbal aspect are mixed up in the apprehended aspect."[13] Dharmakīrti inserts the idea of capability. He says that the content of *kalpanā* is capable of being expressible in language. In this way he tries to accommodate the awareness of children and dumb persons whose thoughts transcend the limits of the given and yet, are not properly speaking linguistic. This leaves scope for asking whether the Buddhists are nominalists or conceptualists.

We feel that the general trend of Buddhist thought is towards nominalism. In the *Vṛtti* we come across such expressions as *sāmānya* involving *saṃketa-smaraṇa* or recollection of a linguistic sign or words. This has also been described as *samayābhoga*, which means fulfillment of a sign.[14] They even compare *sāmānya* with *yadrcchāśabda* or proper names. Like names, these are constructs which refer to objects, although they are in no way a part of reality. A comment from a Nyāya critic of the Buddhist logicians may not be out of place here. Bhāsarvajña says that (just like the Buddhists) they do not accept *buddhi-sāmānya* or thought-universal. Here conceptualism is clearly rejected. It is also to be remembered that the Buddhists explained class awareness negatively, in terms of exclusion only. According to their *apohavāda*, awareness of a universal, say cowness, amounts to denial of non-cows. They do not accept that conceptualistic awareness has any positive content. But, then, it is difficult to understand what exactly Dharmakīrti meant by awareness, which is pre-linguistic, capable of being expressed in language, but nonperceptual.

On the other hand, Śāntarakṣita unambiguously states that *kalpanā* is *abhilāpini pratīti,* or linguistic cognition.[15] The *Vṛtti* says that *kalpanā* grasps the relation between the form involved in the referring term or *vācakākāra* and the referred object or the *vācya.*[16] Here the given is the unique particular that cannot be referred through language. Thus the object and the word collapse into each other in the Buddhist position and they are not talking about any relation between two distincts.

Moreover, the Buddhists hold that the object does not determine the conceptual cognition. Perception, limited to the present, is caused by the momentary real. *Kalpanā* links the past with the present and the present with the future. It assigns continued existence to objects. The object is the fluid series that they call *adhyavaseya* or the object of a judgment.[17] *Nyāyavindu* says that it is about an absent object, so it is not dependent on it. The *Vṛtti* elaborates the same point. It says that the concept is not dependent on the presence or absence of the object. Whether the object is there or it has been destroyed, whether the knower has open eyes or closed ones, the concept remains the same. The percept is influ-

enced by all these factors.[18] The Buddhists consistently deny any essential connection between word and object. Words or concepts are produced by *kalpanā*; they are not aspects of the real. We encounter the real in its concrete particularity through conjunction of sense organs and the real in direct perception. But we never face the universal in the same way. Emphasizing the uniqueness of the real, they argue that to project a universal on a number of particulars is to project an identity, which is not there. This satisfies the traditional definition of error as apprehension of *x* in the seat of non-*x*. So cognition of universal is erroneous.

But the Buddhist does not deny all reality to *sāmānya* and acknowledges their practical usefulness. They describe it as *arūpa nihsvabhava*.[19] It is said to have no form of its own which is cognizable by the senses and therefore it is said to have no essential nature. As we pointed out before, the *sāmānya* does not produce any image, so it is said to be unreal, lacking in causal efficiency. On the other hand, they cannot say that it is nonexistent like the self-contradictory horn of a hare. It has a role to play in our practical dealings.

In this background it is difficult to determine the relation between the particular and the universal. Stcherbatsky holds that "the ultimate end of Buddhist logic is to explain the relation between a moving reality and static constructions of thought."[20] The Buddhists deny almost all possible relations. Nothing in the real world can have two faces, the particular and the universal, for two properties opposed to each other cannot be located in the same place. There cannot be any similarity between the two, because one is real and the other is not. For the same reason the two relations recognized by the Buddhists, identity and causal relation, do not hold between them. Nor is the particular a *vyañjaka* of the universal or the focus through which the latter expresses itself, for even in the absence of the particular the universal is used. When a perceptual judgment takes place, the content is a particular intertwined with the universal. So one might claim that the particular is the *vyañjaka* of the universal. But then, for the cognition of the universal, the presence of the particular is not a necessary condition, and hence is irrelevant for the awareness of the universal.

Some Buddhists suggest that the relation between the two is *sārupya*, which is usually translated as coordination. *Sārūpya* literally means resemblance. J. N. Mohanty says that "for the Buddhist *sārūpya*, though literally meaning 'resemblance', is to be understood as 'similarity between two things absolutely dissimilar' (*atyanta-vilakṣaṇānām sālakṣaṇyam*)."[21] This explains the Buddhist position very accurately, even after severing all possible connections they still want to retain some relation.

The Buddhists had to face another question asked by the opponents. If the universal is purely a product of *kalpanā*, then how is it that we direct it towards the external objects, or how is it that we apply a specific universal to a specific particular and not to others? How do we explain the apparent essential bond between the two? They do not have any clear and consistent answer to this and they appeal to the principle of ignorance. Bimal Matilal comments that an appeal to the principle of ignorance is to acknowledge that it is philosophically unaccountable.[22]

It is clearly discernible that in their ontological analysis, the Buddhists do not accept any connection between the particular real and the conceptual world of experience. It is to be noted that the cognition does not interpret, explain, or amplify the data of experience, but it projects the concepts on the real. The conceptual cognition has been described as *saṃvṛta āropita jñāna*. This means that the projected world of conceptual experience serves to hide and conceal reality.[23] But it has also been called *saṃvyavahārika jñāna* or cognition, which is practically valuable. Here we find that the purely theoretical and the practical are drifting apart. If we looked at the conceptual world as a purely theoretical construct built upon the sensed data, then we could preserve some sort of linkage between the two. But the Buddhists look at the world as a product of imagination, which is not compelled by the inner demand of reality but is produced by some cosmic ignorance. Hence the conceptual scheme has been aptly described as "desire dominated construction," "dispensable imaginative construct" generated by linguistic practice, etc. Here we have to concede that there is an unbridgeable gap between the real and the conceptual.

In fact if the universal were unreal, then the necessary corollary is that the *svalakṣaṇa* alone is real. Some Buddhists uphold this by saying *meyam tvekam svalakṣaṇam* or the object of knowledge is only the self characterized real.[24] Dharmakīrti describes the object of inference as *anartha* or unreal. He holds that inference is to be considered as deviant cognition; it arouses activity towards judged object, which is unreal. We say that it does not possess *yāthārthya* or the property of depicting the object as it is. It fails to grasp the unique real, which excludes every other real by its particularity. The Buddhists do not explain the exact meaning of *yāthārthya*; in fact, they seldom dwell on it. But the prephilosophical idea that cognitions mirror the reality is operative here. To explain the apparent inconsistencies we have to impute to them this *yāthārthya.* The Buddhists assign to mediate knowledge truth as only practical workability, but they also try to anchor this property in some awareness of reality. Further, this position directly contradicts the original Buddhist position proposed by the masters that there are two different types of knowable, the particular and the conceptual, and tagged to these two different types of true cognitions: the perceptual and the inferential. Let us see how they combine the two in their scheme.

III

In Buddhist logic truth has been defined as *avisaṃvādakatva* or nonincoherence.[25] The introduction of two negative epithets is not meant to ensure any logical accuracy or exactness. It does not stand for coherence with any organized body of knowledge. It has been explained as *prāpakatva* or the property of making one reach the object. This again has been explained as *pradarśakatva* or the property of manifesting or exhibiting the object. This is identical with

pravartakatva or the property of moving or directing a person to activity. Their position is that cognition precedes all activity, so cognition is the attainer.

In this background *prāpakatva* might be interpreted in two different ways. Dharmakīrti has tried to preserve and retain the purely theoretical nature of cognition. He reads *prāpakatva* as the property of manifesting the object, which is capable of attainment. He insists that attainment need not mean actual attainment. Cognitions inform, they do not impel, they are *jñāpaka* and not *kāraka.* Perception is *pramā* as it reveals an object regulated by space, time, etc. So also is inference, which reveals an object determined by *hetu.* On the other hand, doubt and error are non-attainers, as they are directed towards unattainables, that is, nonexistent objects. The unattainability of object of doubt might be clear from the form of doubt; but how can the unattainability of the object of error be found out without the help of actual action?

The tilt towards a practical interpretation of *prāpakatva* cannot be overlooked. The object that is attained is as much an object of cognition as of action. According to the Buddhists themselves it is *viṣaya* as well as *artha. Artha* literally means the object of desire. The real object is said to be *arthakriyāsamartha* or capable of satisfying the expectations aroused by the cognition of the object. They have differentiated between the object that is grasped and the object that is attained. The object that is directly encountered in prejudgmental perception is momentary and can never be attained. It has only serial connection with the object that is attained. Instead of reading coherence as that with other cognitions, they look at it as *arthakriyā samvāda* or accordance with the function of the object. Dharmakīrti has acknowledged in *Pramāṇa Vārttika* that the definition of *prāmāṇya* as *avisaṃvādakatva* is *saṃvyavahārika* or belongs to the realm of practice.[26]

All these considerations about truth, the vacillation between the purely theoretical and the practical approaches, affect their final conclusion about the truth of various types of cognition. Perception, which is equivalent of *nirvikalpaka pratyakṣa* of other systems, is said to be *pramā.* It is true not because it has access to the self-definable real but because it possesses non-incoherence. In their discussion of truth, the Buddhists take truth as *avisaṃvādakatva.* This type of *pratyakṣa* is at once *bhāsaka* and *prāpaka*; it manifests the object and also makes attainment of the object possible. The Buddhists are aware that perception itself is dumb; and without the help of the judgmental formulation, left to itself, it fails even to be a proper attainer. Uninterpreted perception is merely *bhāsaka* or manifester, and not even *jñāpaka* or informer. To become the latter, it needs help from imagination. But still it is assigned truth in every sense because of its direct connection with reality.

Surprisingly enough, judgmental perception is exiled from the realm of truth. It is denied truth, not because it involves *kalpanā,* which covers up the unique real, but because the Buddhists supplement the definition of truth as non-incoherence by another clause. The non-incoherence must belong to the cognition by its own right and it must not be a borrowed property. Judgmental perception borrows it from the initial perception, on which it is parasitical and so it is

not *pramā*.[27] Inference, which completely belongs to the realm of *kalpanā,* is said to be *pramā*, as it leads a person to reality.

Here comes our difficulty with the Buddhist position. Cognition does not become true just through its connection with the unique real. It has to be the attainer of a distinct specific object. But space, time, forms, etc., the adjuncts that specify the object, are all superimposed by *kalpanā*. So, after advocating a total disconnection of the unique real from the world of *kalpanā*, they cannot claim that the properties present in the judgmental cognition correspond to those in the object. And as they emphasize the uniqueness of the momentary real, and accept no sharable property of two reals, how can they be sure that the momentary real manifested and the one attained belong to the same series?

Kalpanā has often been compared with the faculty of imagination as found in the philosophies of Hume and Kant, which transform the mutually unrelated sense data into the organized world. Only *kalpanā* could bridge the gulf between the sense data, which is grasped, and the world of thought. But in the Buddhist philosophy, *kalpanā* has not been accorded such a position of honor. Śantarakṣit has claimed that *kalpanā* is the appearance of the denoting name as regulated by the appeared object. However, we have shown earlier that the Buddhists do not accept such a regulation. They seldom accept that the particular is the determinant of the universal. They would rather say that *kalpanā* is not aroused by the object, but is awakened by the traces left by words.[28]

Interestingly, the Vṛttikāra speaks of two different types of *kalpanā* or imagination: one creative and the other erroneous. The creative faculty is responsible for the application of words (*samketa samśrayā kalpanā*); disconnected data are conjoined to create objects to which we apply names and all this is the work of *kalpanā*. But the same faculty is responsible for our perception of sunrays as water (*anyārtha kalpanā*).[29] The Buddhist does not want to recognize any difference between the two; in both the cases imagination is supposed to conceal the exact nature of reality. If they accepted qualitative difference between the two, where one leads to organized practical life and the other is behind failure in practice, then their position would have been easier to decipher.

To sum up: the Buddhists speak about two different types of cognition, perception and inference, or as Stcherbatsky puts it in a slightly different way, immediate and mediate cognitions. Two different ideas about truth are present here. One of them is *yāthārthya* or the non-deviating character of cognitions. It actually stands for the property of grasping the essential nature of object or the object as it is. The Buddhists do not dwell upon the concept of truth as *yāthārthya*, but obviously such a concept is present in their system. Unless we impute to them such a concept of truth, the difference between the *pāramārthika* and the *vyavahārika*, that which is true per se and that which is true for all our practical dealings, cannot satisfactorily be explained. The other concept of truth is *prāmāṇya*, which is the property of leading one to the attainment of the object.

IV

Keeping these two concepts of truth in mind—the *pāramārthika* and the *vyavahārika*—we discuss the truth-value of three types of cognition in their system. First of them is the prepredicative perception, which is true in both the above senses. It has privileged access to the momentary real and, being rooted in reality, is supposed to be the attainer of the real too. Next comes the judgmental perception, which lacks truth in both the above senses. Being tainted with *kalpanā* it transcends reality; and even when it leads to attainment of reality, the attainment is parasitical on the first prejudgmental step, and so it lacks *prāmāṇya* too. And last, inference lacks truth in the first sense, but is the seat of the second. Being a product of *kalpanā* it does not grasp the unique real; but being related to the real indirectly, it is said to be true. It arouses activities that end up in the attainment of the real. Hence there emerges the peculiar position, namely, inference is at once true and untrue. Dharmakīrti clearly says in *Pramāṇavārttika* that it is not dissimilar to erroneous cognitions (being deviant from reality), but, it leads to practical success (which error lacks), and is, in this respect, different from error. *Mithyā jñānāviśeṣe'pi viśeṣo' rthakriyam prati.*[30] Another supporting comment is that even error attains truth by possessing the property of non-incoherence. *Abhiprāyāvisaṃvādādapi bhrānteḥ pramāṇatā.*[31]

Buddhist treatment of error clearly shows that they understand error and truth in two different ways. The *Vṛtti* describes error as cheating.[32] Literally speaking, error is that which deviates from the practically efficient real. This deviation has been understood in two different ways. It can mean failure to lead to the attainment of the object. But error might also mean apprehension of an object in a way that is different from its own form. By contrast, Nyāya and several other schools hold that practical success indicates that the object has been correctly depicted. But the Buddhists hold that the object might be reached even when it has not been correctly manifested; they do not see any essential connection between the two. Bimal Matilal says, "Verbal reports in Nyāya are innocent until proven guilty, while in Buddhism they are always guilty (wrong), although some of them may not mislead us." We can extend this view to all cognitions. This also explains the Buddhist theory of *svataḥ-aprāmāṇyavāda* or the view that all determinate cognitions are essentially erroneous. It is usually held that according to the Buddhists all cognitions are naturally false but some of them gain truth by practical success. Here we should clearly see that two meanings of truth and error present in Buddhist thought, and a confusion of the two, gives rise to such misleading comments about their philosophy. But the point remains that if practical success is not due to the nature of cognition, then the relation between truth and cognition becomes totally accidental. Their claim that there is an intimate connection between the two has not been clearly worked out.

Some speak of the pristine purity of primary perception. But the Buddhists do not look upon perception as the sure and certain foundation of knowledge. They hold that mere freedom from *kalpanā* does not ensure truth for error may

creep in through other holes. They give some examples of disturbing factors such as color-blindness, rapid motion, traveling on a moving ship, and sickness. So it is difficult to say why they accord such a privileged position to prepredicative perception.

In conclusion, I revise my introductory proposal. Instead of saying that the Buddhists deal with the theoretical and the practical aspects of cognition, it is better to say that their main concern is with cognitive experience and corresponding thought and report of it. The first of them is the direct and unique apprehension of the real. They have the valuable insight that experience involves a uniqueness, which thought and language can neither grasp nor communicate. But just because thought fails to report and preserve the unique essence of experience, it cannot be granted a lesser status. They evaluate both experience and thought by the same standard. It would have been interesting if instead of blaming thought of hiding and distorting reality, the Buddhists could work out a proper relationship between the two. Then their attempt to anchor practice in the experience of the real world would have been more successful and the practical and the theoretical would not have drifted apart.

Notes

1. Dharmakīrti, *Nyāyavindu* with *Tīkā* of Dharmottara (Varanasi, India: Chowkhamba Sanskrit Sanstha, 1982), 10.
2. Dharmakīrti, *Nyāyavindu*, 12.
3. Dharmakīrti, *Nyāyavindu*, 23.
4. J. N. Mohanty, *Reason and Tradition in Indian Thought* (Oxford: Clarendon Press, 1992), 240.
5. Dharmakīrti, *Pramāṇavārttika*, with *Vṛtti* of Manorathanandin (Varanasi, India: 1968), II/6.
6. Śantarakṣita, *Tattvasaṃgraha*, with *Pañjikā* of Kamalaśīla ed. Dwarikadas Sastri (Varanasi, India: Bauddha Bharati, 1968), 16.
7. Dharmakīrti, *Nyāyavindu*, 23.
8. Manorathanandin, *Vṛtti*, II/3.
9. Manorathanandin, *Vṛtti*, II/51.
10. Dharmakīrti, *Nyāyavindu*, 24.
11. Manorathanandin, *Vṛtti*, II /6, *vikalpabuddhirastu kalpikā*, II /6.
12. Dharmakīrti, *Nyāyavindu*, 13.
13. T. Stcherbatsky, *Buddhist Logic*, vol. II (New York: Dover, 1962), 19.
14. Manorathanandin, *Vṛtti*, II/5, 6.
15. Śāntarakṣita, *Tattvasaṃgraha*, śloka, 1213.
16. Manorathanandin, *Vṛtti*, II/126.
17. Dharmottara, *Tīka*, 22.
18. Manorathanandin, *Vṛtti*, II/39.
19. Manorathanandin, *Vṛtti*, II/28.
20. Stcherbatsky, *Buddhist Logic*, vol. I, 2.
21. Mohanty, *Reason and Tradition in Indian Thought*, 167.

22. B.K. Matilal, *Perception: An Essay on Classical Indian Theories of Knowledge* (Oxford: Clarendon Press, 1986), 313.
23. Manorathanandin, *Vṛtti*, II/289, 290.
24. Dharmakīrti, *Pramāṇavārttika*, II/53.
25. Dharmakīrti, *Nyāyavindu*, 5.
26. Manorathanandin, *Vṛtti*, I/7.
27. Manorathanandin, *Vṛtti*, I/7.
28. Manorathanandin, *Vṛtti*, *sa ca saṃketasamskāramātrabhāvinī nārthādhīneti* II/6.
29. Manorathanandin, *Vṛtti*, II/290.
30. Manorathanandin, *Vṛtti*, II/55.
31. Dharmakīrti, *Pramāṇavārttika*, II/56.
32. Manorathanandin, *Vṛtti*, II/3.
33. Manorathanandin, *Vṛtti*, II/56, *pararūpeṇa gati brāntiḥ*.

Krishna Chandra Bhattacharyya and *Anekāntavāda*

In the nineteenth century, the confluence of the age-old philosophical traditions of India and the contemporary Western thought currents gave rise to several scholars who were trained in both these disciplines and followed their philosophical inquiries along interesting new dimensions. Most of them used concepts from Western philosophy as tools to understand Indian philosophy in a new light. Krishna Chandra Bhattacharyya (1875-1949) is an exception.[1] He digested well the idealisms of West and East, which include Hegel and Kant, Advaita and Sāmkhya, and whatever he gives to the world are his very own thoughts.

Those who studied philosophy under Krishna Chandra consider him a profound thinker but admit that it is difficult to understand his published works. In a discussion of Krishna Chandra's conception of philosophy, his direct student and a renowned philosopher Ras Vihary Das says, "Krishna Chandra was perhaps the acutest philosophical thinker of modern India" and then adds, "(his) written language is always very terse and sometimes even cryptic."[2] His son Kalidas Bhattacharyya, a highly respected philosopher in his own merit, writes in his preface to *The Fundamentals of K. C. Bhattacharyya's Philosophy*, "his writings are extraordinarily terse" and his "analyses are bafflingly subtle."[3] Yet serious scholars of idealism and phenomenology are invariably attracted to his work. J. N. Mohanty refers to him in his discussion of grades of subjectivity, in his interpretation of Sāmkhya, in his essay on linguistic understanding, and in his analyses of truth.[4]

Gopinath Bhattacharyya says about Krishna Chandra's interpretation of Sāmkhya, Yoga, and Vedānta that it is development in new directions of some fundamental tenets of these schools. "It is development not in the sense of necessary amplification of what is potential therein; it is rather the discovery of new potentialities," he adds.[5] This applies to Krishna Chandra's interpretation of the Jaina theory of *Anekānta*. In fact, instead of saying that it is an interpretation of the old concept, it would be far more accurate to say that it is an extension of

his fundamental position, keeping the Jaina concept in the forefront. In this essay, I present my thoughts on Krishna Chandra's views about *Anekāntavāda* along these lines.

Anekāntavāda does not constitute an integral part of idealism, and is often neglected in the discussion of Krishna Chandra's philosophy. I find his article *The Jaina Theory of Anekānta* interesting in itself. Moreover, I also feel that a good understanding of it may help one to understand his overall idealistic position easily.

Krishna Chandra said that ordinary realism is committed to the conception of a "plurality of determinate truths."[6] We find that this is true of the traditional Jaina concept of *Anekāntavāda*. But Krishna Chandra reads the theory differently. He describes it as ultra realism. His position is that, according to the Jainas, the given can be presented in various ways, all of which need not necessarily be determinate and definite. He explains this by interpreting the seven modes of truth advocated by the Jainas in his own way.

I preface my presentation with two short summaries of Krishna Chandra's views. In the first, I speak of *Anekāntavāda* as it has been developed in the traditional texts. Here the seven *bhangas* have been seen as alternatives; but they are all coordinate and each of them is definite. In the second, I talk about *Anekāntavāda*, as it has been interpreted by Bimal Matilal. I take him to be an ideal interpreter, for he looks at *Anekāntavāda* and the associated views from our position, and consistently brings out various implications, using the contemporary philosophical tools lying at his disposal. In the concluding section I speak of Krishna Chandra.

In the last section of *The Jaina Theory of Anekānta*, Krishna Chandra describes it as a theory of indeterministic truth. He holds that truth need not necessarily be determinate; what is presented in experience can be definitely thinkable or not definitely thinkable. In different papers he speaks of the indefinite. He urges for the "admission of the indefinite logic, side by side with definite position and definite negation."[7] According to him the indefinite has found a place in metaphysics. The list, in which he gives a few examples of the indefinite chosen at random, includes "the 'negative' matter of Plato, the māyā of the Vedāntists, and the śūnyam or 'void' of the Buddhists."[8] He mentions many more. It seems that whatever is indispensable for a particular system of thought, but cannot be defined rationally and definitely, has been termed by him indefinite. He speaks of the indefinite as homeless in logic. However, his search ends in the Jaina system, where the indefinite has been accepted as an integral part of logic.

Krishna Chandra thinks that the seven expressions of the seven-valued logic of the Jainas reflect seven faces of the real and their relationship is not *togetherness* but *alternation*. He comments about Jaina philosophy that "the faith in one truth or even in a plurality of truths, each simply given as determinate, would be rejected by it as a species of intolerance."[9] While this would not be denied by the Jainas, it is to be noted that they accept each of the expressions as determinate, and they do not clarify the exact nature of alternation.

Further, because of their appeal to standpoints (in order to answer the charge of incompatibility) their seven expressions can be interpreted to stand for a collection of truths. From this, Krishna Chandra's position is definitely different. In order to understand him even in broad outlines, we shall have to enter his own realm of thinking and decipher such concepts as "togetherness," "definite-indefinite," "alternation," etc., which he used in his own specific sense. Let us see how far we can understand this highly original thinker.

I

Anekāntavāda and *Syādvāda* are closely associated with each other. *Anekāntavāda* literally means the theory of non-onesidedness. In his introduction to *Anekāntajayapatākā*, the editor says, "*Anekāntavāda* stands for a many-sided exposition."[10] Historically, *Anekāntavāda* originated as a protest against *Ekāntavāda* or the one-sided absolutistic systems, such as Buddhism, Vedānta, etc. But we find that *Anekāntavāda* has an ontological significance and it asserts that reality is non-onesided. In this sense it holds that reality has infinite facets. But this is not mere pluralism. It claims that reality has opposite faces. For example, it is said that the real is *anekātmaka* being both universal and particular or being both substance and attribute.[11] The Jainas not only hold that the real has contrary features, but they also assert that contradictories, such as existence and non-existence, are also aspects of the same real.[12]

Syādvāda, on the other hand, is fully a theory of predication. It recommends that the epithet "*syāt*" should be attached to every expression. *Syāt* is said to be an indeclinable, which literally means "may be."[13] But, "may be" might suggest a subjective sense of uncertainty, which is unwelcome to the Jaina realist. *Syāt* is thus taken to mean "in some respect" in this context. Thus *Syādvāda* asserts that all expressions are relational, being attached to different perspectives. Further, it implies that every predication is true, but it never expresses the whole truth.

We see that Kapadia claims that *Anekāntavāda* and *Syādvāda* are synonyms. He quotes from *Syādvādamañjari* of Mallisen Sury to make his point. The quotation asserts that "*Syāt*, the indeclinable signifies non-onesidedness, so it is *Anekāntavāda*."[14] But this approach overlooks the fact that *Anekāntavāda* has its ontological nuances. Strictly speaking, *Syādvāda* is meant to emphasize the partial and the relational nature of the judgments, and as such it has no necessary connection with *anekānta* reality. But *Syādvāda* is coupled with the seven-valued logic of the Jainas. *Saptabhangīnayavāda* is founded on *anekānta* ontology.

Vādi Devasūri says that a word in expressing its object follows the law of sevenfold predication.[15] *Saptabhangī* is defined as use of seven sorts of expression, regarding one and the same thing, with reference to its one chosen particular aspect, without any inconsistency, by means of affirmation and negation, either severally or jointly, being marked with "in some respects."[16]

Obviously, the apparently inconsistent predications are possible because of the *syāt*. Vādi Devasūri makes it clear that seven types of predication are about each of the infinite faces of the real.[17] So it holds, that the real is infinitefold and its faces are sometimes opposed to one another. The *saptabhangī* is dependent upon both *Syādvāda* and the *anekānta* nature of reality.

In the seven-valued logic the first two forms are positive and negative, "S is" and "S is not," respectively. Naturally these are mutually incompatible. All other criticisms directed against the particular Jaina position are traceable to this fundamental charge of inconsistency. The Jainas assert that in the non-onesided reality these mutually opposed features exist in the same substance, and from different standpoints opposite predications are possible. Through analysis of concrete examples they present their position. From the theory of inference they give their example. It is urged that the *hetu* should have both *sapakṣasattā* and *vipakṣāsattā*, that is, the *hetu* must exist in the *sapakṣa* and not exist in the *vipakṣa*. Thus in different locations existence and nonexistence are features of the same hetu and we can consistently assert that "in some respects the hetu exists" and "in some respects the hetu does not exist."[18]

The *syāt*, which means the indefinite "in some respect," has been amplified to include definite determinants like space, time, substantiality, etc. The list remains open and many other determinants might be added. By varying these determinants, "S is" becomes "S is not." The pitcher, which exists as solid, does not exist as liquid; that which is existent in Kānyakubja is not existent at Mathurā; that which is existent in summer is nonexistent in winter; that which is existent as black is nonexistent as red; and so on. In all these expressions we are talking about reality. Thus both in reality and in corresponding expressions, mutually opposed features are co-present.[19]

In the third form the first two are combined consecutively; this is called *kramārpaṇa*. Because of the time difference, there is no incompatibility. Thus it is said, "in some respect the pitcher exists and it does not exist" or "in some respect, "S is and S is not." In the fourth form or *sahārpaṇa* the first two expressions are to be conjoined simultaneously. It is impossible to say that the pitcher exists and it does not exist, without sacrificing the law of contradiction, unless one is talking figuratively. But the Jainas are doing serious consistent logic, and they say that here the pitcher is inexpressible. As is well known by combining the fourth *bhanga* with the other three, we get the last three forms of the expression: "in some respect S is and is inexpressible," "in some respect, S is not and is inexpressible," and "in some respect, S is and is not and is inexpressible."

The Jainas have further added that none of these seven forms is more basic than the others. One must not hold that the positive forms are more fundamental and the negatives lean on them. A word does not express a negation indirectly. The general tenet is that something can be presented indirectly, only when it has been known directly.[20] Sometimes it is claimed that the fourth predication is absolutely true, whereas the other forms are relatively true, that is, true in some respects only, so it must be assigned a special position. But this is not acceptable

to the Jainas, for according to them an absence of viewpoint is itself a viewpoint and the description "inexpressible" does not exhaustively express the nature of the given.[21] So all the forms of expression are coordinate according to the Jainas.

Further, it is said that the predications are meant to distinguish an object from other objects. Thus each of these expressions indicate the definite and determinate nature of the object.[22]

Both these two points are important for us for we shall see how Bimal Matilal dwells upon both of them and how Krishna Chandra drifted away.

We feel that the Jainas, who claim to be realists, should have worked out the *anekānta* ontology in further detail. The general idea is that these expressions are not merely different subjective ways of knowing reality, but there is some objective reality corresponding to these. What is the exact ontological status of these correlates of the seven forms of expression? If these be *paryāya*, or modes of the real, then the critic would urge that each of them should again be judged, in their own turn, in seven different ways which would naturally lead to infinite regress. The Jainas did not raise this issue. The mutual relation of these expressions was supposed to be alternation; these were presented as alternative descriptions of the same reality. The Jainas do not comment on the nature of this alternation.

II

Bimal Matilal has been interested in the concept of *Anekāntavāda* and has dwelt on it in many places. He makes a number of valuable observations, but here I have picked out only one or two of them, which are relevant for our discussion.

He presents *Anekāntavāda* as a philosophy of synthesis and reconciliation. Like many other commentators, he also maintains "the Jainas carried the principle of non-violence to the intellectual level, and thus propounded their *Anekānta* doctrine."[23] Many, including Krishna Chandra, favor this view. Bimal further continues that the Jainas, like the Buddhists, saw the evils of one-sided philosophies, and while the Buddhists rejected the extreme views and prescribed the middle path, the Jainas held that all rival conclusions might be retained and reconciled, provided they are asserted with proper qualifications and conditionalizations.

By directing our attention to this prescription of the original Jaina theory, he brings out the latent weakness of the Jaina position. He shows that the *syāt* operator does not mean "perhaps" or "may be," it does not indicate any hesitancy on the part of the knowing subject, but it stands for "conditional yes."[24] He shows that the expression "syāt S is" and "syāt S is not" actually stand for "from standpoint 1, S is" and "from standpoint 2, S is not." Thus they can be easily represented by two conditionals, "If m, then S is P" and "If n, then S is not P." So although the pair of categorical propositions looks mutually inconsistent, the conditionals are not at all incompatible with each other. This trans-

lation shows that the charge of incompatibility cannot be leveled against the Jainas. But it also shows that in the sevenfold scheme of propositions, the Jainas are not talking about the same ontological situation. The two expressions, "If m, then S is P" and "If n, then S is not P," have no logical relation at all, the antecedents being different. He clearly shows that the different *bhangas* in the sevenfold scheme are conditionals, having the appearance of categoricals. Variable determinants are hidden behind the same epithet "*syāt*."

Although in their commentaries the Jainas have clearly asserted that the epithet *syāt* stands for the different conditions and different expressions, still the use of the same word *syāt* has often been misleading. Readers are inadvertently led to think that the judgments are made under the same condition. Bimal's discussions bring out this point. Pradeep P. Gokhale says that the specification of the *syāt* amounts to distortion of the original logical form of the *syāt*. He says that "the peculiarity and the beauty of *syādvāda* lies in indicating the existence of *some* standpoint, *some* condition or *some* respect, which makes the given statement true."[25] So he says that Bimal's recommendation that the so-called categoricals in the seven-valued logic are definite conditionals fail to capture the exact implication of *syāt*. He, however, does not deny that here expressions are tied to varying standpoints. So without entering into a critical evaluation of his own scheme, we may say that he would agree with us that even if Bimal's translations distort the original vagueness associated with *syāt,* it establishes that *syādvāda* is a doctrine of standpoints. But we see that it also shows that the judgments do not converge upon the same reality and they cannot be accepted as alternative descriptions of the same reality. So though the charge of incompatibility cannot be leveled against the Jainas, their theory no more remains significantly valuable. The seven *bhangas* become a collection of seven judgments asserted about a pluralistic reality. Their mutual relation can no more be called alternation.

When the Jainas originally talked about different philosophical theories about Reality (with a capital R), their theory made some sense. They held that differences of standpoint, of categorial frameworks, of priorities, accounted for philosophical differences of various theories and with proper explanations these could be reconciled. But the defect of the Jaina position becomes clear through the discussion of empirical propositions.

Bimal Matilal puts his position even more clearly in his last article on *Anekāntavāda*. He shows that indexical elements are responsible for the determination of truth-value, and thus by varying these elements, we can say "yes" and "no" to the same proposition. This is a very consistent and at the same time revealing rendering of the Jaina position that propositions are always tied to standpoints, and no position is absolutely true. But after drawing out many other corollaries of the Jaina proposition, he is aware that in and through his interpretation the core of the *Anekānta* metaphysics is lost, the core which emphasized the "contradictory and opposite sides of the same reality." However, he points out that in spite of all our explanations, we cannot explain away the fourth expression where contradictory predicates are asserted simultaneously of

the same reality, under the same *syāt*, and the predicate emerges as a "separate and non-composite value called *avaktavya*."[26]

He does not himself satisfactorily explain how each expression can be assigned this value without flouting the law of contradiction, and what is the precise nature of the real, which answers this description. Perhaps the *syāt* here stands for the viewpoint of no viewpoint, or the condition of unconditionality. He draws many analogues from modern logic, but he is not fully satisfied with any of these. The Jainas are aware that here opposed predicates clash with each other, they accept it as a standpoint coordinate with other standpoints, but they do not positively explain what this standpoint stands for.

I think that Bimal gives a faithful interpretation of Jaina logic. Here Krishna Chandra's attitude is radically different. He is basically interested in *Anekānta* ontology. Within reality he sees various facets and their mutual relation is indetermination and alternation. He does not speak of empirical standpoints at all. His starting point is that the given real is both particular and universal. Then he turns to the mutual interrelation of these two categories and derives all the seven *bhangas* from it. I turn to Krishna Chandra in the next section.

III

Krishna Chandra is looking for seven ontological faces of reality, which would correspond to the seven *bhangas* of the Jaina logic. The experienced object before all metaphysical dissection has been called the determinate existent. One face of this given object is particularity. This particularity is conferred to the given object by experience. But Krishna Chandra is quite aware that according to realism experience does not constitute objects, but merely discovers. Thus, corresponding to the experience or thought of positing a particular, there must be a face of the real object. This face is called "being" and it corresponds to the first *bhanga* of the *saptabhanginaya*, namely, "S is." But the same determinate existent is existence universal, shorn of all its particularity. Existence or thinghood, being universal is opposed to particularity. The determinate existent has a definite position in experience and the given is experienced as universal existence only through the rejection of its particularity. So the same given real bereft of all particular characters is called negation, by Krishna Chandra. It corresponds to "S is not."

Krishna Chandra here comments that "the same logic is sometimes expressed by saying that a determinate existent A *is* in one respect and *is not* in another."[27] But it is amply clear that this "respect" is very different from the traditional Jaina concept of standpoint. Instead of recommending a shift in the empirical perspective, he is dwelling upon the interrelation of two ontological categories. The Jaina thinker Vādi Deva has said that the real is both universal and particular being infinitefold, but he did not interpret the *bhangas* in this way.

The determinate existent has been described here as "definite definite." The first "definite," or the adjectival definite, indicates the definiteness of experience, it is the objective counterpart of thought. The second "definite," the substantival definite, stands for the content of experience. As the objective face corresponding to the position or assertion of the given as particular and the objective givenness as existence are definitely distinct from each other, their relation is differenced togetherness, or definite distinction. This answers the third *bhanga* of the Jainas, which is "S is and S is not." In traditional thought this is conescutive presentation or *kramārpaṇa*. Krishna Chandra is merely stating here that both the faces are present in the real and he is logically analysing the content and is not talking of temporal consecutiveness.

But in experience the given is not necessarily always definite. When we focus on the clashing nature of two faces, in copresentation or *sahārpaṇa*, the faces tend to erase and cancel each other. The two cannot be present in the real simultaneously; they seem to drive away each other. It is not possible to analyze the content of this expression by using positive assertions; through double negations the content is described as not a particular position, nor nonexistent.[28] This analysis shows that there is an inexplicable surd in the content of the given, but being given in experience, its claim to reality is undeniable. The content is called indefinite; it is described as "definite indefinite" by Krishna Chandra. The experience and its objectivized face are definite, but the content is indefinite; the two incompatibles combine here through the relation of non-distinction. Here Krishna Chandra uses two unusual concepts, the concept of "indefinite" and that of "non-distinction." In the earlier part of the article he analyzes both the concepts.

He develops the concept of indefinite through two illustrations. In the first one he analyzes the concept of knowledge of knowledge. For realism there is no distinction between knowledge and known, for both are equally objective. Pure realism does not accept the difference between contemplating and enjoying; for it, both the object and knowledge belong to the realm of the known. The difficulty arises when we dwell upon the concept of knowledge of knowledge. Do we differentiate between knowledge as known and the object as known? Knowledge has to be known as different and distinct from the known. Krishna Chandra takes here two easy steps: knowledge has to be known as unknown (that is as distinct from known). This is self-contradictory, but yet it is presented in experience; thus it is known as indefinite. Whatever cannot be rationally articulated, but is presented in experience, is said to be indefinite.

He introduces the concept of objective indefinite by referring to Hobhouse. According to Hobhouse, in simple apprehension, what is apprehended is definite, but it has an indefinite background. The indefinite is here apprehended too, but it is apprehended as indefinite. The indefinite which Krishna Chandra introduces in the context of the *Anekānta* reality, corresponds to the *avaktavya* of the seven-valued logic.

While analyzing the different faces of reality and their mutual relation, Krishna Chandra speaks of three basal categories, namely, "distinction, distinc-

tion from distinction as other than distinction, and the indetermination of the two."[29] When the relata are distinct and determinate their relation is distinction. According to Krishna Chandra ordinary realism is satisfied with distinction. In the third mode of reality the relation between the positive and the negative phase is distinction. This has also been described as "differenced togetherness." The relation, which is distinct from distinction, should have been identity. But Krishna Chandra does not accept identity as a determinate relation. By discussing Hegel and Nyāya, Krishna Chandra shows that identity always involves distinction, and here either identity or distinction becomes more prominent than the other. If within identity, both are accepted as coordinate, then the relation should be more aptly called distinction from distinction. The relation between being and negation in the fourth mode is this distinction from distinction, which has also been described as indeterminate distinction or non-distinction.

Krishna Chandra next introduces the third type of relation, which he calls indetermination or alternation. As we have seen, according to Krishna Chandra, the mutual relation of particularity and thinghood is both distinction and non-distinction. As distinct their relation is "differenced togetherness," which corresponds to the third mode; as non-distinct their relation is "undifferenced togetherness," which corresponds to the fourth mode. The relation between each of these modes is alternation or indetermination. He says "particularity and thinghood are in each relation without being in the other relation at the same time."[30] The relation between all the four forms is this relation of indetermination. The whole analysis is ontological, so this relation is to be understood as a relation between the faces themselves.

Krishna Chandra next explains the three other modes of reality. He says that there is a basic distinction between the "definite given" and the "indefinite given." The first three modes are the three faces of the definite. The fourth one is indefinite as such; it is to be combined with the first three modes. In the first, the indefinite itself is taken to be a particular, and as such is to be combined with the definite determinate existent itself.

Thus we have seven modes of truth, which are seven faces of the real, too. These are:

1. Particular position (substantive corresponding to the verb positing)
2. Universal thinghood, which is the negation of the particular.
3. Position and negation, together with their distinction. This is determinate existent.
4. Indefinite, in which the particular and the universal are indistinguishably together. There is no clear-cut distinction between the two, yet they do not collapse into identity.
5. This indefinite as being.
6. This indefinite as many negations together.
7. The indefinite as distinct from determinate existent.

No other eighth mode is possible, as that would be identical with the indefinite.

Krishna Chandra says that each of these modes implies the other modes and implication as objectivized is alternation. Each of these modes is distinct, but as they converge upon the same reality they are also non-distinct. The alternation between the equally undeniable but mutually exclusive faces is said to be the essence of reality. The alternation is not a subjective sense of vacillation or hesitancy, but an objectively real relation.

The concept of indefinite occupies a very important place in Krishna Chandra's philosophy. This becomes especially evident in his interpretation of the last three modes. In the traditional Jaina logic the fifth expression is that the given object is and is indescribable. According to Krishna Chandra the indefinite itself is a being or a particular position. Similarly, in the traditional thought the sixth expression asserts that the given is not and is indescribable, whereas he speaks of it as asserting that the given indefinite is a fusion of many indistinguishable negations.

His theory of expressions just reflects reality. True to his assertion that according to the realists thought only discovers and does not constitute reality, his theory of judgments only reflected the real, so that the role of *syāt* operator is minimal. He answers the charge of incompatibility through the concept of alternation. His position is that the clashing faces of reality are all real if they are given in experience. Their mutual relation is alternation and not co-presence or just togetherness. Thus the charge of contradiction is bypassed through alternation and indetermination.

Here I return to the comment of Gopinath Bhattacharyya, quoted by me in the introduction. Bimal amplified the potentialities present in the traditional *Anekāntavāda*. But Krishna Chandra discovers new potentialities, such that the theory changes beyond recognition. He calls this ultra realism. But if *Anekāntavāda* is different from realism, it is so only after Krishna Chandra's interpretation. Krishna Chandra says that realism believes in a plurality of determinate truths; we have seen that traditional *Anekāntavāda* after Bimal's interpretation is almost reduced to such a theory. Krishna Chandra reads *Anekāntavāda* as a theory of indeterministic truth, which holds that what is presented, is thinkable in alternative modes, definite or indefinite, but this reading is specifically his own contribution.

Notes

1. In a footnote attached to "Acharya Krishna Chandra's Conception of Philosophy" published in the *Journal of Indian Academy of Philosophy*, vol. II, Ras Vihari Das writes, "Many people perhaps do not realize that in India we traditionally refer to our great men by their proper names and not by their surnames as is done in modern Europe. Descartes, Spinoza, Locke, Berkeley, etc., are all surnames, whereas Shankara, Ramanuja, Udayana, Gangesha, Raghunath . . . even Radhakrishnan are all

proper names. The present vogue of referring to people by their surnames appears to be a legacy of Western influence on our culture." Following his footsteps, I have spoken of K.C. Bhattacharyya as Krishna Chandra in this paper.

2. Ras Vihari Das, "Acharya Krishna Chandra's Conception of Philosophy" *Journal of Indian Academy of Philosophy*, vol. II, 1963.

3. Kalidas Bhattacharyya, *The Fundamentals of K. C. Bhattacharyya's Philosophy* (Calcutta, India: Saraswat Library, 1975).

4. J. N. Mohanty, *Reason and Tradition in Indian Thought* (New York: Oxford University Press, 1992), 203-4, 211, 255-6, 147.

5. K.C. Bhattacharyya, *Studies in Philosophy*, vol. I, ed. Gopinath Bhattacharyya (Calcutta, India: Progressive, 1956), xii.

6. K.C. Bhattacharyya, "The Jaina Theory of Anekānta," in *Studies in Philosophy*, vol. I, 331.

7. K.C. Bhattacharyya, "Place of the Indefinite in Logic," in *Studies in Philosophy*, vol. II, ed. Gopinath Bhattacharyya (Calcutta, India: Progressive, 1958), 225.

8. K.C. Bhattacharyya, "Place of the Indefinite in Logic," 225.

9. K.C. Bhattacharyya, "The Jaina Theory of Anekānta," 342.

10. Haribhadra Suri, *Anekāntajayapatākā*, ed. H.R. Kapadia (Baroda, India: Oriental Institute, 1947). ix.

11. Vādi Devasūri, *Pramāṇa-naya-tattvālokālamkāra*, ed. H.S. Bhattacharyya, (Bombay: 1967), *sāmānyaviśeṣādyanekātmakam vastu* Chapter v, Sūtra 1.

12. Haribhadra Suri, *Anekāntajayapatākā*, *vastvekam sadasadrūpam*, 11.

13. Bimal Krishna Matilal, *Logic,Language and Reality* (Delhi: Motilal Banarasidass, 1985). Bimal says that the *syāt* epithet has also been derived in other ways. He breaks it as follows: *as* + potential/optative third form, singular, which indicates probability, 305.

14. Haribhadra, *Anekāntajayapatākā*, quotation from *Syādvādamanjari* of Mallisena, *syādityavyayamanekāntadyotakam. Tatah syādvado'nekāntavadah*, x.

15. Vādi Devasūri, *Pramāṇa-naya-tattvālokālamkāra*, *Sarvatrayam dhvani vidhineṣedhābhyām svārthamabhidadhāana saptabhangamanugacchati*, Sūtra 13.

16. Vādi Devasūri, *Pramāṇa-naya-tattvālokālamkāra*, Sūtra 14.

17. Vādi Devasūri, *Pramāṇa-naya-tattvālokālamkāra*, Sūtra 38.

18. Vādi Devasūri, *Pramāṇa-naya-tattvālokālamkāra*, Sūtra 16.

19. Haribhadra, *Anekāntajayapatākā*, *Svadravyaksetrakalabhavarūpeṇa sad vartate, paradravyakṣetrakālabhavarūpeṇa cāsat. Tataśca saccāsacca bhavati*, 36.

20. Vādi Devasūri, *Pramāṇa-naya-tattvālokālamkāra*, *Kvacit kadācit kathancit prādhānyenapraptipannasya apradhanya anupapatteh*, Sūtra 25.

21. Vādi Devasūri, *Pramāṇa-naya-tattvālokālamkāra*, *Tasyavaktavyaśabdenāpy-avācyatva prasamgāt*, Sūtra 30.

22. Vādi Devasūri, *Pramāṇa-naya-tattvālokālamkāra*: The predication thus indicates the definite and the determinate nature of the thing. Sutra 15.

23. Matilal, *Logic, Language and Reality*, 314.

24. Matilal, *Logic, Language and Reality*, 305.

25. Pradeep P. Gokhale, *The Logical Structure of Syādvada*, JICPR, vol. VIII, no. 3, 1991.

26. Bimal K. Matilal, *Anekanta: Both Yes and No*, JICPR, vol. VIII, no. 2, 1991, 9-10.

27. K.C. Bhattacharyya, "The Jaina Theory of Anekānta," 341.

28. K.C. Bhattacharyya, "The Jaina Theory of Anekānta," 341.

29. K.C. Bhattacharyya, "The Jaina Theory of Anekānta," 340.

30. K.C. Bhattacharyya, "The Jaina Theory of Anekānta," 341.

Mokṣa, the *Parama Puruṣārtha*

In this essay I dwell upon the concept of *mokṣa* as the *parama puruṣārtha*, or the supreme human value. In different philosophical systems it appears in different names, such as *apavarga*, *niḥśreyasa*, *nirvāṇa*, *kaivalya*, *mukti*, etc. These concepts differ from one another in detail, but there is a basic conceptual similarity, which cuts across the ontological commitments of these systems. I have turned my attention to that basic concept.

Mokṣa literally means freedom, and the assurance of freedom is indeed very alluring. Herein lies the popular appeal of *mokṣa*. In philosophical literature *mokṣa* has been classified as a *puruṣārtha*, and *puruṣārtha* literally means the end, which the *puruṣa* desires. To borrow a description from Hiriyanna, it is "human value consciously pursued."[1] It involves a number of features. These have been admirably summed up by Rajendra Prasad, who says, "*Mokṣa* also denotes so many things, e.g., freedom from the chain of birth and death, freedom from suffering, freedom from karma (action), freedom from attachment to the objects of desire, discriminative knowledge that self is completely different from the not-self, eternal bliss, propinquity with god, identity with god, etc."[2] It is to be noted that the last three are entertained only by some schools and are not shared by all. Of all the listed characteristics the basic one is the freedom from suffering. In classical Indian thought *mokṣa* has been defined as complete, total, and final annihilation of sorrow. Avoidance of sorrow being a normal human urge, *mokṣa* is said to be the most coveted end.[3]

For the *mokṣavādins* or the adherents of *mokṣa*, the basic premise is that life is full of sorrow. According to these thinkers the root cause of this sorrow is a misconception that the self is an embodied person and an individual. *Mokṣa* is achieved, when this misconception is destroyed. This leads to the dissolution of the individuality and with that to the destruction of all sorrow. It is the person who is subject to the law of *karma*, and the inviolable chain of birth and rebirth.[4] Thus, *Mokṣa* implies escape from these. I have deliberately avoided these issues in this paper as these do not constitute the core of the concept and unnecessarily

arouse controversial presuppositions, which I do not want to examine here. According to traditional analysis, all the constituents of personality, such as the ego-sense (*ahamkāra*, which literally means the I-maker), and the cognitive, conative, emotive states of awareness belong to the realm of not-self. *Mokṣa*, is said to be founded on *atmajñāna*, which is the knowledge of the self. I have not examined the metaphysics behind this stance, but I have asked whether a person who suffers sorrow can at all accept this ontology and the corresponding theory of value which incorporates *mokṣa* as the *summum bonum*, or not.

My dissatisfaction with the classical concept of *mokṣa* is mainly twofold. First, I hold that the concept of the highest end as freedom from sorrow and that alone is unsatisfactory and partial; it is based upon a one-sided analysis of human nature. Second, such a concept is in a sense suicidal for the individual, and, so, it is neither desirable nor consistently possible for a person to desire *mokṣa*.

Keeping this in mind, I have broken up the discussion into four broad sections. In the first, I have discussed the three other recognized *puruṣārthas*, *dharma*, *artha*, and *kāma*, in order to establish how in their context *puruṣa* means the individualized self. In the second, I have presented the various difficulties that I see in the concept of *mokṣa* as developed in traditional thought. Here I have tried to show that the excessive emphasis on sorrow and the suggestion that our erring sense of identity with the personalized self has to be eliminated in *mokṣa* is not tenable. In the third, I have suggested that it is impossible to formulate the concept of *mokṣa* as a value, without accepting its necessary connection with desire and individuality. In the last section, I have delineated a concept of *mokṣa*, which I find comparatively more satisfying.

I

The concept of *mokṣa* forms an integral part of our traditional culture. In common parlance we often talk of *caturvarga*, or our fourfold scheme of values.

In philosophical literature these have been described as *prayojana*; the latter is defined as the end, which motivates individuals to activity. Uddyotakara, who presents this definition, says that the basic urges, which prompt human activity are the urges for attainment of happiness and avoidance of sorrow. He adds that some thinkers accept *dharma, artha, kāma*, and *mokṣa* as *prayojana*.[5] *Vedānta Paribhāṣā* gives a slightly different definition of *prayojana*, describing it as that which when known is desired as one's own. It also speaks of happiness and absence of sorrow as primary *prayojana*. It also accepts the four recognized ends and places *mokṣa* highest in the hierarchy.[6]

The fourfold scheme is accepted as a convenient classification of values. These are accepted as values because of their relevant connection with happiness and sorrow. *Mokṣa*, as we have already noted, is a value as it puts an end to all sorrow, for all time to come. The term *kāma*, refers as much to desire

as to objects of desire. In the oft-quoted saying "*na jātu kāmaḥ kāmānām upabhogena śāmyati*," which means that desires are not satisfied by enjoyment of the objects of desire, the first *kāma* stands for desire, whereas the second *kāma* stands for the objects of desire. *Kāma* in the restricted sense stands for the objects of sensual desire, but in the extended sense it refers to all objects of physical desire. Such objects, as also the associated feeling of pleasantness, are covered by the term *kāma* in the theory of *puruṣārtha*. *Kāma* is primary value as it directly produces happiness or is naturally pleasant, whereas *artha*, or wealth, is accepted as a secondary value as it helps satisfaction of *kāma*. *Dharma* is also a secondary value and is furthest removed from these, as it is expected to produce happiness in some distant future.

So all these four ends are accepted as values, because they somehow satisfy the basic human urges for attainment of happiness and/or avoidance of sorrow. But this similarity is superficial. The person who desires *kāma* and *artha*, the physical and the economic value, is the socially situated natural man, an embodied person who interacts with many such agents. These two are essentially connected with *dharma*, the moral value. The general trend is *dharmādarthaścakāmaśca*, which literally means that from *dharma* comes *artha* and *kāma*.[7] It actually implies that wealth and objects of physical desire become value only when these are sanctioned by *dharma*. That these two have no similarity with *mokṣa* is quite apparent. These two only temporarily satisfy human desires; but *mokṣa* annihilates these desires themselves through dissolution of personality. *Mokṣa* does not stand for a life of unalloyed joy (as it is commonly supposed to be) where all our desires are satisfied. Such a life is promised in heaven, and heaven, even if it exists, is far from *mokṣa*. There are a handful of *ānanda-mokṣavādins*, who hold that *mokṣa* is a state of bliss; but to most thinkers *mokṣa* is as much a negation of all sorrow as of all happiness. According to all thinkers, in *mokṣa* there is no pain of thwarted desires, because it is a state of desirelessness. The *ānandamokṣavādins* also do not define *ānanda* as an emotion arising out of satisfaction of desires, but they look at desirelessness as a positive state. And they have all looked at *mokṣa* as involving virtual dissolution of personality. Thus there is an unbridgeable gulf between *mokṣa* and these two values, and if *mokṣa* is a *puruṣārtha*, it is so in a very different sense. It remains for us to find out the position of *mokṣa* as a value vis-à-vis *dharma*.

Here I have made two statements, which require clarification and justification. I have said that *mokṣa* is qualitatively distinct from other *puruṣārtha*s as first, it involves desirelessness, and second, it recommends dissolution of personality. Both these points will be discussed in the next two sections. However, it is to be noted that this directly clashes with the opinion of Rajendra Prasad.[8] In his excellent analysis of the *puruṣārtha*s, he lays down the main features of *dharma*, *artha*, and *kāma*, the *trivarga* (the threefold values). With great expertise and insight, he discusses their interrelationship, and he shows that these are social and functional in nature. He shows how *artha* is a means to *kāma*, and *kāma* is to be regulated by *dharma*, and *dharma* being

totally a social value, these two are also so. He argues that *dharma* is social, because the *dharmic* obligations are socially allotted, and observance of *dharma* is a necessary condition of social stability and harmony. I agree fully with this analysis, though I have some reservations about the totally social interpretation of *dharma*. I shall come back to this later. According to Rajendra Prasad, the basic difference between the *trivarga* and *mokṣa* is that the former are social in nature, while the latter is personalistic. But, Rajendra Prasad has also said that *mokṣa* is similar to the *trivarga* because although some interpreters hold that *mokṣa* involves dissolution of personality, actually it does not. On this point I would definitely disagree with him. In my next section I shall try to establish my position. He also suggested that the theory of *puruṣārtha* should be restructured "so as to include the concept of *mokṣa* in that of *kāma*."[9] This, I also think is impossible. *Kāma* stands for the satisfaction of all physical desires, or as he himself says "it is a categorial representation or hypostatization of a man's appetitive life."[10] But *mokṣa* looks at desire as bondage, it has prescribed desirelessness as the highest value, so the restructuring has to be concretely worked out before this inclusion.

Before turning to these issues let me give a brief exposition of *dharma*. It has been defined in various allied senses in different systems of thought. In some it means the objective value produced by performance of duty.[11] In another system *dharma* stands for some property produced in the self by performance of duty.[12] In still another simply the practice of the injunctions has been called *dharma*.[13] The source of the obligatoriness of duties might be the scriptures; thus *dharma* has been technically defined as *codanā lakṣanạ dharma* or ends sanctioned by the injunctions and prohibitions of the *śruti*. Similarly the moral rules tabulated in the *smṛti* of Manu, etc., as also the socio-ethical rules present there, have been accepted as *dharma*. Again, the traditionally preserved moral codes as expressed in the behavior of the *śiṣṭa*, the knowledgeable good person, are said to be ideal and trend setting. Manu says that in matters of conflict a person may appeal to his conscience as a last resort.

Dharma as much stands for rituals, as for a large body of ethical virtues. Some of the moral duties were called *sāmānyadharma* and these were obligatory for one "in virtue of his being simply a member of the human species."[14] Some of these are truth, nonviolence, non-appropriation of the riches of others, protection of the distressed, etc. These are definitely social morality. It may be rejoined that these are not directed towards improvement of the society and that these are actually personal excellences. But it is clear that even if these are personal excellences, they are so of a social man. The bulk of these virtues emerge in situations involving the interaction of individuals. In the epics these have been presented through different parables and have been portrayed as relativistic and situation bound. The virtue, which is introduced in a story, is emphasized as the highest virtue. Thus in one story, nonviolence, in another truth, in still another charity has been focused upon as the highest virtue. In contrast, *viśeṣa dharma* refers to rituals and moral rules obligatory for different social groups.

These are *varṇa dharma*, or duties assigned to people belonging to different castes; *āśrama dharma*, or duties tied to different stages of life; or *kula dharma*, or duties obligatory to people belonging to different families, etc. They have enumerated the various obligations of a man as indebtedness to gods (*devaṛṇa*), to his forefathers (*pitṛṛṇa*), to his fellow individuals (*nṛṛṇa*), to the learned men of the past (*ṛṣi ṛṇa*), and even to the animal world (*paśu ṛṇa*). An individual is seen here not only as a part of the society but also as a part of nature. Thus it is his duty to work for the well-being and sustenance of all. So a person who practices *dharma* is a socially situated natural man.

Through the following three alternatives we may formulate the exact relation between *dharma* and *mokṣa*:

a. *Dharma* is practiced for the attainment of various extraneous ends,
b. *Dharma* is self-rewarding as a value
c. *Dharma* is a necessary pre-requisite for the realization of *mokṣa.*

a. Because we have presented *dharma* as a social virtue, it must not be thought that it was consciously directed towards the sustenance and well-balanced development of the society. To individuals *dharma* were prescriptive personal rules, but they were so framed that they automatically led to a smooth and proper working of the society. But some thinkers, especially those preoccupied with the *smṛtis*, held that observance of *dharma* ensured a journey to heaven after death, or achievement of certain excellences in the next life.

Let me explain the position more clearly. *Dharma* as a value, sanctioned by various scriptural injunctions and prohibitions is linked with various duties such as *nityakarma* (daily necessary duties), *naimittika karma* (occasional duties), *kāmyakarma* (conditional duties), etc. These duties are desire bound, for, by their performance, a person either goes to heaven or gets some other rewards. Manu, for example, says that by performance of *dharma* codified in the *śruti* or *smṛti* a person acquires fame in this life and goes to heaven hereafter. Gautama asserts that performance of *dharma* would determine a man's family, appearence, intelligence, wealth, learning, etc. in his next birth.[15] Some have claimed that the daily necessary duties should be likened to the unconditional moral laws as by their performance a person does not earn any reward. But then it has been amply made clear that these actions are negatively connected with results, as their nonperformance would be met with punishment.

Under this interpretation *dharma* being directed towards some achievable end and being necessarily connected with socially situated persons is absolutely different from *mokṣa*. If after entertaining this view *dharma* is described as a necessary condition of *mokṣa*, then that would be an artificial imposition from outside.

b. This view was held by the early Prābhākaras. Injunctions were considered self-validating. But injunctions become *dharma* only when they are supposed not to produce unhappiness in excess of happiness. So *dharma* is in a sense tied to happiness and the reference to an end is in-built in the very concept

of *dharma*. Even then they held that the accomplishment of the dictates of injunction is itself *dharma* and there is no ulterior end. As expected, such a view of *dharma* is complete in itself and does not point to any further *puruṣārtha* or *mokṣa*. For them, *niyogasiddhi*, or realization of the imperative, is the highest end. As Rajendra Prasad comments, "dharmic life is an end in itself."[16]

On rare occasions the idea of *dharma* as intrinsically valuable emerged in the epics. In the Yudhisṭhira Draupadī Samvāda in the Vanaparva in the Mahābhārata, the former derides people, who perform *dharma* seeking the results, that is, the future well being of the performer as the *dharma-vāṇijyaka* or trader of morality. He speaks of himself as one, who performs sacrifices or practices charity because those are his duties.[17] Unfortunately, in these texts the connection of such *dharma* with *mokṣa* has not been systematically worked out. It is interesting to note that the epics often speak of *trivarga*, or the first three values. Thus, in the Rāmāyana, Lava and Kuśa propose to sing the story of the epic, which would lead to the enhancement of *dharma*, *artha*, and *kāma*. In the Mahābhārata, the Pāṇdavas have often been addressed as people well versed in these three values. This absence of reference to the concept of *mokṣa* might be the result of an historical accident that the concept originated much later. But in view of the fact that they have mentioned *mokṣa* elsewhere, this might mean that *mokṣa*, as a value, is fundamentally different from other values.

This is my response to Rajendra Prasad's suggestion. When he asserts that *dharma*, *artha*, and *kāma* constitute a well-knit trio, I agree with him. When he declares that *trivarga* scheme seems to be quite self-complete and *mokṣa* does not fill up a gap, I accept him.[18] But it is to be remembered that the traditionalists present *mokṣa* as a transcendental value, qualitatively different from the mundane values and (as I hold) as an alternative to these. So we must examine the concept of *mokṣa* more thoroughly before totally rejecting it, or incorporating it in the three-member set.

In any case, under this interpretation, there is no logical connection between *dharma* and *mokṣa*.

c. *Dharma* is accepted as a necessary prerequisite of *mokṣa* in many systems of thought, especially in Sāmkhya-Yoga and Vedānta. It is held that purification of mind is necessary for the realization of *mokṣa*, which is achieved through practice of *dharma*. There are eight steps of Yoga of which the final one is *mokṣa*. The first two steps are *yama* and *niyama*, which cover some of the moral precepts, which come under *dharma*. Now this *dharma*, which is a means to *mokṣa* and the concept of *dharma*, which we have been developing as an independent value, which regulates and perfects *kāma* and *artha* are two distinct disciplines, because the attitudes behind them are different. The second one is necessary for the proper development of a well-balanced social individual. The first is a discipline, which prepares the aspirant for *mokṣa*, for self-realization, encouraging dissociation from natural and socio-ethical life. I shall come back to this later.

II

In Indian philosophical literature we come across a peculiar preoccupation with sorrow. There are comments on the sorrowfulness of life, classification of various types of sorrow, ingenious arguments presented to focus on the supremacy of sorrow in life. The whole of Buddhist philosophy is the development in the background of four noble truths, the first of which is the essential sorrowfulness of life. From Buddha through various thinkers up to the recent past, this trend has been alive. Here I would like to speak of an argument given by Schopenhauer, mentioned by Tilak in his commentary on the Gitā. Schopenhauer states that when our desires are satisfied we are happy; but desire itself is unpleasant in nature and some of our desires are certain to remain unfulfilled. So if we present the situation in the form of a fraction, that is, satisfied desire/ desire as such, the denominator would necessarily be greater than the numerator. This expression is supposed to represent the overall sorrowfulness of life. I do not think that this is a persuasive argument and perhaps only by comparing satisfied desires with thwarted desires can we get a correct picture. But here I do not want to establish the sorrowfulness of life; I only want to show how our traditional thinkers harped upon the predominance of sorrow in life.

In the background of such an analysis of life, *mokṣa* is presented as the supreme end. All our classical thinkers agree in defining *mokṣa* as permanent, complete, and necessary annihilation of sorrow. They assert that whereas our ordinary attempts to destroy sorrow sometimes fail, in *mokṣa* there is necessary removal of sorrow or *aikāntika duhkhaniṣedha*, and whereas in our mundane life, we destroy one sorrow to face some other sorrow from some other quarter, in *mokṣa* the eradication of sorrow is total or there is *ātyantika duhkhaniṣedha*. So *mokṣa* is basically a negative state. (I shall discuss the exceptions later.) The Naiyāyikas have discussed the nature of this absence threadbare. *Mokṣa* roots out all future sorrow, thus it can claim to be prior absence or *prāgabhāva*. Prior absence is antecedent absence, and it is supposed to precede the future emergence of the negatum. But *mokṣa* totally rules out the possibility of any future sorrow. The Mīmāmsakas have tried to retain the description by calling it *paṇda prāgabhāva*, or futile prior absence. The Naiyāyikas have preferred to describe it as destructional absence or *dhamsābhāva*. They hold that the removal of every particular sorrow is destructional, but this absence is very special in as much as it is non-contemporaneous with any other sorrow.[19] Thus *mokṣa* is destructional sorrow and the destruction of the very possibility of sorrow.

The totally negative character of *mokṣa* deserves special consideration. When Rajendra Prasad comments on the similarity of *mokṣa* and *kāma*, he asserts, "the essential characteristic of *mokṣa* is satisfyingness or absence of disagreeableness which is also the result of the fulfillment of any normal desire."[20] But this absence of disagreeableness present in *mokṣa* is qualitatively different from such states emerging out of satisfaction of desires. It is not just removal of

a want or destruction of a sorrow, but it is destruction of the very possibility of sorrow. Hence it is fundamentally different from *trivarga*.

Here naturally we ask, how is the very possibility of sorrow destroyed? The answer is that in spite of the mutually opposed analyses of self, all the schools have agreed in rejecting the reality of the individuated self. They all agree that our sense of identity with the natural social person is erroneous and the root cause of all our sorrow. Human desires traceable to the ego-sense are said to be the chains, which constitute bondage.[21] And all these schools recommend not expansion and transcendence but rejection and nullification of individuality. Rajendra Prasad differentiates between personalistic value and egoistic value.[22] He states that *mokṣa* is a state of egolessness, but in *mokṣa* the personality is retained, since it is the person, the individual, the self, which is said to be liberated.[23] According to him "to say that the (*mukta*) liberated is egoless is to say that his apparent, crude, or undesirable ego is effaced or sublimated for the liberation of the genuine, refined or desirable ego."[24] My point is that while this type of *mokṣa* is desirable, the way in which our classical thinkers have treated the concept amounts to virtual dissolution of personality. They often say that *ātmā* or self is free, but I do not think that this *ātmā* is the individual.[25] So, if my position is accepted, then *puruṣa* has to pay too dear a price to achieve the *parama puruṣārtha*. But let me discuss this in more detail.

In our traditional thought sorrow has been treated in at least in three different ways. First, different types of sorrow have been enlisted and classified, as we find in Sāmkhya. Second, suffering and happiness have been accepted as opposites, but happiness has been shown to be invariably associated with sorrow, and the overall sorrowfulness of life has been projected, as we find in Nyāya. Third, everything in life has been called transitory and momentary and therefore painful, as we find in Buddhism. In this section I propose to explore these three alternatives.

Let me consider the second alternative first. The main trend of the Naiyāyikas is to endorse a purely negative view of *mokṣa*. (Bhāsarvajña, the Naiyāyika influenced by the Śaiva School, is an important exception.) The Nyāya sūtras dwell on the predominance of sorrow in life, and then define *mokṣa* as final deliverance from suffering. The Naiyāyikas have looked at sorrow from three different angles. First, they have said that there is both joy and sorrow in life. Life is compared to poisoned rice sweetened with honey. In life joy and woe are woven fine but as *vivekahāna* is not possible, or as it is not possible to separate happiness from sorrow and enjoy it, therefore to uproot sorrow men agree to forego happiness.[26] Second, they have emphasized the predominance of sorrow in life. The Naiyāyika tells us that if we weigh sorrow and happiness in a scale we find that sorrow is heavier, as happiness has sorrow as its invariable associate. The Naiyāyika goes on to say that sorrow pervades our life. To seek happiness is an unpleasant experience; if we fail to achieve our desired goal we feel sorrow, if we realize it partially we are dissatisfied; to attain our goals we have to encounter many hurdles and even when we get the much

striven for object, we are always apprehensive that we shall have to part with it in future. Thus sorrow is said to be ingrained in happiness.[27] Nyāya does not deny the reality of happiness in life. It is said to be *sarvajantupratyakṣa*, or directly experienced by all. But Nyāya holds that it partakes of the nature of suffering being invariably present with it. Nyāyabhāṣya says that life is sorrowful not because there is absence of happiness, but because there is presence and association of sorrow.[28] Curiously enough, at least in one important passage, the Naiyāyika (precisely speaking Vācaspati Miśra) asserts that sorrow and happiness are invariably related and vice versa.[29] This means that both happiness and sorrow are present in the same locus, or they are experienced by the same person, or both are caused by the same factors.

Keeping this third position in mind the critic might say that this does not prove the predominance of sorrow over happiness in life. The optimist can well emphasize the brighter side of life. The Naiyāyikas himself has said that love of happiness and aversion to pain are the twin basic urges which activate men; now, the onus lies with him to explain why the *mumukṣu*, that is, the person who desires *mokṣa*, foregoes this natural love of happiness and develops an aversion for it. Once the Naiyāyikas admits that happiness is invariably related with sorrow and vice versa, it is arbitrary for him to say that the highest value is geared to one part of the assertion, namely, happiness is necessarily connected with sorrow. Similarly, it can be argued against the first and the second argument that once the reality of happiness is admitted, it is unjustified to say that the urge for happiness should be given up, just because pure happiness cannot be extracted or just because happiness is necessarily associated with sorrow. In spite of all their sophistications, can they give a satisfactory answer to the question put forward by the Cārvākas, namely, who gives up rice being afraid of husk, or who gives up fish being afraid of bones?

According to Nyāya the root cause of our sorrow is our extraneous identification of ourselves, with the psychophysical complex, the personality constituted of our body, our sense organs, our *manas*, etc. Nyāya holds that through the knowledge of reality, our *ahamkāra*, or the ego-sense, or the sense of individuality conditioned by defects, is removed.[30] The Vaiśeṣikas say that in *mokṣa* the connection of self with all its special properties, such as awareness, suffering, happiness, desire, aversion, etc., is severed. It is continuation of the bare self which would never die, never grow old.[31] The Naiyāyika describe this final end as destruction of all sorrow and destruction of all awareness of sorrow.[32] The supposed opponent describes this state as end of all activity, all happiness, all awareness. I feel like supporting them in exclaiming that such *mokṣa* is terrible. Identifying life with sorrow, the Naiyāyika describes *mokṣa* as the end of this life and the end of the possibility of any future life.[33] The Naiyāyika have defended their position by saying that when life becomes unbearable because of suffering, even death is welcome to a person. But can suicide be the supreme value in life? Can such *mokṣa* help us to regulate and reorient life positively? Does such *mokṣa* add a new dimension to life? To my mind it looks like pure escapism.

It is to be noted that Nyāya does not speak of end of self in *mokṣa*. The self-substance retains certain properties such as number, infinite magnitude, etc.; but being devoid of specific properties such as awareness, desire, happiness, etc., which I consider to be the essential constituents of self, it is virtually dead to me. It is also interesting to note that Nyāya sees in *mokṣa* rectification of an error. It is erroneous to maintain the ego-sense, and this is corrected in *mokṣa*. But *mokṣa* is not identical with this knowledge. The knowledge has only instrumental value, as through a number of steps (i.e., destruction of defects, of all actions, of the birth cycle) it ultimately leads to annihilation of sorrow. But, as I have already suggested, the Nyāya theory of *mokṣa* as the highest value does not do justice to the richness of human experience.

Now let us turn to the first alternative exemplified in Sāmkhya. The ontological commitments of Sāmkhya are diametrically opposed to those of Nyāya, yet there is the same emphasis on suffering. There is the same rejection of the empirical ego-sense of persons as erroneous and the same concept of *mokṣa* as transcendence of activity and agency. The very first Sāmkhya Sūtra defines *parama puruṣārtha* as complete annihilation of sorrow. Sāmkhya classifies suffering under three heads. First, it speaks of sorrow pertaining to the self, where the self means the individual, or the psychophysical complex. These are the sorrows associated with fever, anger, jealousy, etc. Second, there are sorrows rooted in natural factors such as those caused by fire, snakebite, etc. Last, they have spoken of sorrows, traceable to demons, earthquakes, floods, etc., which they have described as sorrows caused by extra-natural factors. According to Sāmkhya, we suffer all these sorrows because we confuse the *puruṣa* or the self, which is contentless consciousness, with the individual persons, who are evolutes of *prakṛti*. Sorrows actually belong to the psychophysical complex, but they are projected as belonging to the self. The self is nothing but the pure subject. All activity belongs to the realm of the object, and to the objective world belong all actions and all sorrows associated with it. *Mokṣa* is *vivekakhyāti* or the cognition of the subject and the object in their proper perspective. Sāmkhya considers it erroneous to hold that the self is an agent and in *mokṣa* this sense of agency is dispelled. *Mokṣa* is also called *kaivalya* where the self, who is as a matter of fact unrelated, is realized as unrelated.

We have seen that the sorrows, which they have listed, affect the mind-body complex, which we call the individual. The more intense is our attachment to and our sense of identity with this individuated self, the more intensely we would feel this sorrow. But a person, who feels identified with this self, would welcome the well-being of that self; why would he seek de-individuation, which is the essence of *mokṣa*? The natural man as affected by sorrow would like complete destruction of sorrow, but he would like to remain a natural man. He would either try to get rid of his particular problems (which he is constantly trying to), or he would seek unmixed pleasure, but why would he try to transcend this level? There is a qualitative difference between our particular

attempts to remove particular sorrow and the attempt to remove all sorrow through *mokṣa.* In the first, the sense of individuality is retained; in the other, it is rejected. It is difficult to see why the agent, because of the sorrows associated with his individuality, should be ready to forego his sense of individuality itself. All the constituents that make up our personality, such as *buddhi* or intellect, *ahamkāra* or the ego-sense/the I-maker, the *manas*, the five sense organs, the five organs of action or the whole psycho-physical complex called a person, is a superimposition on the unrelated pure self, and the pure self is only a witness. I hold that the desire to get rid of sorrow cannot solely motivate a person to realize the pure self.

The following diagram clarifies my position:

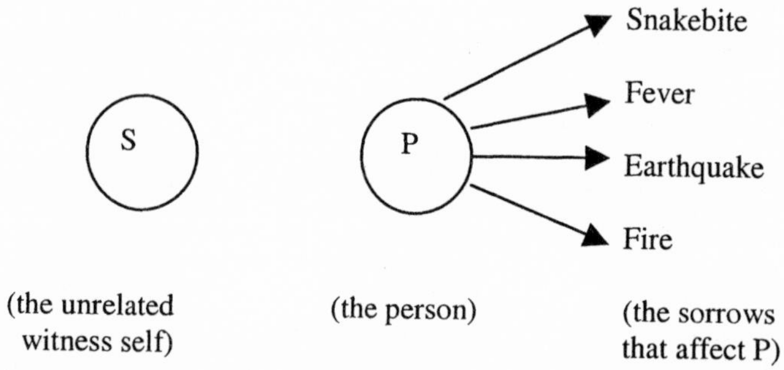

P is the person affected by the various sorrows. Sāmkhya maintains that the actual self is S, the pure unrelated principle of consciousness, and asks us to realize that sorrows belong to P, the not-self, and not to the self. This realization is said to be *mokṣa*. But my point is that if sorrows were the problem of P, why would he accept the dissolution of P-hood as the solution of this problem? Sorrowfulness of life is presented in a particular framework of which personhood is a necessary feature, and eradication of sorrow should be within the same framework. Here, instead of explaining the problem, Sāmkhya explains it away.

If I am permitted to introduce a classification of evil from a totally different system of thought, then I would like to recall Leibnitz's. He speaks of three types of evil—physical evil or suffering, moral evil or sin, and metaphysical evil or imperfection. Here the Sāmkhya thinkers give a list of suffering, analogous to physical evil, but they seek to root out such evil through metaphysical perfection. But, I feel that if only sorrow is felt at the metaphysical level it would lead to yearning for *mokṣa*.

To sum up, my dissatisfaction with Sāmkhya is twofold. First, the way in which they present *mokṣa* as freedom from sorrow is not persuasive. Second, their analysis of self as consciousness only is virtually equivalent to dissolution of personality. They have tried to retain individuality of selves by accepting

bahupuruṣavāda, or the theory of plurality of selves. But in the absence of a principle of discernibility it has remained an inexplicable inconsistency in Sāmkhya. This free self as pure consciousness is as much antiegoistic as anti-individualistic.

Let us turn to the last view, where sorrow has been linked to the transitoriness of life. The Buddha's first noble truth asserts the sorrowfulness of life. He speaks of sorrow, which is traceable to disease, old age, death, presence of hated objects, parting with desired ones, unpleasantness arising out of thwarted desires, etc. His point is that everything, which we experience, has been produced by something and hence it is transitory and liable to destruction. His *anityavāda*, or the theory of transitoriness, leads to *kṣaṇikavāda* or the theory of momentariness, and the resultant *nairātmyavāda* or the no-self theory. Buddhism asserts that as there is no persistent self or stable object, so all our desires, cravings, attachments to permanent life are baseless. To realize this is to attain *nirvāṇa* or *mokṣa.* Whether *nirvāṇa* stands for total annihilation without any residue or for complete cessation of all desires commensurate with a peaceful changeless continuity is controversial in Buddhist literature. But it is beyond all controversy that in *nirvāṇa* there is complete destruction of all sorrow. Unlike Nyāya or Sāmkhya, Buddhism does not accept the existence of a permanent self; but like them it holds that our idea that there is individuated abiding self is erroneous. It is the root cause of all our sorrow, and the dissociation from such a self is *mokṣa*. Different schools of Buddhism, with the most diverse ontologies, have all agreed to deny the reality of the personal self. The Buddha himself denied the existence of the self-substance and replaced it by five *skandhas* or *nāma-rūpa*, which is the psychophysical complex. Then, under the *samyag smṛti*, he preached *kāyānusmṛti*, where he urges the seeker of freedom should remember that the body is reducible to thirty-two constituent elements without any residue, so that the ego-sense and the sense of *I* and *mine* are unfounded. This thought is foundational for later Buddhist schools and they have emphasized it in various ways. *Therāvāda*, for example, speaks of chains of *samyojana*, and freedom is freedom from these chains. The first of these chains is *satkāyadṛṣṭi*, or personality belief, the belief that there are persons, whereas there are only *skandhas* or constituent conditions. The *vijñānavādin*s speak of *kleśāvaraṇa,* which are impediments to freedom. The main point is that there is no self but an ever-continuing stream of conscious states. Different defects, which breed the belief that there are persons, are *ātmadṛṣṭi*, which is *satkāyadṛṣṭi*, as explained above. Then there are *ātmamoha*, or the unfounded belief that there is a self; *ātmamāna* or self-conceit; *ātmaprema* or love of personal self, etc. But the *arhat* has rectified all these errors so that there is end of all sorrow with the end of belief in personality.[34] Vasubandhu would say that there is nondual de-individualized continuity forever. It is comparable to the Nyāya theory of *ahamkāra nivṛtti* or the Sāmkhya projection of *mokṣa* as the realization of the pure unrelated self.

Thus far I have criticized the traditional schools because they have spoken of *mokṣa* as dissolution of personality. This means that I have taken for granted that our basic awareness of ourselves is as persons. When our classical thinkers assert that the empirical personality is not tenable in the last analysis, their theory of value is parasitical on their ontology. But then *mokṣa* should not be presented primarily as a value involving destruction of sorrow; it is to be considered as an unpalatable but necessary corollary of their respective metaphysics. I have shown that the other three *puruṣārtha*s are based on the concept of *puruṣa* as a person. If the personality is nullified, *mokṣa* does not remain a human value. This would become clearer in what follows.

III

Mokṣa has been categorized as *puruṣārtha*, and *puruṣārtha* has been defined as an end, which is desired. In this context my discomfort is twofold. First, as I hold that it is impossible to flesh out the concept of *mokṣa* as a value, without a reference to a person who desires it? Second, *mokṣa* is defined as a state of desirelessness, but this clashes with the idea of *mokṣa* as an end, which is desired. It is to be noted that our classical thinkers were aware of both these difficulties. Let me dwell upon these at some length.

Mokṣa has been presented as an end to be realized or achieved. It is true that the Advaita Vedāntin do not accept this end-like nature of *mokṣa*. But then, in a sense they admitted it by introducing the twin concepts of *prāptasya prāpti* or the attainment of that which is already attained and *parihṛta parihāra* or the rejection of that, which has been already rejected.[35] By describing *mokṣa* as the realization of an end, which is eternally realized, they make room for some sort of attainment. The concept of an end is closely connected with that of a voluntary action. A quick survey of their analysis of voluntary action, even in very broad outlines, might prove rewarding.

There might be two different types of analysis of voluntary action, the Nyāya type and the Mīmāmsā type. The simplest definition of voluntary action is that it is preceded by *svecchā*, or desire of the agent. Nyāya has spoken of a number of necessary conditions of voluntary action. One of them is *kṛtisādhyatājñāna*, or the awareness that the action can be performed. But the really important factor is *iṣṭasādhanatājñāna*, or the awareness that the action would be conducive to good. But this good is relative and it has been explained as the good of the agent. Thus here a reference to the agent is unavoidable. The Prābhākaras also accept *kṛtisādhyatājñāna*, but instead of turning to the results of the action or projection of the goodness to be produced, they hold that the sense of duty is more important here. Thus they speak of *kāryatājñāna*, or the awareness that a certain action is one's duty, as a necessary condition of voluntary action. But this awareness moves an agent only after it refers to the agent. This stage is called *svaviśeṣaṇatayā pratisandhānam*, or projection of the

proposed end as qualifying the agent. Action proper must be preceded by ideal appropriation of the action by the agent. Gāgābhatta, belonging to the Bhātta tradition, distinguishes between the two senses of *kāryatājñāna*.[36] They may be just the rational awareness that a certain action is one's duty. But when it is accepted as one's duty, that is, when it is morally accepted, then only does it become morally obligatory. Thus the role of the agent here is decisive. Such an agent has to be a person and an individual and it is inconsistent for him to desire dissolution of personality.

Now, let us turn to the concept of *mokṣa* as a state of desirelessness. Being apprehensive that a purely negative view of *mokṣa* would fail to motivate people, a group of thinkers have presented a positive concept. The proponents of such a view have been a section of the Buddhists, one or two Naiyāyikas and the different schools of Vedānta. The bulk of the Naiyāyikas and the Mīmāmsakas have been their opponents, Without entering into their maze of arguments and counterarguments, we can say that the main point raised by the critics of the positive view is that if *mokṣa* is a pleasant state it would be desired, but desire itself is a bondage, and desire for eternal happiness is no exception. Thinkers belonging to the negative schools argue that *mokṣa* does not cease to be a *puruṣārtha*, even if there is absence of bliss and desire for bliss; they hold that through destruction of sorrow, it becomes *puruṣārtha*.

The traditional tirade against desire deserves certain considerations. Desire has been criticized on various grounds, of which, the most widely prevalent one is pragmatic. The oft-repeated couplet that desire cannot be satiated by fulfillment of desire, just as fire cannot be extinguished if it is fed with ghee, express this stance. Another such couplet asserts that when a person's desire for an object is satisfied, he would be troubled instantly by some other desire. But it is to be remembered that thinkers outside our own tradition have not looked at desire as so pernicious. In fact, some thinkers hold that through our desires we expand our personality. However, the Indian attitude is that our desires are necessarily egocentric, and clinging to such ego is typical of the man in bondage. The liberated man is expected to have snapped the fetters of desire. Thus the free man has been described as *akāma*, or desireless; as *āptakāma*, or one whose desires have been satisfied; as *niṣkāma*, or one who has given up all desires; and as *ātmakāma*, or one who is satisfied with the highest metaphysical self, etc.[37] In this background, my comment to both the opponent and exponent of the negative view of *mokṣa* is that their position vis-à-vis desire is the same as the desire to get rid of all sorrow is as much a desire as the desire to realize pure bliss. So if desire is bondage then both the views are equally deplorable.

The traditional thinkers have tried to save the situation in different ways. The supporters of the positive view say that the seeker of *mokṣa* does not desire bliss, but necessarily gets it in the form of peace and contentment associated with the sense of perfection. Further, they all hold that the desire for the total annihilation of sorrow is not ordinary desire, it is not aversion or *dveṣa*, but is *vairāgya* or the sense of renunciation. *Vairāgya* is said to be qualitatively

different from desire. But most of these philosophers trace *vairāgya* to the sense of sorrow and thus fail to work out this qualitative difference. The Naiyāyika, for example, has spoken of *nirveda*, which literally means lack of interest in pleasure and the acknowledged means of pleasure. This leads to *vairāgya*, which is defined as distaste for the objects of enjoyment, even when they are presented.[38] But then, these do not significantly improve the situation, as these states are traced to the awareness that life is full of sorrow. Ultimately, the sense of sorrow is considered to be the most overwhelming emotion of life, and I think that this evaluation is one-sided and partial.

Śamkara, in his commentary on the Brahma-Sūtras, has given a slightly different meaning of *vairāgya*. The prerequisites to be fulfilled by the seeker of freedom are fourfold. The first of them is *nityānitya-vastuviveka*, which literally means an awareness of the distinction between things eternal and non-eternal. The second is *vairāgya*, which has been expanded as detachment from the results of the work done here and hereafter. These have been traced to the unbearability of suffering. They together highlight the awareness of the emptiness and hollowness of mundane life coupled with the belief in eternal life. The second condition stands for distaste for the results of all actions and thus it covers both happiness and sorrow. In other words, it means a devaluation of all mundane values. The third condition stands for a number of physical and mental disciplines, which include *titikṣā*, or forbearance of suffering, without any regret or attempt to overcome it.[39] This leads to *mumuksuatva*, or intense urge for freedom. I am not claiming that the Advaitins have not looked at *mokṣa* as annihilation of all sorrow. Vedānta Paribhāṣā describes *mokṣa* as *niratiśaya sukha* or maximum happiness, and as *śokanivṛtti* or the end of all suffering. But it has to be acknowledged that with Śamkara it is more a transcendence of empirical life and realization of the super-personal self than destruction of sorrow.

But then it is well known that Advaita Vedānta looks at deindividualized continuation as the *summum bonum* of life. It speaks of total dissolution of personality. Śamkara's position has been described as involving "the expansion of the I-consciousness to the extent of infinity," where there is "ruthless ignoring of the individuality of man."[40] So, though Śamkara has given a new explanation about the urge for freedom, his concept of *mokṣa* fails to satisfy us.

In the traditional concept of *mokṣa*, that is, in the definition of *mokṣa* as destruction of all sorrow and desire and in the rejection of individuality as erroneous, I see a denial of naturality. As a creature of nature, a person has various conscious experiences and *mokṣa* is transcendence of all these. Śamkara has said that *pramāṇa-prameya vyavahāra* is *naisargika*, or the cognitive relation with the objective world is natural, which the individual shares with the lower animals, and in *mokṣa* this is transcended. The Mīmāmsakas have said that the experienced world chains up a person through three factors: through the body, which is the seat of experience; through the sense organs, which are the instruments of experience; and through color, sound, etc., which are objects of experience.[41] In *mokṣa*, these chains are snapped, that is, all natural experiences

are expunged. As a creature of nature a person has various conscious experiences, such as cognition, emotion, conation, etc. These are said to be founded in our erring sense of identity with the natural person. *Mokṣa* is transcendence of all these.

Mokṣa, as a *puruṣārtha* is qualitatively different from other *puruṣārthas*. The others serve as incentive to the natural, socially situated, ego-bound agent, whereas *mokṣa* demands virtual dissolution of that ego. (The Advaitins have admitted the diametrically opposite nature of the two types of value in their differentiation of the *pravṛtti mārga*, which is the life of action and the *nivṛtti mārga*, which is the life of renunciation). According to the traditional thinkers the natural man is not the self. For some schools, the rectification of this error that the individual is the self is *mokṣa*. According to others, there is a super-personal self, and to realize such a self as true self is *mokṣa*. They have presented *mokṣa* as transcendence of the limits of nature. My suggestion is that instead of looking at this transcendence as nullification of personality and radical de-individuation, it is possible to look at it as a continuous process of expansion. Such a concept is present in the writings of Kalidas Bhattacharyya. In my last section I would like to turn to him.

IV

Kalidas Bhattacharyya has added a new dimension to our traditional concept of *mokṣa*.[42] In many of his later works he has been occupied with the concept of freedom. While retaining the old structure, he has injected new meaning into the concept of *mokṣa*. He looks at man as at once natural and transnatural, as one who is an integral part of nature but at the same time as one who has transcended the barriers of naturality. Here he differs from the thinkers who look at man as merely a part of nature, that is, as an efficient animal. Bhattacharyya means by nature the domain strictly determined by space, time and causality. Because of such determination, our physical, organic and even psychical behavior is often predictable and calculable. Man rises above nature by his conscious refusal to submit to these determinations. The reflective consciousness is an essential ingredient of freedom. So not through mere indeterminacy, but through self-conscious refusal, man rises above nature. Man is thus born free; but this freedom is to be developed and expanded. This withdrawal from nature or dissociation from nature has been described as negative freedom. It is to be supplemented by the infinitely rich concept of positive freedom. He presents his theory of freedom through the twin concepts of "freedom from" and "freedom to."

The self-awareness of consciousness is one face of positive freedom, but still it is "freedom from." In some places he means by "freedom from," "the conscious non-submission to the natural determinants." All the philosophers,

who have spoken of freedom as dissociation, such as the Advaitins, who have spoken of dissociated consciousness in itself as the highest ideal or the Mahāyāna Buddhists, who have emphasized the dissociation in itself, have endorsed the different versions of "freedom from." But Bhattacharyya holds that "freedom to," which means "free dealing with nature and its items," is superior to this freedom.[43] Instead of canceling and nullifying nature, he prescribes a return to nature with a changed attitude.

Bhattacharyya has described in detail the various alternative forms of this freedom. Such dealing with nature may be cognitive, conative, or emotive. Free cognition is not merely blind interaction with nature in terms of causation, or mere recording of presentations after mechanical submission to nature. Through universalization and theory construction and speculative metaphysics, which are the gradual unfolding of reason, free cognition expresses itself. On the emotional side, human experience is no more limited to the personal experience of anger, attraction, hatred, etc., which are the instinctive calculable responses. Free emotion expresses itself through the various experiences of art and religion. Free conation finds expression in organization of social norms and various rationalistic ethics. To me, this concept of freedom is very valuable, as it does not involve any rejection of life and nature. The free life is seen as continuous with life of nature, so that the reorientation of life in the light of freedom is possible. This is neither dissolution nor nullification of natural life, nor again acceptance of such life as final.

I would like to turn to the traditional concept of *mokṣa*, in light of these observations. Bhattacharyya often comes very near the traditional thinkers, as for example when he speaks of "every man's authentic awareness of himself as free."[44] Here he is talking the language of Advaita Vedānta. But when he speaks of freedom as that which is opposed to strict causal determination, he has drifted away. Bhattacharyya classifies philosophers into two groups: the naturalists and the transcendentalists. He places Nyāya and Mīmāmsakas under the first group. According to him the naturalists look at human life as an integral part of nature, such that everything is controlled by the compulsive forces of nature and all human activity is predictable. For him conscious transcendence of naturalism is freedom. In traditional thought, the acceptance of personality woven around the finite I-consciousness as real and final is bondage. None of the schools accept the natural, relational, individuated self as ultimately real. Thus I would say that as far as *mokṣa* is concerned, none of the traditional schools, not even Nyāya and Mīmāmsaka is naturalist; they all deny the reality of natural persons. According to them this realization is *mokṣa*.

The traditionalists have recommended contentless expansion, which is like a circle, which has neither any center nor any circumference. But following the footsteps of Bhattacharyya, we can think of *mokṣa* as a finite-centric extension of life beyond the limits of naturality. Such life would be a continuous process of expansion, not without the *I*, but without the animal-like clinging to the *I*. The I-maker is to be retained, for the core is necessary for the continuation of life. Freedom is freedom from blind attachment to it. Such a concept of freedom is

valuable, as it does not involve a rejection of life, individuality or nature. The free self is seen as continuous with the ego, so reorientation of life and free dealing with nature is possible. Here transcendence of naturality is the awareness of the futility of the totally ego-bound life. It finds expression in "better understanding, appreciation or reorganization of Nature" and personality.[45]

The most pertinent question here is, in what sense is this concept preferable to the traditional one? I have argued that the concept of *mokṣa* as entertained in traditional thought falls short of our expectations, on three grounds. First, it looks upon *mokṣa* merely as freedom from sorrow; this approach is one-sided and partial. Here the urge for *mokṣa* is conditioned by awareness of the hollowness of the totally naturalistic life and a desire for expansion and free expression in different facets of life. This transcendence of naturalism is present in man, and it calls for further development and refinement. Second, traditional thought demands dissolution of individuality, whereas this concept recommends retention of individuality and transformation and further development of personality through cultivation of the higher values of life. This concept does not demand total rejection of the I-consciousness or the ego-sense, but it speaks for the destruction of the blind attachment to the *I*, so that the *I* does not remain the only propelling factor in human activity. Animal-like clinging to *I* is to be rejected as pernicious, ego-bound values are to be given up. As Bhattacharyya has shown, it is possible to inculcate the higher values of life only after transcending these attachments. The development of the higher values requires some amount of dissociation from too great an attachment to the ego.

I have said that two different types of analysis of voluntary action are possible, and both of them necessarily refer to the ego. The one says that the awareness of the goodness that the act is to produce is the determinant of the act, while the other asserts that the very acceptance of the act as duty is the most important necessary condition. Under both analyses reference to the person or the moral agent is unavoidable. But if personal attachments were erased, then it would be possible for the agent to take the correct moral decision. Bhattacharyya has said that in the realm of science also, for proper development, the personal factor should be wiped away.

My last point was that the traditionalists held that in *mokṣa* either the very personality of the *puruṣa* is dissolved or the individual self continues, but all his connections with experience are severed. They looked upon desire as bondage. But the revised view is opposed to totally ego-bound desires and not to any and every desire. Desire for happiness and aversion towards sorrow might be the two basic urges which control our activity. But freedom is connected with a third urge, which is at once awareness of our finitude and the urge to transcend the limits of a life controlled completely by these two natural urges and an intense desire for self-expression through various finer values. Thus under this view, there is no inconsistency in the *desire* for the highest value. Here *mokṣa* is neither *nirvāṇa* or end of life nor is it *kaivalya* or a state of unrelatedness, but it is *niḥśreyasa* or the highest good.

Another pertinent question is: is this concept practicable? Or, is it not true that the ego-bound life is the only possible kind of life? Is it possible to live a totally dissociated life, in which the center of all experience is the ego, yet where there is no attachment to it? Here, my suggestion would be that even if it is impossible to actualize such a life, it should at least be accepted as the regulative ideal. That man practices some amount of dissociation is our common experience.

I would like to add that the idea of this type of freedom is not foreign to our tradition. The life of the *jivanmukta* is something like this. But *jivanmukti* is accepted in traditional thought as an intermediate stage in which life is continued, before death ushers in *mahāparinirvāṇa* or *videhamukti*, which we have discussed as *mokṣa* above. But I feel that the dissociated life of the *jivanmukta* should be accepted as the highest ideal and there should be emphasis on the positive aspect of life. Such positive freedom might find expression in various ways. Bhattacharyya himself has mentioned *niṣkāma karma*. Only if a person has transcended his attachment to the ego is it possible for him to perform *niṣkāma karma*. The duties of a person might be determined by the concrete social situation, yet only if he is properly *niskāma*, only if his actions are not determined by egocentric desires are his actions totally free. The *Bhagavadgītā* repeatedly says that the ideal person should be *nirmama* and *nirahamkāra*, or he should do away with the sense of *mine* and *me*. But this does not mean end of life. Kṛṣṇa instructs Arjuna to return to life in its full glory, after being dissociated from the narrow ego. Or, let us take the case of a real devotee. By complete surrender to the divine will, one no longer clings to the natural ego, yet one can lead a full life.[46] Or again personal emotions bound up with the individual agents become *rasa* when the personal elements are expunged and the emotions are universalized. Even in our cognitive life, such free relation with objects of awareness is possible. Our senses are naturally directed towards the external world and through them we become an integral part of nature, which exercises its sway over us. But the Gītā says that after complete withdrawal or inwardization and discipline of the senses it is possible to dwell freely on the objects of awareness, that is, without blind involvement and objective compulsion, and by so dwelling a person achieves a life of contentment.[47]

Here *mokṣa* is the return of the self to natural life after overcoming its animal entanglement with nature. This is positive freedom. In this sense *mokṣa* can claim to be the *parama puruṣārtha*.

Now, what would be the connection of *mokṣa* with the other three values? *Dharma* would definitely be the expression of this *mokṣa*, for by overcoming our natural propensities, it is best possible to do our duties. But such *dharma* is not to be interpreted merely "as an important factor in the maintenance of social stability and harmony."[48] Practiced in the correct attitude it is the expression of the sense of goodness present in man. *Artha* and *kāma*, however, would be reduced to secondary means necessary for the sustenance of the agent. Being totally social and natural in character, they do not have any direct connection with the development of the free life of a person.

Notes

1. M. Hiriyanna, *The Quest after Perfection* (Mysore, India: Kavyalaya Publishers, 1952), 22.

2. Rajendra Prasad, "Theory of Purusartha," in *Karma, Causation and Retributive Morality* (New Delhi: ICPR, 1989), 279.

3. I have deliberately characterized *mokṣa* as a coveted end, without entering into the controversy as to whether this end is the normally desired one or whether it is normatively desirable. To ask this question is to introduce the distinction between description and evaluation, which is present in Indian tradition only in a subdued form, in the shape of a distinction between the *śreya* and the *preya*, or the pleasant one and the better one. The *puruṣārtha*s have been presented as ends which motivate men to activity, and in that sense they are the desired goals. But they have also discussed why and under what restrictions these ends become desirable. The general attitude towards *mokṣa* is that the wise desire it and it is the highest desirable goal.

4. To explain the continuity of personality after death, in the absence of the physical body, they hold that a subtle body remains, which is not destroyed in death.

5. Uddyotkara, *Nyāyavārttika*, ed. by P.V.P. Dvivedin (New Delhi, 1986), *Kim punaḥ prayojanamiti. Yena prayuktaḥ puruṣaḥ pravartate tata prayojanamiti laukiko-'yamarthaḥ. Kena prayujyate. Dharmārthakāmamokṣaiḥ iti kecit. Bayantu paśyāmaḥ sukhaduhkhāptahānibhyām.*

6. Dharmarājādhvarindra, *Vedānta Paribhāsā*, ed. Srimohan Tarkavedantatirtha (Calcutta: Samskrita Pustaka Bhandar, 1970), *Yadavagatam sat svavrttitayeṣyate tat prayojanami . . . Tatra sukhaduhkhābhāvau mukhye prayojane.* 168 & *Iha khalu dharmārthakāmamoksākhyeṣu caturvidha puruṣārtheṣu mokṣa eva parama puruṣārtha* 3.

7. It is very interesting to note that for Yudhisṭhira—the king, the knowledgeable one, the epitome of virtue—all these three values are equally important. Thus Nārada, while instructing Yudhisṭhira, asserts that he hopes that the latter with expertise would divide his time and aspire after all three values, *dharma*, *artha*, and *kāma*. He continues to hope that Yudhisṭhira would not neglect *dharma* by running after *artha*, or *artha* by running after *dharma*, or both by running after *kāma*. The attitude is that if one is assured that *dharma* would not be transgressed then all are equally important.

Mahābhārata, Sabhāparva, V:
Kvacidarthañca dharmañca kāmañca jayatām vara.
Vibhajya kale kalañja samam varada sevase. 20.
Kvacidarthena vā dharmam dharmenārthamathāpi vā
Ubhau vā prītisārena na kāmena prabādhase. 19.

8. Prasad, *Puruṣārtha*, 279, 283-84.

9. Prasad, *Puruṣārtha*, 302.

10. Prasad, *Puruṣārtha*, 278.

11. S. K. Maitra, *The Ethics of the Hindus* (Calcutta, India: University of Calcutta, 1956), 84.

12. Maitra, *Ethics*, 85-86.

13. Maitra, *Ethics*, 91.

14. Prasad, *Purusārtha*, 278.

15. Madhusūdana Sarasvati, Commentary on the *Śrimadbhagavadgītā*, ed. Nalini-kanta Brahma (Calcutta: Navabharat Publishers, 1986), commentary on 18/45.

16. Prasad, *Puruṣārtha*, 299; Maitra, *Ethics*, 153.

17. *Mahābhārata, Vanaparva*, XXVII:
Dharmavāṇijyaka hīno jaghanyo armavādinām. 5.
Dharmam carāmi suśroni na armaphalakāraṇāt. 4.
Nāham dharmaphalānveṣi rājaputri carāmyuta.
Dadāmi deyamityeva yaje yaṣṭavyamityuta. 2.

18. Prasad, *Puruṣārtha*, 283, 298.

19. *Nyāyadarśana*, Sūtra and Bhāṣya, ed. Phanibhusana Tarkavagisa, with commentary (Calcutta: Pascim Banga Rajya Pustak Parsad, 1988), 427.

20. Prasad, *Purusārtha*, 302.

21. Uddyotkara, *Vārttika*, *rāgadveṣau hi bandhanamiti*, 1/1/22.

22. Prasad, *Puruṣārtha*, 295.

23. Prasad, *Puruṣārtha*, 295.

24. Prasad, *Puruṣārtha*, 295.

25. Some schools of Vedānta, especially the Viśiṣṭādvaita School, speak for retention of personality in *moksą*. But usually they introduce the concept of God in heaven so that the discussion tends to be more theological than philosophical. Because of my limited knowledge, I dare not discuss these.

26. *Nyāyadarśana*, *Bhāṣya*, *Aniṣṭahānāya ghaṭamānanam iṣṭamapi jahāti. Vivekahānasyā-śakyatvāditi*, 1/1/22.

27. *Nyāyadarśana*, 4/1/56.

28. *Nyāyadarśana*, *Duhhkhānuṣangāt duhkhamjanmeti na sukhasyābhāvāt*, 4/1/57.

29. *Nyāyadarśana*, *Tātparyatīkā*, *Anuṣango'vinābhāvah.Tatsvarupamāha yatraikam sukham vā duhkham vā tatretarat duhkham vā sukham vā*, , 1/1/22.

30. *Nyāyadarśana*, *Doṣanimittānām tattvajnānādahamkāranivṛtti*, 4/2.

31. *Nyāyadarśana*, *Tadabhayamajaramamṛtyupadamiti*, 1/1/2.

32. *Nyāyadarśana*, *Bhāṣya*, *Sarvaduhkhocchedam sarvaduhkhāsamvidam*, 1/1/2.

33. *Nyāyadarśana*, *Bhāṣya*, *Upāttasya janmano hānam anyasya cānupadanam*, 1/1/22.

34. Vasubandhu, *Vijñaptimātratāsiddhi*, ed. Sukomol Chaudhuri (Calcutta: Sanskrit College, 1975), 106, 119, 121.

35. Dharmarāja, *Paribhāṣā*, *Loke'pi prāptaprāpti parihṛta-parihārayo prayojanatvam dṛṣṭameva. Evam prāptasyānandasya prāptih;parihṛtasyānarthasya nivṛttir moksaḥ prayojanam*. 169.

36. The two forms are: (i) *Mayā idam kartum śakyate;* (ii) *Mayā idam avaśyam kartavyam.*

37. *Bṛhadāraṇyaka Upaniṣad*, ed. Swami Gambhirananda (Calcutta: Udbodhan Karyalaya, 1944), *So'yam Yo'kāmo niṣkāma āptakāma ātmakāma na tasya prāṇa utkrāmati*. 4/46.

38. *Nyāyadarśana*, *sarvam duhkhenānuviddhamiti paśyan duhkham jihāsur janmani duhkhadarśī nirvidyate nirvinno virajyate virakto vimucyate*. 1/1/21.

39. Bharatiya Darśanakoṣa (Vedānta) (Calcutta: Sanskrit College, 1981), on *Titikṣā*, 64; on *sādhanacatuṣṭaya*, 145-146.

40. N. V. Banerji, The Concept of Philosophy (Calcutta: University of Calcutta, 1968), 50.

41. Pārthasārathi Miśra, *Śastradīpikā*, ed. Lakṣmaṇ Sastri Dravida, (India: Chowkhamba, 1913) *Tredhā hi prapañcam puruṣam badhṇāti . . . bhogāyatanam śarīram bhogasādhanānīndriyāni bhogyah śabdadayoh viṣayah. . . . tadasya trividhasyāpi bandhasyātyantika vilayo mokṣaḥ.*

42. Kalidas Bhattacharyya dwells upon the concept of *mokṣa* in the following articles (among others): *Bhāratiya Sanskriti O Anekānta Vedānta* (Burdwan, India: Burdwan

University Press, 1982); "Notions of Freedom Compared and Evaluated" in *Communication, Identity and Self-Expression: Essays in Memory of S. N. Ganguly*, ed. S. P. Banerji, etc. (Delhi, India: Oxford University Press, 1984); "My Reactions" in *Philosophy of Kalidas Bhattacharyya*, ed. Daya Krishna (Pune, India: University of Poona, 1985), I.P.Q. publication, no. 9.

43. Bhattacharyya, Notions of Freedom, 106.
44. Bhattacharyya, Notions of Freedom, 114.
45. Bhattacharyya, Notions of Freedom, 114.
46. Daya Krishna, "The Myth of the Purusarthas," in *Indian Philosophy, A Counter Perspective* (New Delhi: Oxford University Press, 1991) Daya Krishna, speaks of Bhakti as *sakāma karma*. He says that the devotee, as the servant of God, wants to be born again and again, to be in his service, to do his work, to sing his praises. But I have argued that *sakāma karma* stands for egocentric desireful action, and this type of desire is a superior form of desire, purged of egocentric elements. It does not contradict the *niṣkāma karma* thesis.
47. Madhusūdana, *Gītā*, II/64.
48. Prasad, *Puruṣārtha*, 283.

Svadharma

Our pre-philosophical moral life is often regulated by traditional norms and rules, which we unquestionably imbibe from the society. The concept of *svadharma* highlighted in the *Bhagavadgītā* is one such ethical concept. It has been used and misused in the Hindu Society from the distant past till the recent times. Yet situations arise in life that lead us to reinterpret such tenets to suit our changed social milieu. *Svadharma* is no exception. Arjuna had uncritically accepted it. But at the beginning of the battle of Kurukṣetra, being plunged into moral predicament, he questioned its moral authority, and Kṛṣṇa discussed its essence, to show its obligatoriness. Many serious scholars from the nineteenth and the early twentieth centuries, after coming in contact with the Western thought currents, reexamined their own tradition; and in the process they turned to the *Gītā* and adopted *svadharma* to suit their changed times. Even a few decades back, thinkers from divergent disciplines were trying to interpret the concept in their own way.[1]

In this essay, I attempt to examine *svadharma* from my own time and place. I have two main concerns. First, I apprehend that although the term "*sva-dharma*" has been retained, its import has changed with time and in the literature of the recent past, it has changed radically. I want to examine this. Second, I submit, that it is a mistake to look at it as an ethical theory complete in itself. It should be viewed as an integral part of a wider canvas, which is the total attitude towards life prescribed in the *Gītā*. Originally, it was meant to be so, and even in its modern formulation, it has to be thus considered, to be a significant ethical view.

I

A person, as a human being, is expected to practice and respect some moral tenets. These universal codes of conduct are called *sāmānyadharma*. But a

person has special faces too, as a member of a certain class, family, group, etc. The moral rules linked to these particular aspects of personality are called *viśeṣa dharma*. The former are normally expected to be practiced by all ethically conscious individuals. The *Gītā* has prescribed a few. Foremost among these are *maitri* and *karuṇā*, or friendliness and compassion.[2] It also recommends charity, forgiveness, penance, etc. But it attaches utmost importance to a special type of *viśeṣadharma* called *svadharma*. It stands for the specific duties determined by the class to which the individual belongs and his particular station in life. Or *svadharma* is identical with *varṇāśramadharma*.

Traditionally, the *varṇa* system was an economic principle meant to help the proper functioning and preservation of society. It recognized four functions of a social man in the community: "the religious and intellectual, the political, the economic and the servile functions."[3] The society was partitioned into four marked classes, and each class was expected to take up a profession commensurate with these functions. Membership of these classes was determinable by birth, which made the system easy, convenient, and manageable. Again, each individual's life was supposed to be divided into four sections, and his duties were relative to that period in life. The four periods were: first, the educative life of the unmarried student or the period of training; second, the life of the married householder or the period of work; third, the life of retirement after completion of all the moral and social duties or the period of retreat; and, last, the life of the mendicant seeking mystic emancipation or the period of renunciation. The duties obligatory during these periods are called *āśramadharma*. As *āśramadharma* is not controversial it is seldom discussed, and the focus of all the controversies is *svadharma* as *varṇadharma*. As a socio-economic concept the *varṇa* system degenerated into rigid casteism, but the *Gītā* brings out the moral nuances.

Most interestingly, *Gītā* prefaces the moral discussion by presenting an analysis of self. The self is depicted as transcendental, infinite, and beyond all characterization. It is unborn, perpetual, and eternal. It has no beginning, no end in time, and no limit in space. It has no physical identity, being described as uncleavable, non-inflammable, unwettable, and undryable. Conceptually it is unthinkable, indefinable, etc. It is beyond all specifications. Such an ontological entity is not a person. In fact it might be identical in all beings. Such a self cannot be a moral agent.

But when Kṛṣṇa speaks of *svadharma*, that is, moral duties of *sva* or self, this self is a particular person. He is a natural human being. He is a socially situated individual, and his moral duties are socially defined codes of conduct. Śamkara clearly explains that *svadharma* is identical with the moral duties of the agent, which, in the present context, is the duty of a warrior or participation in war.[4] *Svadharma* is synonymous with *svakarma*, and Madhusūdana means by it actions and duties enjoined by *varṇāśrama*.[5] The emphasis is on *varṇa*. When Kṛṣṇa asserts that Arjuna should not hesitate to participate in the war, for nothing else can be a superior duty for him as a warrior, he is obviously referring to *varṇadharma*. Or again, when Kṛṣṇa says that if Arjuna fails to join

this righteous war, he would lose his reputation and also fail to perform his *svadharma*, he is definitely speaking of *varṇadharma*.[6] But Kṛṣna gives a twist, so that many modern thinkers feel that, in the *Gītā*, *varṇadharma* is seen in such a way, that the moral duties of this person are determined more by his specific nature than by his identity as the member of a class.

Arjuna faces a moral dilemma. There are many ways to solve such a dilemma. If both the alternatives are equally strong morally, then they are often dispersed on nonmoral grounds. Kṛṣṇa tried this, when he ordered Arjuna to fight, saying "Dying you will attain heaven, winning you will have the enjoyment of the earth."[7] Another way to get over the problem is to show that one of the alternatives is not morally viable. Kṛṣṇa does this, too. He says that Arjuna is presenting his nonmoral grievances in moral garb and is thus trying to shirk his duties. It might appear that Kṛṣṇa is trying to explain away the situation instead of explaining it. But this is not entirely true. It does not matter if Arjuna's grievances are genuine or not. It is immaterial whether Arjuna considers that participation in war means violation of some universal moral codes. Independent of these considerations, Kṛṣṇa emphasizes the importance of the concept of *svadharma* throughout the text. Universal moral rules are indeed honored and respected. But in real-life situations, the dictates of *svadharma* are supreme and can never be questioned. The *Gītā* gives a formula for concrete working of practical morality. The context-free universally accepted moral rules have exceptions and are often outweighed by moral considerations tied to particular actual situations. The *Gītā* has given codes to help a person in such situations, which are linked to his *varṇa* and *āśrama*. The *sva* or the moral agent is looked upon as a representative of a *varṇa* or a class, and, concordant with this *varṇa* and *āśrama* or his station in life, a person's duties are determined. The *Gītā* specially emphasizes that the duties enjoined by *varnāśrama* might contradict the universal duties, yet that does not destroy their moral obligatoriness. Thus Madhusūdana comments that war is apparently immoral as it involves injury to life, but here it is morally justified being sanctioned by the codes of *svadharma*.[8]

The *Gītā* firmly asserts that one should observe the specific duties and it is morally wrong to swerve from these rules and accept duties obligatory for persons belonging to another *varṇa* or *āśrama*.[9]

It is to be noted that Kṛṣṇa never said that the *varṇa* divisions are hereditary. It would be wrong to turn to the *Gītā* for a divine sanction of rigid casteism. But why did Kṛṣṇa never say that caste or *varṇa* is determined by birth? Was it too obvious to be mentioned? Or do we today think that it was too obvious because of our long history of rigid casteism and because we always turn to the text borrowing our vision from the traditional commentators? Perhaps Kṛṣṇa was aware of the innate irrationality of the situation, that *varṇa*, which is supposed to regulate the whole life of an individual, is solely determinable by the accident of birth. He tried to rationalize the concept and add a dimension to it by introducing two new determinants: quality and action. He asserts that the

fourfold order was created by me, according to the divisions of quality (*guṇa*) and active function (*karma*).[10]

The qualities or *guṇas* were supposed to be of three basic types—*sattva*, *rajas*, and *tamas*. In the *Gītā* these *guṇas* have been described basically by "their psychological action in man."[11] Very broadly speaking *sattva* stands for knowledge and contentment, *rajas* for creative endeavor, attachment, affection, and activity and *tamas* for ignorance and inertia. By considering the preponderance of one or another of these qualities, individuals were classified into four distinct sections. Now if these *guṇas* are accepted as psychological technical terms used in that society, then we can say that men were classified into four groups according to their temperamental leanings and psychic make-up. *Varṇa* differences have been explained in this way. Those in whom *sattva* predominates are brāhmins. In *kṣatriyas rajas* predominates and there is a touch of *sattva* left. Similarly, the *vaiśyas* and the *śūdras* are naturally supposed to possess different psychological make up. These groups have naturally different food habits, different attitudes towards sacrifices, different attitudes for practicing charity and austerity. Actions and actors, firmness and happiness are all different in different types of persons. They form personality types who are different from each other in every way. But the interesting aspect of this doctrine is that even in morality the duties and obligations, imperatives and virtues of these typical groups are different. The virtues expected of a brāhmin, in whom *sattva* predominates, are serenity, self-control, austerity, purity, forbearance, uprightness, wisdom, knowledge, and faith.[12] The *kṣatriya*, in whom *rajas* predominates and there is a touch of *sattva* left, is supposed to possess heroism, vigor, steadiness, resourcefulness, not fleeing ever in battle, generosity, and leadership.[13] These list of virtues show how the economic theory of social prudence was turning into a socio-ethical principle in the *Gītā*. The list of *karma*s does not comprise external functions tied to vocation and profession, but these are moral virtues. As Sri Aurobindo pointed out, the work of the brāhmin according to the *Gītā*, is not teaching or priesthood, but calm, self control, purity, etc.[14]

These are called *natural* in the individual. These have been described as "*sahaja karma*," "*svabhāvaja karma*," or "*svabhāva niyata karma*."[15] *Sahaja* literally means "something born with" and there is scope for interpreting it as hereditarily transmitted work. But *svabhāvaja* means "born of inner nature" and *svabhāvaniyata* means "something regulated by inner nature" and thus interpreting *sahaja* in the same vein, we can say that *svadharma* stands for duties and virtues, which express the inner nature of the agent. The *Gītā* profusely praises performance of these natural duties. To swerve from one's own nature and be attracted by the mission of life natural for others have been called derogatory. It asserts that in human situations, performance of *svadharma* might be associated with moral disvalue (as for example, even the morally justified war involves loss of life), but such defects must not deter a person from observing *svadharma*.[16] It is even claimed that by practicing such morality a person attains perfection and such practice is the highest homage to God.[17]

Madhusūdana's commentary on the relevant *ślokas* is interesting. He quotes a number of authorities, such as Gautama, Vaśiṣtha, Āpasthambha, Manu, etc. He also gives a detailed list of *karmas* specific for different classes listed by these thinkers. According to almost all of them learning, charity, and sacrifice are common functions obligatory for the first three classes. According to Gautama, priesthood, teaching, etc. for brāhmins or protection of the wronged one and punishment for the wrongdoer for the *kṣatriya* are special functions, which they need not necessarily practice, yet they could turn to these if they wanted to earn their livelihood. Vaśiṣtha recognizes these specific functions as *svadharma*, but comments that these are optional and could be relied upon for subsistence. Again virtues listed in the *Gītā* as *svadharma* for brāhmins, have been described as specific for brāhmins and universal for others. By universal they mean the virtues which should be cultivated by all, irrespective of their *varṇa* and *āśrama*. According to Yājñyabalkya these are natural for brāhmins, while conditional for others.[18] The implication of all this is that brāhmins, in whom *sattva* is naturally dominant, would automatically cultivate these virtues; but if under exceptional circumstances *sattva* predominates in persons belonging to other *varṇas*, they would also cultivate these. The flexibility of the list and the inclusion of the professional functions show a clear departure from the position assumed in the *Gītā*. These thinkers certainly did not hold that the *varṇa* divisions were to be made on consideration of psychical makeup and function; the ethical orientation attempted in the *Gītā* is absent; and they held that *varṇa* is determinable by birth.

According to the conservatives, the *varṇa* system was rigid and unchangeable, because it was a divine command. As we have already mentioned Kṛṣṇa had said that he created the fourfold order, according to the difference of quality and action. Some have attached importance to the last explicatory part of the line, which gives a rational twist to the divine command, laying bare the grounds for the relativization of morality. Ānandagiri, for example, says that due to the qualitative difference of individuals their actions were different and that is how the fourfold order was created.[19] But the others turn to the first part of the quoted line. Śaṃkara emphasizes God's agency and asserts that God created the fourfold order. He supplements his position with quotation from the śruti.[20] As if the sanction of the whole system lay in its being a divine command. The conservatives believed in a pre-established harmony between a person's natural leanings and his birth in a particular *varṇa*. People born in specific *varṇas* were supposed to possess naturally the temperament suitable to that *varṇa* and the *varṇa* determined the duties. Thus by conveniently incorporating a number of presuppositions, the *svadharma* was given a tenable look, the pivotal among these being the idea that the individuals belonging to different *varṇas* form natural classes determinable by birth.

In the concluding section of the *Gītā*, it has been said that the duties of brāhmin, *kṣatriya*, *vaiśya*, and *śūdra* has been systematically divided corresponding to the *svabhāvaprabhavaih gunaih*. Here two factors are mentioned, which determine *svadharma*, namely, the nature of the agent and his qualities,

but the interrelation of the two is not made clear. The phrase is ambivalent, and Madhusūdana himself gives two alternative explanations, which would severally favor two opposite interpretations of *svadharma*. It may mean that the duties have been classified according to the predominance of the *guṇas*, such as *sattva*, etc., which are also the ground of the specific nature of the agent. Here the duties are directly linked with the psychical makeup and the essential nature of the agent. This is consonant with the lenient modern interpretation of *svadharma*. But then Madhusūdana also suggests that *svabhāva* might stand for nature, which is determined by the *samskāras* or tendencies accumulated in the previous life, which have become active for expression and fruition. Here the appeal is to the law of *karma* and birth in a specific family is not considered to be an accident. The *svabhāva* is the ground of the *guṇas* or qualities, and these *guṇa*s determine the duties.[21] It is well known that, according to these traditionals, these *samskāras* are held responsible for birth in a specific *varṇa*. This explanation of the phrase is consistent with the conservative theory of the *varṇa* system explicated above and corresponding rigid classification of duties.

To sum up, the ethical theory of *svadharma*, as enunciated in the *Gītā*, and as traditionally interpreted, implied the following: First, the actions of the agents must be regulated by the general motive of the welfare of the society; second, the society is divided into four natural classes and each individual is of a type who represent a class and as such the virtues associated with that class are expected of him, and the duties obligatory for that class are obligatory for him; and finally, the ethical life is always an expression of the essential nature of the agent.

The first of these has not been explicitly stated in the *Gītā*. But the *varṇa* system was originally designed to ensure proper functioning of the society. In fact one of Arjuna's basic objections was that his performance of duty would lead to the destruction of the social structure. In answer to that Kṛṣṇa has projected the fourfold *varṇa* system, with its classification of morality, as the ideal. If some of the virtues obligatory for brāhmins are directed towards achievement of personal perfection, such as serenity, self-control, etc., his other virtues such as charity, teaching, and so forth, and virtues expected of *kṣatriyas*, *vaiśyas*, and *śūdras*, are definitely those expected of a social man and are directed towards a balanced sustenance of the society. The idea of the overall good of the community is present as a backdrop to all these discussions. In fact the concept of *lokasamgraha* has been praised in the *Gītā*. It means inspiring individuals to perform their duty and preventing others from swerving from the path of duty, which obviously is a social concept.[22] Many modern interpreters of the *Gītā*, such as Bal Gangadhar Tilak, have looked at *svadharma* as essentially connected with the good of all.

Every modern thinker, including Tilak, Bankim Chandra Chatterjee, etc. has rejected the second clause about natural class. However, most of them have spoken about some sort of class system in the society. But in their attempt to extract the essence of the *Gītā* and rehabilitate it, they have attached great importance to the third position.

Bankim, for example, tries to establish that even original class difference was based on qualitative differences. He suggests that the Ṛk, which asserts that the brāhmins formed the mouth of the *puruṣa*, etc., is actually allegorical.[23] He quotes from Gautama Saṃhitā, which defines brāhmins in terms of the virtues associated with them. In the course of time, the society has become complex; there are societies other than the Hindu society which have a different classificatory structure. There is nothing sacrosanct about the fourfold order, and it might have to be replaced by fivefold or sixfold classes. But when a person accepts an order, either by heritage or by personal decision, the duties associated with that order becomes his *svadharma*.[24] According to him, this is the essence of *svadharma*. Kṛṣṇa identified *svadharma* with *varṇāśramadharma*, prevalent in the then society. Under the changed circumstances, it has to be understood differently. So we see that he has drifted away from the natural-class theory and concedes that *svadharma* might be a matter of personal choice.

Tilak, a great exponent of action, also speaks in the same strain. He emphatically asserts that the ethics preached in the *Gītā* is not essentially connected with the fourfold order present in that society. According to him, the society might belong either to the Hindus or to the foreigners, it may be ancient or modern, it may belong either to the east or to the west, if the fourfold order is present in that society then according to that order, or if any other system is operative in that society then commensurate with that system, whatever duty falls in the agent's lot, or whatever he accepts as his own, becomes his *svadharma*. And the *Gītā* asserts that the agent has no right to desert this duty for personal gains and so change the course of his action.[25] So Tilak too admits that *svadharma* has no essential connection with the fourfold order, and he also makes room for personal decision.

Girindra Śekhar Basu tried to combine the first and the third point. He looked at *svadharma* as the duty determined by the general motive of the good of the society and at the same time he held that it must accord with the individual nature. He acknowledged that the class difference is there, but then he held that the classification is necessary for the moral and material progress of people.[26] A person accepts a set of duties as his own, because of his mental makeup. He gives concrete examples. Droṇa, though he was born a brāhmin, led the life of a kṣatriya, and realized his potentialities. If he chose the typical life of a brāhmin, he would have failed to perform his *svadharma*. Lineage or family does not determine *svadharma*. At the same time, the good of the society as such is the criterion of morality for him. He relates the story of Śarvilaka, the murderer; he robbed and killed men, saying that this was his family profession, his *svadharma*. The author comments that Śarvilaka, Arjuna, and the common hangman all take life. The action of the first man is not justified, as it is not performed for the good of the society, whereas the actions of the last two are justified as those are done for the good of the society.

So the modern interpreters of the *Gītā* tend to hold that whatever the structure of the society, class difference would always be there. But, I think, that this postulate is not essential for their understanding of *svadharma*. First, they have

been flexible about the number of classes. Second, they have all accepted the possibility of choice. The modern version of *svadharma* demands that once a person is committed to a particular way of life, the duties associated with that life, the duties which promote social good, become obligatory for him. In fact they all agree that these duties are not determined by birth in a certain class or family, but these are self-chosen duties. The *Gītā* texts are essentially elastic, and they have allowed various interpretations. According to the traditional commentators, in the strictly structured society, *svadharma* stood for hard and fast tabulated rules. Madhusūdana explicitly states that one should perform the actions enjoined by the *varṇa* and *āsrama* and must not indulge in self-chosen actions.[27] The *sva* here is seen as a representative of a class, whereas in modern thought the *sva* is a person. The ambivalence is present in the writings of Radhakrishnan, too. First, he says that there are four broad types of nature and answering to them are four kinds of social living. A little later he asserts: "The emphasis on *svabhāva* indicates that human beings are to be treated as individuals and not as types."[28]

The emphasis on the third alternative is most marked in the writings of Sri Aurobindo. According to him there are four distinct orders of the active nature and the fourfold order corresponds to this.[29] But then, according to him, Kṛṣṇa accepted the system and gave it a profound turn and it is not bound up with the transience of a particular social form and order. Sri Aurobindo continues that the *Gītā* is not concerned with the validity of the Aryan social order, but it portrays the relation of a man's outward life with his inward being. He emphasizes authenticity in moral life. For him the *sva* is a person, and *dharma* stands for moral virtues and duties and thus *svadharma* is meant to emphasize that the virtues translate the inner potentialities into action. He turns to the assertion in the *Gītā*, "devoted each to his own duty, man attains perfection."[30] Coupling this with another declaration, namely, "the Lord abides in the heart of all beings,"[31] Sri Aurobindo concludes that all human activity must issue from one's essential nature. A person's native divinity or perfection should find expression through these. He describes *svadharma* action as an "authentic movement, not what is imposed (on it) from outside" with "terrible weight of external necessity."[32] It is development from within of the true personality of an individual.

Here *svadharma* has been adopted in such a way that, as a moral concept, its essence has changed beyond recognition. Initially, it stood for an ethical precept, which prescribed rules of conduct that differentiated the right from the wrong. In modern thought, it has become a part of a perfectionistic ethics that looks at morality as constituted of freely chosen actions, which reveal the inborn latent essence of man. However, it has to be admitted that, though originally the *Gītā* was meant to provide the first type of ethics, the roots of this later interpretation are also traceable in the text itself. In the traditional form, it was easily workable, but being tied to the natural class hypothesis it was totally unjustifiable. In its modern version, it is personalistic and relativistic. It stands for authenticity and sincere working out of an ideal to which a person is committed. As such it is subject to all the advantages and disadvantages of relativistic ethics.

But if this modern form is relativistic, was not the *svadharma* tenet in its original form relativistic too? It held that under the same circumstances what is right for one might be wrong for another. (I take this to be the clear implication of the oft-repeated assertion, that it is better to die performing *svadharma* than switch over to *paradharma*.) Instead of looking at morality as relative to person, this theory looks at morality as relative to a class. Some may want to say that this relativism is actually parasitical on one common good, namely, good of the society as a whole. But if such good was considered to be foundational, the conception of it should have been developed further and in detail. However, we find that it is only vaguely present in the discourse. Merely by appealing to the good of the society, one cannot achieve the much longed for objectivity. The *svadharma* tenet, whether in its traditional form or in its rehabilitated version, can at most claim to give a general directive or guideline to moral life, but it falls short of being a complete ethical theory. It is not complete because neither universalization nor critical appraisal nor solution of a moral dilemma are possible with this theory. It so happened that Arjuna was alternating between *svadharma* and *paradharma*. But if he wavered between two horns justifiable by *svadharma* itself, then how could the enigma be solved? In fact, according to Madhusūdana, Arjuna was wavering between two sets of alternatives—the first one being, "Should they (the enemies, who were his near and dear ones) be killed or should they be protected?" The second set was "Is it right to actively protect the world or is it right to opt for a life of renunciation?" The alternatives of the first set being sanctioned by the *svadharma*, how could one decide which of them was right? One would have to look elsewhere for moral guidance. Not any and every war, but participation in a war enjoined by duty has been acclaimed as the highest duty for a ksatriya.[33] But what is the mark of such a righteous war? At this juncture, I would like to introduce my second point.

II

The concept of *svadharma* constitutes only a part of the total ethics enunciated in the *Gītā*. For its proper evaluation, we should therefore see it as a part of a wider canvas. Proper performance of *svadharma* requires that it should be associated with the moral virtues commended in the text. Like the refrain of a song, throughout the text Kṛṣṇa repeats that the ideal person, the person firmly founded in wisdom, is expected to be *nirmama* and *nirahamkāra*, that is, one who has transcended the bounds of possessive sentiments (centered around the *mine*) and one who has inculcated impersonal outlook. Neither personal emotions nor expected results should influence his activities. He should be the equal-minded one who has transcended natural relativities like cold and heat, and also emotional relativities like joy and sorrow, victory and defeat, gain and loss. The *Gītā* mentions disvalues such as fear, rage, desire, greed, etc., each of which arises out of excessive attachment to the ego.[34] The *Gītā* has identified different

types of ideal life as suitable for persons with different empirical leanings, and yet the above-mentioned virtues are the common factors which form an integral part of any and every ideal life.

So the import of the above discussion is as follows:

If a person is hesitant to perform the duties which naturally appeal to him as a socially situated person, then one or the other factor suggested above are disturbing him. These are either excessive attachment to the ego or self-bound emotions such as happiness or sorrow or expectation of projected results. These are the factors which debar us from taking the proper moral decision. Purged of these, with complete intellectual honesty, it would be easier to perceive oneself objectively as an individual who is also an integral part of the social situation. From that standpoint it would be easier to judge the concrete duties obligatory for an individual, the duties which are good for the society and which are in consonance with the essential nature of the moral agent. Realization of such duties would constitute fulfillment of one's *svadharma*.

Some thinkers, such as the followers of Śamkara, would detect an incompatibility between *svadharma* interpreted in this way and moral discipline. They would say that the *svadharma* tenet is based upon the concept of a man as a natural individual, who is an integral part of the society, whereas the above mentioned discipline is necessary for the realization of the trans-social, trans-natural self. They see an unbridgeable gulf between *pravṛtti mārga* and the *nivṛtti mārga*—the path of renunciation and the path of action. Because of this standpoint, Madhusūdana, as mentioned above, juxtaposed two horns of a dilemma. I believe, however, that for the *Gītā*, there is no basic inconsistency between the two and the pursuit of freedom does not mean a negation of the socio-ethical life. Instead of preaching renunciation of social duties, the *Gītā* redefined social duties to show that it stands for an attitude of detachment towards life.

The above concept of duty should also be admitted as the total thrust of the text. Arjuna, being a warrior by caste, nature, and temperament, accepted participation in war as his *svadharma*. But face to face with his opponents he was shocked to realize that war meant death of all his near and dear ones—many generations of his relations, his friends, and his teachers. The blood-smeared victory, which he could visualize, was not the end he coveted. He refused to fight and presented a series of objections to justify his stance. These have been read as "solid moral reasons" by M. M. Agrawal.[35] But to my mind these appear as pretexts, used to dress up his unwillingness to fight and give it a moral look, rather than serving as moral grounds which motivated him. He was afraid that war would lead to complete destruction of the social structure, particularly of his family and clan. He was apprehensive that under such circumstances women would become corrupt and in the absence of proper successors to perform the necessary rites the peace of his forefathers in heaven would be disturbed and, thus being responsible for all these misdeeds, he would be placed in hell hereafter.

Had Kṛṣṇa considered these to be serious moral objections he would have seriously examined them. He could have presented a hierarchy of moral rules showing the superiority of *svadharma* over these. Or he could have subsumed *svadharma* and these considerations under some overarching moral law suggesting their compatibility. But Kṛṣṇa did neither. He dismissed summarily all these objections as unfounded. If Arjuna was afraid that he would be banished to hell, Kṛṣṇa retorted that in this rightful battle victory meant sovereignty over earth and death meant a straight journey to heaven.

But Kṛṣṇa takes infinite care to show that Arjuna's attitude towards life is wrong. Arjuna's emotions and personal attachments were disturbing him. Arjuna was succumbing to emotions. He was afraid of the possible disastrous results of the war. Some commentators have analyzed Arjuna's dilemma as a conflict between *svadharma* and *sāmānyadharma*, which is the universally valued ethical virtues of love and *ahimsā*. Madhusūdana points out that Dhṛtarāṣtra thought that being overpowered by the generally accepted moral tenet that *ahimsā* is the highest virtue, Arjuna had refused to fight.[36] But it is to be remembered that Arjuna never spoke of such universal virtue. As Radhakrishnan remarks, "it is not slaughter, but slaughter of ones own people that causes distress and anxiety to Arjuna."[37] His attitude towards his opponents was not one of love and kindness; rather, he said that, although they were assassins or who were fit to be killed according to the then accepted moral codes, he was still hesitant to kill them, as they were his own relatives. It was not a conflict between different kinds of moral duties; Arjuna's vision was blurred by non-moral considerations. Arjuna describes himself as one who is unsure about his moral duties. But Kṛṣṇa treats it as a case of confusion. By discussing the relevant issues, and by recommending the ideal attitude towards life, Kṛṣṇa was cleansing Arjuna's mind so that he could take the proper decision. If a person pays no attention to the expected results, abandons attachments, is of an even mind in success and failure, then what could be the motive for an action? The only motive would be the thought that to perform such and such action is one's duty, and that action has been described as the best type of action.

In this essay I have tried to show that the teachings of the *Gītā* in general and the *svadharma* tenet formulated therein are exceedingly elastic. It is possible to understand them in our own way yet it would not be (to borrow a phrase from Sri Aurobindo), "a reading of the modern mind into an ancient book."[38] In this connection, my observations are that, although in the *Gītā* the *svadharma* tenet has been presented as integrally connected with the fourfold order, the connection is superficial. In fact the *varṇa* system itself is a transient feature of a changing society. But the reference to the *varṇa* system makes it clear that *svadharma* stands for duties obligatory for a socially situated person and, as such, duties vary from person to person. Originally the *varṇa* system was supposed to capture this variation but through stratification of the *varṇa* order it has drifted away from this original position and has deteriorated into casteism, an artificial imposition from outside. It is more important to realize that the duties express the essential nature of man, and one should be true to that nature.

The *Gītā* and the commentaries remind us that *svadharma* has to be performed in the proper spirit. I have tried to show that the moral attitude prescribed in the *Gītā* frees the action of its subjectivity and relativity and ensures its ethical nature. *Svadharma*, thus interpreted, can claim to be a complete moral theory.

Notes

1. This long list includes Bankim Chandra Chattopadhyaya, Balgangadhar Tilak, Sri Aurobindo, S. Radhakrishnan, Girindra Sekhar Basu, Buddhadev Basu, and many other scholars and thinkers. Their backgrounds have been truly varied. Bankim was a civil servant; he is often considered modern India's first major writer. Tilak edited a newspaper and was a freedom fighter. Sri Aurobindo began as a freedom fighter and became a yogin and a vedic scholar in his later life. Radhakrishnan was a professor of philosophy who went on to become the president of India. Girindra Sekhar, who corresponded with Sigmund Freud, introduced psychoanalysis to India. Buddhadev, a professor of literature, was also a noted writer. All of them are respected for both the breadth of their thinking and the depth of their scholarship.

2. *Bhagavadgītā*, XII/13.

3. Sri Aurobindo, *Essays on Gītā* (Pondicherry, India: Sri Aurobindo Ashram 1959) 594.

4. Śamkara, *Commentary* on *Gītā*, with *Sub-commentary* by Ānandagiri on *Gītā*, ed. Pramathanath Tarkabhusana (Calcutta, India: 1986), *svadharmamapi svo dharmaḥ kṣatriyasya dharmaḥ yuddham*, II/31.

5. Madhusūdana Sarasvati, *Commentary on the Bhagavadgīta*, ed. Nalinikanta Brahma (Calcutta: Navabharata Publishers, 1986), *Svakarmaṇā prativarṇāśrama-vihitena*. XVIII/47.

6. *Gītā*, II/31 and 33.

7. *Gītā*, II/37.

8. Madhusūdana, *Commentary*, . . . *himsādimatvepi yuddhasya svadharmatvenā-dharmatvābhāva*.

9. *Gītā*, III/35; XVIII/47.

10. *Gītā*, IV/13.

11. Sri Aurobindo, *Gītā*, 477.

12. *Gītā*, XVIII/42.

13. *Gītā*, XVIII/43.

14. Sri Aurobindo, *Gītā*, 599.

15. *Gītā*, XVIII/42-48.

16. *Gītā*, XVIII/48.

17. *Gītā*, XVIII/46.

18. Madhusūdana, *Commentary*, on XVIII/41.

19. Śamkara, *Commentary* on *Gītā*, ed. Pramathanath Tarkabhusana (Calcutta, India: 1986), *guṇavibhāgena karmavibhāgaḥ tena cāturvarṇasya sṛṣṭim*, IV/14.

20. Śamkara, Commentary, *Cāturvarṇyam mayā īśvarena sṛṣṭam upāditam*, IV/14.

21. Madhusūdana, *Commentary*, XVIII/41.

22. Madhusūdana, *Commentary*, *Lokānām sve dharme pravartanam unmārgāt nivartanañca lokasaṃgrahaḥ*, III/20.

23. Bankim Chandra Chattopadhyaya, *Srimad Bhagavadgītā*, included in the collected works, vol. II, iv/13, 770.
24. Bankim, *Gītā*, 693-695.
25. Balgangadhar Tilak, *Gītārahasya*, Translated by Jyotirindranath Tagore, New edition, ed. Dhyanesh Narayan Chakrabarti (Calcutta: Progressive Book Forum, 1983).
26. Girindra Sekhar Basu, *Bhagavadgītā*, (Calcutta, 1948).
27. Madhusūdana, *Commentary, Sve sve tattadvarṇāśramavihite na tu svecchā-mātrakṛte karmaniśrutismṛtyudite abhirataḥ samyaganusṭhānaparah samsiddhim*, XVIII/45.
28. S. Radhakrishnan, *Bhagavadgītā* (London: George Allen & Unwin, 2nd ed., 5th impression, 1958), 365.
29. Sri Aurobindo, *Gītā*, 591, 598.
30. *Gītā*, XVIII/45.
31. *Gītā*, XVIII/61.
32. Sri Aurobindo, *Gītā*, 591, 601.
33. Madhusūdana, Commentary, II/7.
34. *Gītā*, II/37, XVI/21.
35. M. M. Agarwal, "Arjuna's Moral Predicament" in *Moral Dilemmas in the Mahabharata*, ed. B. K. Matilal (Shimla, India: Institute of Advanced Study, 1989), 132.
36. Madhusūdana, Commentary, II/1.
37. *Gītā*, II/26.
38. Sri Aurobindo, *Gītā*, 40.

Niṣkāma Karma

Niṣkāma Karma is perhaps the most important and interesting concept of the *Bhagavadgītā*. It is not only the core concept of the *Karma Yoga* but also all other *yogas* are founded on it. *Karma* means action, so *Niṣkāma Karma* translates as desireless action. But desire has been accepted as the most important ingredient of all actions by all the schools of Indian thought. Undoubtedly Kṛṣṇa is introducing a new concept here, action not produced by any desire, and it calls for discussion. It is true that Kant has made us aware of the absolute and unconditional nature of ethical imperatives. Yet, reading Kant into the *Gītā* is, I think, simplifying the matter too much. *Niṣkāma Karma* needs to be analyzed on the basis of a background in Indian theories.

So, I have devoted the first section to some preliminary discussion of factors accepted as essential components of action by various schools. In the second section I have analyzed the concept of *Nīṣkāma Karma* and the allied concepts, which help us to understand the core concept in its fullness. In the last section I have tried to show why I consider it to be the central thought of the *Gītā*. I have also referred to some relevant issues. Throughout the whole discussion my underlying aim has been to find out whether *Niṣkāma Karma* is psychologically feasible or not, and, if it is feasible, then what is its ethical value.

I

Action is something on which cognition, emotion, memory of the past, and expectation for the future, converge. A broad outline of the structure of action is as follows. This is more or less accepted by all, but it varies from system to system in detail and emphasis. Desire is the basis of all action. It is primarily

directed towards the fruits of action and secondarily towards the means, which lead to the realization of those fruits.

Fruits of action are awareness of *sukha*, or pleasure or happiness, and *duhkhābhāva*, or absence of pain.[1] Happiness is defined in Nyāya as a quality of the self that is felt as pleasant. Pain is that which is felt as unpleasant; but absence of pain, the desired end, being negative in character is not a quality of self. These two are ends in themselves or are desired for their own sake. Nyāya says that these desires are not subsidiary to any other desire. Desire for ends is preceded by cognition of these ends.

The desire is next extended to the means, which would help us to achieve the goal. It is preceded by *iṣṭasādhanatājñāna*, or the knowledge that the action is conducive to good. First, there is knowledge that certain ends are good or *iṣṭa*; then, there is awareness of the means, which would lead to the realization of those ends. It involves memory of the past, when similar means were instrumental in producing the desired good. This good is not any impersonal good, it is good or wellbeing of the agent. After this, the action is undertaken, if powerful sense of repulsion does not intervene. There is always the proviso that if the good is accompanied by evil, then there has to be a balance of good over evil. If the overall good produced by the action is outweighed by unwelcome results, then the action is not undertaken. Their stock example is that a person does not eat rice which is mixed with honey and poison. In fact Arjuna was thinking in this way. Arjuna refused to fight because he thought and said that the war would involve cruelty and would lead to disastrous results. He was thinking under the consequential scheme, which is natural.

Such a desire becomes *cikīrṣā*, or the desire to act, when it is supplemented by *kṛtisādhyatājñāna*, or the knowledge that the action can be performed. Even when a person desires rain he cannot act to produce it, because it is beyond one's capacity to do so. It is to be noted that whereas the *iṣṭasādhanatājñāna* looks at the action as a means, *kṛtisādhyatājñāna* treats it as an end. So these two cognitions produce volition, or the will to do. This has been termed *prayatna*, or *kṛti*. *Pravṛtti*, or the will to act, and *nivṛtti*, or will to renounce action, fall under *kṛti*. *Kṛti* produces *ceṣṭā*, or effort and then finally emerges action. Effort can be of the body, of language, of mind. Correspondingly, action can be physical, linguistic, or mental.

It is to be noted that Nyāya has also said that the springs of action are *doṣas* or faults. These are *rāga*, or attraction, *dveṣa*, or repulsion, and *moha*, or false knowledge. The last one underlies the first two. Actions are undertaken for fruits, which are pleasure and pain, and actions combined with *doṣas* produce these.[2] According to Nyāya, actions arising out of scriptural injunctions also have the same structure. Nyāya strongly feels that no one would undertake these actions unless he is absolutely assured about the end, even when the end is imperceptible. The Bhāṭṭas also agree with Nyāya. They hold that the ordinary commands work when they point out the end to be achieved and the scriptural imperatives also reveal the goal through the meaning of injunctions.

The Prābhākaras do not accept this analysis of action. The real spring of action is the knowledge that it can be done. About past actions one is fully aware of the necessary relation between means and ends, yet no action takes place. So *iṣṭasādhanatājñāna* fails to produce action here. *Kāryatājñāna*, or the awareness that it can be done, produces action. Mere desire fails to produce action, as, for example, a person does not act to acquire the moon because it is beyond one's capacity to do so. *Kāryatā* is explained through two adjectives. First, it is that which can be performed. Second, it embodies that which is aimed at by the will. Further, the self has to appropriate ideally the action as qualifying himself. This grounding of the action in self, together with the idea that the action can be done and should be done, leads to the emergence of action.[3] So we find that the Prābhākaras reject the *iṣṭasādhanatājñāna* of Nyāya, virtually incorporates *kṛtisādhyatājñāna*, and emphasizes the decision of the agent. It is to be noted that the Hindu thinkers do not always emphasize the difference between *can* and *ought*. In the works of Gāgā Bhaṭṭa we come across a clear formulation of this difference. In the typical Bhāṭṭa fashion he looks at both the subject and the object of action, the agent and the action itself. When the emphasis is on the action, the agent says, "I can do this." Here the emphasis is on inherent objective practicableness. When the emphasis is on the agent, the decision is that, "I should do this" or "this is my duty." This is internalization of the imperative.

The Prābhākaras were interested in the *ought* that comes from the scripture. The sense of ought emerge from the very form of the verb involved in the injunction. The suffixes, such as *lot, lin, tavya*, express the order, and the specific root determines the specific action. Some thinkers see in the Prābhākara philosophy a reflection of the duty for duty's sake theory of the *Gītā*. They do not speak of the goal, but they hold that the very form of the imperative moves a person to action. But my point is that they were thinking under the ritualistic scheme, where the idea of goal is built into the very idea of scriptural action. They accept the classification of vedic *karma* into *nitya* or obligatory, *kāmya* or desired by condition, *pratiṣiddha* or prohibited action, etc. Obligatory actions are said to be binding on individuals, although they do not yield any result. But even obligatory actions are connected negatively with results, for their non-performance leads to sin. So in their analysis all actions are goal oriented. Madhusūdana Sarasvati makes this very clear. An action which does not yield any fruit is never undertaken. This holds good about the *nitya karma*, too. Just as a mango tree planted for fruits yields shadow, sweet fragrance, etc. as by-products, so also *nitya karma*, performed as obligatory action, leads to production of some value.[4]

We might say that all the systems would agree that the desire for the goal moves a person to act; the individual agent, his desire or attraction, and dislike for the fruits, which are *sukha* and *duhkha*, moves a person to action. Almost all these factors are denied in the concept of *niṣkāma karma*. We shall try to find out what this means exactly.

With these preliminary comments, let me turn to *niṣkāma karma* itself.

II

Kṛṣṇa says: "You have right to action and never to the fruits (*phala*) of action; do not be the cause of the fruits (*phala*) of action, do not be attached to non-action."[5] Here the commentators have to explain the apparently self-contradictory order, expressed in the last line, namely, work, but do not produce the results. The last half of the last line says that action should not be given up. The *Gītā*'s attitude has always been that total renunciation of action is neither possible nor desirable. Some amount of action is necessary, even for continuation of life.[6] It is not possible to assert that action is the root of all bondage, so I shall abstain from all activity; this very assertion involves some action on the part of the speaker, which is as good as any positive physical action. Some conservative traditional thinkers tend to think that in the *Gītā* action stands for the scriptural injunctions and prohibitions; but my reading is that that the *Gītā* means by *karma* any and every action, and the *karma yoga* demands revision of our fundamental attitude towards life, through every action. Undoubtedly, the *Gītā* is discussing primarily the scriptural injunctions and all ethical imperatives, for it starts with Arjuna's moral dilemma; but later on the discussion is extended to all other actions. The *Gītā* gives a list of actions, which include seeing, hearing, touching, smelling, eating, going, sleeping, breathing, speaking, excreting, grasping, and opening and closing of the eye-lids.[7] When the Gītā discusses *karma*, I think it refers to all these.

Nor can Kṛṣṇa advise Arjuna: "do not consider yourself to be a cause of the fruits or consequences of your action." He himself has given an analysis of the causal conditions of an action. These conditions are *kartā*, or the doer, or the agent; *adhisṭhāna*, or the location of an action; *karaṇa*, or the instruments involved; *ceṣṭā*, or the effort given by the agent; and *daiva*, the unknown factor.[8] These factors are supposed to determine the nature and success of every action. So how can it be possible for the agent to be not the cause of the conesquences of an action?

A consistent interpretation of this couplet demands that we should see the ambiguity present in the term *phala* or fruits. The vagueness of meaning is responsible for confusion. At least three different meanings are discernible here. First, any thing produced, any natural perceptible consequence of an act can be called the fruit of an action. The Bhāratīya Darśana Koṣa has accepted this meaning, among others.[9] Acceptance of this meaning leads to misinterpretation of the message of the Gītā. Some critics have said that the Gītā preaches indifference towards the physical results of an action; it favors half-hearted action. I think that the Gītā does not accept this meaning. This meaning makes performance of action psychologically impossible. In fact, the *Gītā* derides action done without prior calculation of the expected results.[10]

Second, the fruits might stand for the pleasure and pain produced by an action. In the first section I quoted the Nyāyasūtra, which asserts this meaning.

The Darśana Koṣa mentions both the first and the second meaning. This meaning fits in well with the ethics preached in the *Gītā*. As we shall see, Kṛṣṇa has repeatedly said that do not be attached to pleasure or pain, be equal-minded. I think that the thrust of the couplet is that the agent must totally dissociate himself from expected emotions.

A third meaning is also possible, in which the fruits stand for the imperceptible results of an action, which lead to heaven and hell and determine one's life in the next birth. This meaning was highly favored by the traditional commentators. It is to be remembered that when the *niṣkāma karma* theory was formulated, the law of *karma* reigned supreme. It stands for an all-pervasive moral order which embodies the principle of universal justice, involving retribution. I feel that it was introduced to explain the inequalities found among men. It is held that every ethical or scriptural action produces some unseen consequences together with the natural results. These imperceptible consequences have been variously called *dharma, adharma, samskāra*, etc. Parents, natural intelligence and personality, birth in a specific family, complexion, physical stature, and such other facts of life, which we have to accept and cannot choose, are said to be produced by actions done in our last life. These stored up conesquences which are imperceptible are called fruits of action. So, we might say that an action produces a direct natural result, which affects a person emotionally by producing pleasure or pain; it also produces some imperceptible consequences. These might be called the *karmic* consequences of action. In fact, traditional commentators, such as Madhusūdana, accept the third sense. This is the typical meaning of *phala*. So, according to the conservative commentators this couplet means that one should not perform any work or the prescribed duties for the sake of the karmic consequences.

Niṣkāma karma is seen as a tool to be free from the consequences of one's action. When Kṛṣṇa advises Arjuna to discard desire for the fruits of action, he uses the term in the second or the third sense, and not in the first. The commentators have seldom dwelt upon the exact meaning of the term. Let us turn to some usages. Madhusūdana says that the fruits of an action are bound to follow from it. Here any one of the three senses is possible. Again he says that fruitless actions are never undertaken; here the context shows that he is using the term in the first sense, that is, in the sense of natural consequences.[11]

In the *Gītā* we can differentiate between two strands of discussion. One is ethical. It is to be noted that the problem with which the *Gītā* starts is an ethical problem; Arjuna did not know which action to choose. In this context, the second sense is very relevant. We shall see later that, irrespective of the exact meaning of the term *phala*, the *Gītā* preaches an ethics, which advises the agent not to be influenced by the desire for absence of pain or pleasure. The other one is directed towards *mokṣa*. In this context, the third meaning gains importance. The discussion of *mokṣa* is not very prominent here, but reference to *mokṣa* is indeed not absent. The *Gītā* asserts that, by discarding the fruits of action, a man achieves freedom from the chain of birth.[12] It is held that to experience the fruits

of action a person passes through the cycle of death and rebirth. Here, fruits definitely stand for the third meaning.

Madhusūdana has clearly explained that when a person acts *desiring* the fruits, he becomes a producer of those fruits; this is the clue behind the advice that do not be a cause of the consequences of an action.[13] Or in other words it is accepted that the agent is the cause of the natural consequences of an action; but if the action is ethically sound, that is, if the action is not performed by the agent for the pleasure or pain which it produces, then the agent is not cause of the fruits. Automatically, he is free from the karmic consequences of those actions. So the advice does not imply that actions should be given up.

Daya Krishna has argued that "if it is action performed from desire, that is, *sakāma karma* which leads to bondage, then there is no reason to believe that desire or *kāma* by itself would lead to bondage."[14] He goes on that if desire gives rise to bondage, then action would become redundant unless it is held that action produces a bondage of a different kind. He is dwelling upon the relevance and importance of desirelessness here. But my point is Kṛṣṇa has made it clear that action by itself is neutral, it does not necessarily produce bondage. Also, action cannot be completely given up; some amount of action is necessary for continuation of life. Herein lies the importance of *niṣkāma karma*. *Kāma* leads to bondage and by giving up desires and working from the sense of duty, or in other ways, which is not tainted by desire, one works at the same time is not held in bondage. When *karma* is performed in the desireless way, it loses its sting.

Niṣkāma karma theory expects the agent to work, discarding the expectation of pleasure or pain, and the sense of attachment to these results. According to the analysis given in the *Gītā*, it is not action, but attachment to action, that binds a person. So this is a way to achieve freedom. If an agent does not work for pleasure and pain, he is not a cause of pleasure and pain or of the associated *karmic* consequences. His actions would not lead to *dharma* or *adharma*, which lead to rebirth. *Niskāma karma* has been praised throughout. It is the inferior, who is. motivated by the benefits of action;[15] wise men act renouncing such interest.[16] Such statements are repeated like the refrain of a song.

We find that Arjuna was thinking under the ordinary scheme of action. Arjuna refused to fight because his emotions overpowered him. He judged that the consequence of war would be more evil than good, involving the death of all his near and dear ones. Arjuna's actions would involve cruelty, which is *adharma*, and he would go straight to hell after death. This war would lead to destruction of his family. But then, if expectation of happiness and absence of pain is rejected as motive, there would be complete absence of action. Kṛṣṇa introduces here his new ethical theory. Actions should arise out of the sense of duty of the agent. Emotions are not determinants of action; these should be brushed aside. Arjuna is told *yuddhāya yujjyasva*,[17] or fight, because fighting is your duty, or *kāryam karma samācara*,[18] or perform the action, which is your duty. Here he is presenting something like the duty for duty's sake theory. No ulterior motive should influence the decision of the agent.

The Hindu scriptures presented two ways of life. First, there is the path of action, or the *pravṛtti mārga*, which emphasizes the performance of rituals and actions prescribed by the scriptures; this assures good life in future either in heaven or in the next life. Kṛṣṇa has blamed such a mode of life. In flowery language the ritualistic parts of the Veda describe the happiness in heaven. Arjuna is asked to renounce this. The other is *nivṛtti mārga*, or the path of renunciation, which prescribes complete renunciation of action. The *Gītā* combines the two by holding that it is not action, but the desire for the fruits, which causes bondage. So the ideal life is practice of desireless action. In this context Hiriyanna's comment has become a cliché, namely, "the *Gītā* teachings stands not for renunciation *of* action, but for renunciation *in* action."[19]

Now let us turn to the other allied concepts through which the *niṣkāma* attitude unfolds itself.

One of them is equal-mindedness. In the second chapter, Kṛṣṇa introduces the idea of equal-mindedness in a very interesting way. He is scolding Arjuna for not wanting to join the battle, saying that his enemies, who have held him in great esteem, would now deride him and call him a coward. Retaining the light conversational tone he says that if Arjuna is killed in battle, he would go straight to heaven, and if he wins he would enjoy the sovereignty over earth.[20] He is standing here on the platform of desireful action. Then, radically changing his viewpoint Kṛṣṇa says, "Equalizing both pleasure and pain, both gain and loss, both victory and defeat, join the battle for battle's sake (i.e., accepting the battle itself as your duty, and not for any other ulterior motive) and you would incur no sin."[21] This couplet at once brings out the difference between desireful action and desireless action. Ordinarily an action is undertaken to achieve pleasure and avoid pain; in this particular case it is either victory, which is gain or defeat, which is loss. Kṛṣṇa says that a duty is to be performed, because it is the agent's duty. The agent should act without being affected by the opposite emotions. The consequences would follow naturally; there would be either victory or defeat. But on the moral level, the action would be barren; there would be no sin, no hell, and no continuance of life after death.

Madhusūdana gives an interesting explanation of the above situation. Arjuna did not want to fight. His argument is that if he is engaged in battle, because he wanted to go to heaven, then the action would be called *kāmya-karma*, or optional action, and it is better to avoid it if it involves sin. Now, if, on the other hand, the motive were winning the kingdom, then the end being perceptible, it would be an ordinary political action. But, such action must be sanctioned by morality; this one would never be so sanctioned, because it involves loss of life. So, Arjuna faces a dilemma in which both alternatives are equally distasteful. He wants to get out of the situation, by refusing to fight. But, even then, war is thrust upon him, as *svadharma*, and hence obligatory and compulsory. Under the circumstances refusal to fight would lead to sin, involving rejection of obligatory action. But taking part in the battle would also be sinful because it involves cruelty. The only way to steer clear of sin is to give up the old scheme and be equal-minded towards both the alternatives.[22]

Kṛṣṇa says *samatvam yogaḥ ucyate* or equal-mindedness is yoga.[23] Hiriyanna speaks of *samatvam* as equanimity or balance of mind. In this context different types of opposite pairs have been mentioned in the *Gītā*. The above analysis is present in Karmayoga. In Dhyānayoga, Arjuna is told to be equal-minded towards praise and insult. In Bhaktiyoga, the agent is described as one who neither rejoices nor hates nor grieves nor desires. He is the same to foe and friend, and is unperturbed in honor and dishonor, pleasure and pain, praise and censure, success and failure. In our ordinary life, individuals are always wavering between the opposite alternatives. Every action is closely connected with pleasure-pain, attraction-repulsion, and success-failure. These are natural for man; these are determinants of all actions. Anticipating happiness, we act; we shun an action if there is the possibility of sorrow. This structure is so clearly visible, in Arjuna's despondency. Possible death of his own people, possibility of the destruction of the society, possibility of his going to hell is influencing his decision of not joining the battle. Here Kṛṣṇa says that these opposite emotions are not determinants of action, they should be brushed aside.

In this discussion we are mainly talking about pleasure and pain; one who is not influenced by these dualities is praised as one who has transcended the dualities. Other such relative pairs also boil down to pain and pleasure. The ideal person has been described, among other things, as one who is beyond the opposing dual factors known as pleasure and pain.[24] I see here a definite difference from the classical Indian thought. There, *mokṣa,* the highest goal, is defined as complete destruction of pain and the possibility of future pain. Here, pain is accepted as a fact, which should not influence the decision of the agent when he is confused about his duty. Pain should be faced with an attitude of neutrality.

Among others, I find two pairs relatively interesting. One is cold and heat.[25] These sensations arise out of sense object contact. Here instead of talking directly about pain and pleasure, Kṛṣṇa is talking about the instruments which would lead to those ends. The thrust of this is that pain and pleasure, arising out of our contact with the objective world, are to be treated as equals, they must not influence our actions. Another one is *śubhāśubha*—good and evil. These terms have to be understood in a very narrow sense simply as beneficial and harmful and not in any specific moral sense.

Another way of looking at the same ideal is through the concept of detachment. Every type of action should be performed in a detached way. If a person is not exceedingly happy when he attains something and is not dejected when he fails to attain his goal, then he is accepted as non-attached. Madhusūdana Sarasvati explains non-attachment as absence of desire for the fruits of action and absence of the sense of agency.[26] The Advaitins have emphasized this last clause. We shall try to discuss this later. Non-attachment constitutes the core of the *niṣkāma* attitude. Attachment chains a person in every way. If a person is absorbed in an object and is constantly thinking about it, he becomes attached to it. This attachment arouses desire, and when this desire is thwarted the result is anger. Anger leads to delusion of values, and memory lapse. This destroys our normal assertive faculty called reason and then there is destruction.[27] But if a

person is not swayed by attachment and aversion, he has control over his senses; he acquires the rare ability to dwell on the object, without being regulated by it.[28] He is free from attachment or aversion, he has self-control, and he dwells on objects with contentment.

This concept of non-attachment has given rise to a number of wrong interpretations. It has often been translated as disinterestedness, indifference, etc. I think that a more appropriate term is neutrality, not towards the actual conesquences of an action but towards the emotions aroused. A person acts to produce results, so it is meaningless to say that he is not keen to produce them. Only it is demanded that he should not aim at self-centered gains. Non-attachment does not mean half-hearted attitude towards actions. The ideal agent is described as *dhrtyutsāha samanvitam*, that is, as a person who works with zeal and patience.[29] Such a person is not an indifferent worker. The *Gītā* does not propagate a negative ethics.

This takes us to the fundamental and very important concept of the *Gītā*, which I have called *anahamvāda*. In chapter II the ideal man has been called *sthitaprajña*, or a person of unwavering wisdom. He is *nirmama* and *nirahamkāra*, or he has transcended the possessive instinct associated with the ego, and he is aware that the self is not identical with the ego-sense.[30] Such a person is *anahamvādin*. This idea occurs again in III/30, where the doer is described as one who has renounced all expectations and possessiveness.[31] Again the devotee is described as free from possessiveness and egoism.[32] Here, the term *nirahamkāra* has highly controversial implications. The extremists take it to mean a person who does not feel any identity with the ego-sense; he has realized his identity with the super-personal self or *ātman*. It can also stand for simple overcoming of the excessive attachment of the ego and many of the modern thinkers would take this meaning. The *Gītā* gives a description of a person who is the limit of self-love. He is called a demonic character, with a false sense of self-importance. He has insatiable desire, he is given to lust and sensual pleasure, he is mad with the idea of power. He says: "This today has been gained by me; this particular end I will get; this wealth is mine and that wealth also will be mine; the enemy has been killed by me; and the others also I will kill; I am the lord, I am the enjoyer, I have satisfied my ambitions, I am powerful and happy; I am rich and well-born; who else is like me?" Such a person is deluded and is given to lustful gratifications.[33] The *Gītā* mentions many vices, but then those which are emphasized are traceable to this self attachment. The three infernal gates are lust, hate, and greed.[34] Desire and anger are looked upon as all-devouring, all-vitiating enemies.[35] The ideal man is told to relinquish egoism, power, arrogance, desire, anger, possessiveness.[36] These tracts are easily understandable without any reference to the reality of the changeless self. The *Gītā* is asking Arjuna to give up excessive self-centeredness. Here the terms *nirmama* and *nirahamkāra* can be understood in the ordinary sense. We shall see that up to the end the *Gītā* has retained the idea of action. Action requires the presence of some type of agency. Here we can interpret the *Gītā* to imply that a refined sense of agency has to be retained.

This idea is the foundation of the *Gītā* teachings. The metaphysical background of the *Gītā* is the idea that in each individual, two selves are intertwined together. One of them is the beginningless, endless, changeless self that is described by the *Gītā* in the second chapter. The other is the personal ego. All our shortcomings, our tensions and desires, hopes and failures are traceable to our sense of identification with this limited ego. If this sense of identity were destroyed, then the equal-mindedness, detachment, neutrality recommended in the *Gītā* would automatically follow. Once the myth of individuality is exploded, there would be no transmigration and rebirth, no journey to heaven and hell. The conservative thinkers, especially the Advaitins, have looked upon the *Gītā* in this way. Here the term *ahamkāra* is used in the specific sense in which it has been used in the Advaita philosophy.

But I think that this specific metaphysical background is not that important. Had it been so, then *naiṣkarmya* or complete cessation of all work, would have been the teaching of the *Gītā*. Kṛṣṇa says that complete cessation of work is neither possible nor desirable. He says that not even for a single moment can one ever remain engaged in non-activity. One should always act, for action is better than non-action.[37] By controlling the organs of physical action, if a person indulges in mental activity, he does not attain cessation of action.[38] He does not encourage Arjuna to renounce the world. He tells Arjuna to return to work with a changed attitude. The Advaitins say that Arjuna belongs morally to a comparatively lower state, or he is an ordinary man belonging to the mundane world, so he is not fit to receive the highest teachings, and so the prescriptions have been suitably modified. But then Arjuna represents the common man and the teachings are meant for men like him. Kṛṣṇa never says that there are two types of teachings; rather, he says that these are meant for all, including women, *vaiśya*, and *śūdra*! The Advaitins assert that Kṛṣṇa is asking Arjuna to transcend totally the sense of individuality. But how can action be possible without any sense of agency? At the most it can be said that Kṛṣṇa is asking Arjuna to transcend excessive self-centeredness.

The *Gītā* does not speak of total rejection of action for any one. Arjuna is asked to act. Kings like Janaka have reached the state of perfection through action.[39] Kṛṣṇa says about himself that he works. He has nothing more to accomplish which he would like to realize through action, so his action does not fall into the consequential scheme of *sakāma karma*, or desireful action. He has no duty whatsoever in the three worlds, so he is not obliged to work. Still he works and he works for *lokasamgraha*, for inspiring laymen to work. He says that if God does not work, the creation would be disintegrated.[40] Benefit of the people can be called a motive here; but according to the *Gītā* a desire is a desire when it aims only at self-centered gains. In a sense this can be called the culmination of *niṣkāma karma* practice. Here actions flow spontaneously, without any external obligation, for the good of all.

Further, if the *Gītā* is interested in the changeless self, it has dwelt at length on individuals, too. Persons have been classified into three types according to their psychical constitution, personality and temperament. This classification is

said to be natural. But we shall see that it is valuational, too. Starting with their different food habits, nature of sacrifice, penance, charity, action, agency, zeal, pleasure, etc. they have all been differentiated and classified. A brief perusal of some of these would show that the concepts which involve the *niṣkāma* attitude in some way or another have been called praiseworthy. Even virtues are not called morally laudable if they are not practiced in the *niṣkāma* way.

Sacrifice, penance, and charity were accepted as universal virtues. Kṛṣṇa never spoke against the prevalent customs, but often reinterpreted them. He has dwelt on sacrifice and has shown that *jñāna*, seen as a sacrifice, is the best of all.[41] The Mīmāmsakas unconditionally prescribed all the above three. The *Gītā* shows how the same virtue practiced in a special way becomes morally superior. To show this it falls back upon this classification. The *sāttvika* (translated as pure-clear) perform sacrifice, with no desire for the benefits of the sacrifice, accepting the injunctions of the scriptures, taking the sacrifice as one's duty. The *rājasika* (translated as active-passionate) offers the sacrifices, expecting returns, which are the fruits of action; they also perform for the sake of egoistic show. The *tāmasika* (translated as inert-dark) perform sacrifice, which does not conform to the scriptural rules.[42] There is no distribution of food, no sacred chant; it is devoid of faith and without any token gift for the superior.[43] This structure is maintained all through. The ideal person, the *sāttvika* man has *niṣkāma* attitude, the *rājasika* does not. The *tāmasika* goes against all prevalent norms.

Kṛṣṇa speaks of penance of body, mind, and speech. By the *sāttvika* these are practiced without any desire for gain, by the *rājasika* for gaining fame and name, involving showmanship, and by the *tāmasika* out of obstinacy, involving self-torture.[44]

Even charity, which is universally acclaimed as a virtue, is thus scrutinized and classified. The *sāttvika* gives, accepting the practice as his duty, and gives to one from whom he expects no return. Three other clauses are added—the gift must be given to the deserving person in the right time and place. The *rājasika* gives, expecting return benefit, with an aim to earn the fruits of the action. He also practices charity reluctantly. The *tāmasika* gives at a wrong place and/or time, to the wrong person, and gives disdainfully and patronizingly.[45]

Continuing the discussion, Kṛṣṇa comes to two very important concepts, namely, *sannyāsa* and *tyāga*. The Sāmkhyas have said that all actions should be given up, because actions constitute the chains of bondage. The Mīmāmsakas hold that the actions ordered by the scriptures should never be given up, for they purify the mind. The *Gītā* gives new definitions. Renunciation does not mean total renunciation; it means that of desire prompted action. *Tyāga* does not stand for relinquishing all responsibilities of life; it means that of the fruits of action.[46] In this sense both the above should be practiced by all and are practiced by the *sāttvika* people. Earlier, he has already said that one who acts without clinging to the fruits of action, accepting the action as his duty, is the true *sannyāsin* or renouncer.[47] The term is not applicable to one who has discarded the sacrificial fire or the scriptural rituals obligatory for a householder. The same spirit is

present here. It is the *rājasiika* and the *tāmasika* persons who believe in giving up all actions. The difference between the two is that the first gives up action being afraid of the pain and physical exertion involved. The second gives up because he is foolish and deluded. The *sāttvika*, the ideal one, acts properly. He accepts the action as his duty; he gives up attachment and expectation of the fruits of action. Thus, according to the *Gītā*, the person who acts in the ideal way is the person who has renounced attachment.[48]

Two other concepts are relevant here. One is that of the doer and the other is action. The *sāttvika* action is obligatory; after recognizing its imperative character it is performed without attachment, it is not moved by attraction or repulsion, or by the desire for the fruits of action. It is the same as *niṣkāma* action. The *rājasika* action is prompted by the desires of the ego-centered agent and involves great strain. The *tāmasika* action springs from the delusion of values of the agent, who does not pre-consider the future results, the loss or injury involved in the action or his own capacity to perform.[49] This last line is significant. It is often held that the *Gītā* says that the agent should act without caring for the consequences. But it should be clear now that the agent is expected to consider the possible consequences; only it is said that the personal gains should not be the deciding factor.

The description of the doer corresponds to this. The *sāttvika*, or the ideal doer, is free from attachment; he does not cling to the narrow ego, is endowed with firmness and zeal, and is unmoved by success and failure. The *rājasika* is prompted by desire for fruits, he is greedy, cruel, and passes through moods of exaltation and depression. The *tāmasa* person is, among other things, deceitful, malicious, lazy, despondent and procrastinating.[50] So the common idea, that the *sāttvika* person is a non-doer, is wrong. He works; he is not greedy for the results and at the same time he is not lazy.

The above clearly shows that the *niṣkāma* attitude constitutes the core of morality prescribed here. According to the orthodox commentators, it is derivable from the metaphysical background. This background is more Sāmkhya than Advaita, that is, even if the self is considered to be pure consciousness, the object is not devalued. *Prakṛti* is as real as the *puruṣa*. In the beginning the *Gītā* speaks of the pure self; but later on it discusses the individuals and their differences. If the *niṣkāma* attitude is traced to *puruṣa,* the content of duty is determined by personality. I feel that the content together with the attitude makes up the ethics of the *Gītā*. In the concept of *niṣkāma karma* we find retention of action, and rejection of that part which causes bondage. Kṛṣṇa introduced the concept of *niṣkāma karma* when the *law of karma* reigned supreme. By performing *niṣkāma karma* a person was to be liberated from the endless cycle of death and birth.

I feel that these commentators have excessively focused on the metaphysical position, which emphasizes the reality of the changeless self. We can ask: Is it a necessary condition of the ethics of the *Gītā*? I think that it is not. We have said that the teachings of the *Gītā* can be divided into two sections. One is simply ethical; it is directed at solving Arjuna's moral dilemma. It does not

require the background at all. The concepts of performance of duty without expectation of the benefits of action, of equal-mindedness and neutrality to the expected results and associated emotions, and the idea of transcendence of egoism and possessiveness are all understandable, without any reference to such a self. The other is spiritual; it aims at *mokṣa.* It is interested about the place of God in life. For those discussions the idea of the changeless self is somewhat relevant. However, it is to be remembered that the *Gītā* is theistic, and the spiritual tracts cannot totally do away with the idea of person and individual.

We can also ask whether the idea of such a changeless self is sufficient to issue the ethics of the *Gītā* or not. Again, I think that it is not. If one does not accept the reality of individual persons, then the concept of *niṣkāma karma* becomes meaningless. As we have already noted, had the transcendental self been the only reality, the corresponding ethical imperative would have been complete renunciation of all action. It might be asked that why is the ethics of the *Gītā* prefaced by a description of the changeless self at all? I feel that Arjuna was refusing to fight because he was afraid of death. Kṛṣṇa states that death is inescapable and natural (and if one accepts the law of *karma,* then rebirth is natural too). The inevitability of death and the powerlessness of the individual is vividly shown in the terrifying sublime vision of God in the *Gītā.* He shows that this must not influence the ethical life of an individual.

Here the question is: can the ethics be satisfactorily rehabilitated after being severed from that metaphysics. I feel that it is possible. Kṛṣṇa is simply asking Arjuna to transcend excessive attachment to the ego. Arjuna was suffering from this. Madhusūdana Sarasvati says that Arjuna refused to fight against his friends and relatives because his rational sight was blurred by his attachment to the ego.[51] Radhakrishnan said that Arjuna was not hesitant to kill people, but he was most unwilling to kill his *own* people. He says, "it is not slaughter, but slaughter of one's own people that causes distress and anxiety to Arjuna."[52] When an agent is free from his egocentric motives, when personal considerations do not interfere, it is easier to observe one's duties, and the judgments are rational and clear. The basic premise of morality is that the moral agent should look at himself as any other person, without assigning to himself a special seat. As long as the agent is engrossed with himself, his personal pleasure and pain, desires and expectations would regulate his actions. His personal gains would determine his decisions. But if he wants to search for the morally good, he has to transcend the limits of egoism and be equal-minded and detached. The *Gītā* is not asking much. This can well be a deontological ethical position.

III

The *Gītā* has spoken of a number of yogas, of which the Karmayoga, the Jñānayoga, and the Bhaktiyoga are most important. The commentators have chosen from these and have attached prime importance to the yoga of their

choice. Śamkara speaks of supremacy of *jñāna*. He criticizes the view that a combination of *jñāna* and action leads to the highest end. His point is that *jñāna* and *karma* are radically different from each other, so how can the two be combined? He admits that the *Gītā* has spoken of action, too, but he holds, that as a matter of fact, action is subsidiary to *jñāna*. It leads to purification of mind, which ultimately leads to *mokṣa*. *Jñāna*, according to the Advaitins, is the ultimate realization that individuals are identical with *ātman*, the eternal changeless self. Such a self has been depicted in the second chapter. In Balgangadhara Tilak we find a strong supporter of *karma*. To quote him, "Gītā has expounded nothing but the doctrine of Action combined with Knowledge."[53] Or in other words, *jñāna* is ancillary to action, and is that which makes *niṣkāma karma* possible. Sri Aurobindo, among the moderns, represents the *bhakti* cult. He holds that love of God and total surrender to the Almighty leads to the best form of life. According to him, "living consciously in the Divine and acting from that consciousness" is the highest ideal to be realized.[54]

But I feel that these views are all one-sided. I have called the *niṣkāma* attitude the core concept. Practice of *niṣkāma karma* is Karmayoga. The other two yogas also accept this core concept as an integral part of their position. They should be treated as alternative disciplines, with difference of emphasis. These differences have been necessary to accommodate the difference in temperament of the individuals. Basically, the *Gītā* prescribes a radical reorientation of life, which can be achieved in various ways. These ways share one common precept and that is the development of *niṣkāma* attitude.

Let us turn to the *Gītā* itself. Kṛṣṇa in different contexts praises the yoga, which he is elaborating as the best one. In the first few chapters he praises action. Then he says that *jñāna* is the best, nothing is equal to *jñāna* in purity, all actions end in *jñāna*.[55] Again, there is a clear and bold declaration that the yogin is better than the *tapasvin*, or the man who practices penance, the wise man and the active one, so Arjuna should become a yogin.[56] In chapter XII, he says that one who is devoted to him is dear to him. These statements confuse us, and fortunately they confused Arjuna too. He tells Kṛṣṇa, "By words that appear to be mixed up, you seem to confound my reasons."[57] But clarificatory statements are also there. Kṛṣṇa declares that only children think that knowledge and action are different, not the well-informed ones.[58] Again he urges that the same end is reached by the man of action and the man of knowledge; so he who considers the two to be identical has proper insight.[59] Again, it is said that renunciation and practice of action are identical, for one cannot be an ideal actor or yogin without renunciation of desire.[60] But, what appeals to me most, is where he says that the path of wisdom is for the *sāmkhyas*, the path of action is for the yogins.[61] So I feel that all the yogas are equally important, and they are alternatives, *niṣkāma* attitude as foundation common to all. The *Gītā* says that Yoga is a rational way of action,[62] and I think that *niṣkāma* attitude is that rationality.

It is the responsibility of the yogas to explain the way in which the *Gītā* advocates retention of the sense of agency in their discipline. The Advaitins say

that, after the highest realization about the nature of self, the sense of agency is completely destroyed. *Niṣkāma karma* is meant for people belonging to lower strata, who practice it for *cittaśuddhi*, or purification of mind. They interpret the term *nirahamkāra* in the technical sense in which it is used in Advaita philosophy. There are lines which support such a stance. For example, the *Gītā* says that to see a person as a non-doer is to see correctly.

The followers of Karmayoga feel that *niṣkāma karma* is the means as well as the end. In the center of all their activity, there is the universe, and they replace the *I* by *all.* Thus they work not for achieving personal ends, but for the good of all. There are lines which support such a position, too. We have already spoken of Janaka, who achieved perfection through *niṣkāma karma*. According to the *Gīta*, Kṛṣṇa, the God, works and he works for *lokasamgraha* or good of all.[63] According to Madhusūdana, inspiring men to perform their duty, and preventing others from swerving from that path, is *lokasamgraha.* In the closing chapter, the *Gītā* says that devoted each to his own occupation, a man reaches perfection. Performance of one's own action is to be seen as worship of God, which leads to perfection.[64]

The devotee completely surrenders to the Will of God. It is the easiest way for the believer to go beyond self-centeredness. He submits totally to God and he looks at all his work as God's work. One of the couplets, which endorse this view, asserts that God is present in the heart of every individual and to understand this is to understand the mystery of life.[65]

The *niṣkāma karma* has been liked by classical commentators because they thought that it combines the good points of both *pravṛtti mārga*, the positive way of action, and *nivṛtti mārga*, or the negative way of inaction, and it shows a good practicable way of realizing freedom. Some modern thinkers like it because of its practical benefits. Vinoba Bhave, for example, thinks that it improves the quality of action. He says that it leads to the realization that an action is much more enjoyable than the results attained. When a person is not disturbed by the thought of success or failure of his achievement, his concentration on the work itself is much better. The attitude of Budhadev Basu is similar. But I think that these are the secondary benefits, which follow from the practice of this concept; in itself it can be appreciated just as an ethical theory.

Girindra Sekhar Basu has given a very different explanation. Five factors are responsible for the production of the result and only the unwise claim the total responsibility of action. The *Gītā* points out the defect of such a one-sided approach. This interpretation is traceable to a simple understanding of XVIII/16.

We find here that the natural man is the limited man and the limits are the limits of desire. To transcend naturality, he must transcend desire and his emotional entanglement in personal gains and losses. This would give him the taste of freedom. The scriptures talk of total transcendence of naturality. After discussing in detail the nature of individuals in terms of *guṇas*, which are natural components constitutive of man, Kṛṣṇa speaks of the *guṇātīta* or one, who is beyond all the *guṇas.* But here we are entering the realm of mysticism. For the

ordinary thinker, it is beyond conception, an ever-receding ideal. In fact, rejecting the literal meaning, the *guṇātīta* has been described as on who is totally detached by Madhusūdana. Curiously, we come across a declaration in the *Gītā* itself, namely, that neither in this world nor among the gods in heaven is there a single individual who is free from these three *guṇas*![66]

I have said in the first section that *niṣkāma karma* involves negation of almost all the components considered to be essential for action. It definitely denies the role of emotion, both as the expected end serving as the spring of action and also as influencing the personality of the agent after action. Actions should spring from the sense of duty. It replaces the desire for the fruits of action. *Sthitaprajña*, the ideal man firmly established in wisdom, is lauded as one who is not disturbed by desires. Pain does not create any tension in him; happiness does not arouse any desire in him. With complete control over himself, he attains tranquillity and peace. He is likened to the sea, which is not disturbed by the rivers, which empty their water into it without destroying its calmness.

However, desire in one form cannot be got rid of. It is the desire for desirelessness. Daya Krishna describes it as "a second order desire with respect to all first order desires. It tries to suggest how desires 'ought' to be desired."[67] The fundamental urge for perfection has to be there, whatever its form; it might be the desire for purification of mind or it might be the desire for *mokṣa*. For this reason Daya thinks that *niṣkāma karma* involves a conditional ought, conditioned by the "desire to be free from the consequences of one's actions." Later on he presents the position of the opponent. The opponent says: "It may be argued that consequences inevitably bind one, and that as no one desires bondage, the imperative for *niṣkāma karma* is essentially unconditional."[68] Daya counters this by asserting that it is not clear why all forms of bondage should be treated as intrinsically undesirable, and why all consequences should inevitably bind one. Bhakti movement illustrates his point. The devotee wants to be born again and again, to be in the Lord's service, to do his work, to sing his praises. So he enjoys his bondage created by devotion and love of God. Against this, my point is that the intrinsic undesirability of bondage is the basic premise here; and it is also taken for granted that consequences of action bind men. I feel that the desire of the devotee is necessarily *niṣkāma*, for desire, which leads to continuation of life—the desire, which has to be expunged—is self-centered desire. Desire of the devotee is basically different from this. Such desire presupposes complete surrender to God's will, and complete transcendence of the narrow self. The actions of the devotee are comparable to the playful actions of God, called Līlā, which flows out of joy for the creation of the world. These actions are ends in themselves and there is nothing external to be achieved. So the desire of the devotee does not contradict the tenet of *niṣkāma karma*.

Further, the role of individual as an agent cannot be overlooked. The extremists want to say that complete deindividuation is the ideal laid down in the *Gītā.* Again, I feel that the *Gītā* advocates transcendence of total ego-centeredness and rejection of the possessive instinct, but not total rejection of

the sense of agency. If *nirahamkāra* means rejection of excessive attachment to the ego, then that is understandable, but if it means complete destruction of the sense of ego, then in the absence of a sense of agency actions become impossible. On the one hand, the *Gītā* says that total renunciation of action is neither possible nor desirable, on the other hand, it declares that to see a person as a non-doer is to see correctly. Here we come face to face with the glaring ambiguity present in the *Gītā*. It does not try to solve the riddle. Modern thinkers have not taken these precepts literally; Hiriyanna, for example, holds that absolutely motiveless actions are impossible, ego-bound motives are to be renounced.

Actually, the *Gītā* praises the *niṣkāma* attitude, in which each and every action has to be performed in that spirit. Though Kṛṣṇa originally asked Arjuna to assume the *niṣkāma* attitude to solve his practical moral dilemma, the underlying aim is always there. In the very beginning Arjuna is asking, which is the better one?[69] The context suggests that he was asking which of the two alternatives is better. The conservative commentators read this by saying that he was asking what is the ultimate goal of life. I feel that Kṛṣṇa suggested that this principle would help one to solve ordinary moral problems and, when followed stringently, it would lead to the ultimate liberation.

By this time it should be clear that the *niṣkāma karma* theory of the *Gītā* is not the Indian version of the duty for duty's sake theory of Kant. Duty for the sake of duty has been prescribed here, but some thinkers feel that the element of conditionality is important in *Gītā*. In various places various ends have been suggested. *Niṣkāma karma* leads to purification of mind; it leads to attainment of *mokṣa*, and also to *lokasamgraha*, or good of all. However, such conditionality is inescapable in every ethics. The motive to be good, in some form or other, conditions all moral actions. But there is another difference. In Kantian ethics the categorical imperatives and the hypothetical imperatives coexist side by side. But in *Gītā*, although *niṣkāma* concept is introduced initially to solve an ethical problem, later on this is extended to each and every action. The *Gītā* is asking for a reorientation of the whole life. This becomes obvious when the agent is considered to be a devotee. What you do, what you eat, what you offer, what you give, what austerity you practice, let it be done as an offering to me.[70] Here the *Gītā* no longer is limited to the solution of moral dilemmas, it is talking about life itself. The principle that organizes life would also solve its specific problems.

Sometimes we feel bewildered when we face the fierce determinism of the *Gītā*. There is a natural determinism, for Kṛṣṇa says that the *guṇas* constitute one's nature and it is impossible to go against them. Nature compels one to act consistently with one's temperament, even when one wishes to defy it. Arjuna cannot avoid fighting as he is a warrior by birth, which means that *rajas* predominates his nature.

Naturalistic analysis of the ethical properties, that is, analysis of personality and moral value by tracing them to the *guṇas*, leads to another inconsistency. It is sometimes asked: can a warrior fight with a *niṣkāma* attitude? This apparently

innocent question conceals an important anomaly present in this ethics. Here two principles have been introduced, both of which are explainable in terms of the *guṇas*. A person should observe *svadharma*. *Svadharma* is equivalent to *varṇāśramadharma*. *Varṇa* differences are determined by inherent constitution explainable in terms of the preponderance of *guṇas*. Again, the *Gītā* preaches that every person should practice his duties in the *niṣkāma* way. But *niṣkāma* attitude is present only in persons in whom *sattva* predominates. A brahmin is naturally *sāttvika*, and it is naturally possible for him to develop *niṣkāma* attitude. He can observe both the precepts consistently. What about a *kṣatriya*? How can Arjuna, who is a warrior by nature and in whom *rajas* predominates, practice *niṣkāma karma*?

The answer comes from Madhusūdana. He is aware of these difficulties. He says that if human actions were totally determined by nature, then all these *śāstras* involving injunctions and prohibitions would be meaningless. His answer is that nature leads a person in certain ways, but it is possible to transcend nature and chose the right alternative. The message of the *Gītā* is that actions should not be propelled by attraction and repulsion, which is natural, but should be determined by the sense of duty. To follow the call of duty is to rise above natural determinism.

So Arjuna, who is a warrior by nature, cannot give up the duties of a warrior; but he has every right to perform *niṣkāma karma*. I have said that the *guṇas* are as much psychological concepts as they are valuational ones. *Gītā* should have observed the difference. *Guṇas*, as natural principles, determine the personality of the agent and the content of duty. But the attitude, which constitutes the core of the ethics, should not be tied to the *guṇas*. Every one has the right to be a better person, to inculcate the *niṣkāma* attitude. The epics accept this. Persons from different *varṇas* are accepted as ideal person; a hunter, a home-maker lady, a butcher are morally appreciated because they practice *svadharma*. In spite of their different professions they are accepted as *sāttvika*.

The *Gītā* talks of the determinism of the divine will too. God dwells at the heart of all individuals and causes all men to work, as if mounted on a machine.[71] In front of these determinisms, the whole of the *Gītā* and its message looks meaningless. But there is one redeeming couplet. In the end, Kṛṣṇa says, that he has told Arjuna the entire secret; now, after considering all the pros and cons, without any omission, he should do as he likes. Even if the freedom of will is not there, the sense of freedom is there which guarantees possibility of ethics. Against divine determinism, Madhusudana's advice is to take refuge in Him, and He would show the way.[72]

I would like to end this discussion by commenting upon a comment on the *Gītā*. I give a free translation from Bengali of this comment. The *Gītā* is responsible for all the sorrows of India. It has done a great disservice by making men renounce action and seek freedom. The whole country followed the tenet "Be the incidental cause, O Sabyasāchi" (which means here, be an apparent cause only).[73] This statement rests upon a gross misunderstanding of the message of the *Gītā*. It speaks sarcastically about the determinism present in the

Gītā. But in the history of philosophy serious thinkers such as Spinoza, Russell, and Freud, have shown how determinism can accommodate ethics. Arjuna wanted to renounce action and Kṛṣṇa sought successfully to make him act. Tilak calls it the gospel of action; Hiriyanna says that it teaches renunciation in action. I hope my discussion will have cleared up this kind of misunderstanding.

Notes

1. Vātsyāyana, *Nyāyabhāṣya*, ed. Phanibhusana Tarkavagisa (Calcutta: Bangiya Sahitya Parisad, 1937), *Sukhaduhkhasamvedanam phalam*, 1/1/20.
2. *Nyāya sūtra, Pravartanālakṣaṇa doṣaḥ*, 1/1/18.
3. Śalikanātha Miśra, *Prakaraṇapañcikā*, ed. Subrahmaniya Sastri (Varanasi, India: Benares Hindu University), *Sa yāvanmama kāryeyamiti naivā-vadhāryate tāvat kadāpi me tatra pravṛtti na bhaviṣyati.*
4. Madhusūdana Sarasvati, *Commentary* on *Śrīmadbhagavad Gītā*, ed. Nalinikanta Brahma (Calcutta: Navabharat Publishers, 1986), 220-221.
5. *Gītā*, II/47.
6. *Gītā*, III/8.
7. *Gītā*, V/8,9.
8. *Gītā*, XVIII/14.
9. *Bhāratīya Darśana Koṣa*, compiled by Srimohana Bhattacharya and Dinesh Chandra Bhattacharya Sastri, (Calcutta: Sanskrit College, 1978), Vol. I, 115.
10. *Gītā*, XVIII/25.
11. Madhusūdana, *Commentary*, 1104.
12. *Gītā*, II/51.
13. Madhusūdana, *Commentary*, *phalakāmanayā hi karma kurvan phalasya hetur-utpadako bhavati*, 245.
14. Daya Krishna, "The Myth of the Puruṣārthas" in *Indian Philosophy, A Counter Perspective* (Oxford: Oxford University Press, 1991), 193.
15. *Gītā*, II/49.
16. *Gītā*, II/51.
17. *Gītā*, II/38.
18. *Gītā*, III/19.
19. M. Hiriyanna, *Outlines of Indian Philosophy* (London: George Allen & Unwin, 1932), 121.
20. *Gītā*, II/35-37.
21. *Gītā*, II/38.
22. Madhusūdana, *Commentary*, 219-221.
23. *Gītā*, II/48.
24. *Gītā*, XV/5.
25. *Gītā*, II/14, VI/7.
26. Madhusūdana, *Commentary*, 246.
27. *Gītā*, II/62-63.
28. *Gītā*, II/65.
29. *Gītā*, XVIII/26.
30. *Gītā*, II/71.

31. *Gītā*, XVI/13-15.
32. *Gītā*, III/30.
33. *Gītā*, XII/13.
34. *Gītā*, XVI/21.
35. *Gītā*, III/37.
36. *Gītā*, XVIII/53.
37. *Gītā*, III/8.
38. *Gītā*, III/5, 6.
39. *Gītā*, III/20.
40. *Gītā*, III/21-23.
41. *Gītā*, IV/33.
42. The translations have sometimes been taken from the *Bhagavad Gīta*, translated by Nataraja Guru (New Delhi: D. K. Printworld, 1993).
43. *Gītā*, XVII/11-13.
44. *Gītā*, XVII/17-19.
45. *Gītā*, XVII/20-22.
46. *Gītā*, XVIII/2.
47. *Gītā*, VI/1.
48. *Gītā*, XVIII/7-9.
49. *Gītā*, XVIII/23-25.
50. *Gītā*, XVIII/26-28.
51. *Gītā* M, 60.
52. S. Radhakrishnan, *The Bhagavad Gītā* (London: George Allen & Unwin, 2nd ed., 5th impression, 1958), 89.
53. Balgangadhar Tilak, *Srimad Bhagavad Gītā Rahasya or Karma Yoga Sastra,* translated by Bhal Chandra Sukhthankar (Poona, India: 1935), 431.
54. Sri Aurobindo, *Essays on the Gita* (Pondicherry, India: Sri Aurobindo Ashram, 1959), 33.
55. *Gītā*, IV/33.
56. *Gītā*, VI/46.
57. *Gītā*, V/1.
58. *Gītā*, V/4.
59. *Gītā*, V/5.
60. *Gītā*, VI/2.
61. *Gītā*, III/3.
62. *Gītā*, II/50.
63. *Gītā*, III/20.
64. *Gītā*, XVIII/45-46.
65. *Gītā*, XVIII/61.
66. *Gītā*, XVIII/40.
67. Daya, "The Myth of Puruṣārthas," 192.
68. Daya, "The Myth of Puruṣārthas," 192.
69. *Gītā*, II/7.
70. *Gītā*, IX/27.
71. *Gītā*, XVIII/59-61.
72. Madhusūdana, *Commentary*, 336-339 and 1230-1232.
73. A. K. Bandyopadhyaya, *Pauranika* (Calcutta: Firma K. L. M. Private Ltd., 1979), 332.

In Search of Egoism and Altruism in Hindu Thought

Cross-cultural dialogues are encouraged these days but often we find that certain concepts are irretrievably culture bound. In this essay I try to find out whether the Indian values are basically similar to Western values or not. Egoism and altruism are quite well known concepts in Western thought. Egoism drives much of our thoughts and actions. It seems to me that altruism is a foundational concept in Christian ethics. So, I chose to search for these concepts in Indian philosophy and Hindu thought. Even at the risk of telling you the results of my findings now, I have to admit that I failed to find any paramount importance of these concepts in Hindu thought. That does not mean that these concepts are not there. They are very much present in theological and philosophical writings; but there is a basic difference of approach, and in this essay I want to focus upon that difference.

The *Concise Oxford Dictionary* defines *egoism* as a theory that treats self-interest as foundation of morality. Altruism, on the other hand, holds that regard for others is the guiding principle of action. So egoism and altruism are looked upon as opposed to each other. It is even believed that our natural propensities are egoistic, and altruistic virtues are thrust upon us for the maintenance of social stability and harmony. But Hinduism has not recognized any clear-cut difference between the two. Virtues have not been categorized as altruistic and egoistic; nor has there been any evaluative comparison of these two separate theories. Rather, Hinduism has favored a fusion of the two, in which altruistic virtues are prescribed as essential for betterment of personality. Self-perfection constituted the core of Indian morality, which ultimately ends in self-realization or *mokṣa*.

It is to be remembered that Hinduism has no founder. It is a religion of natural origin. The Hindus like to describe their religion as *sanātana dharma*, or eternal religion. It is a religion of natural growth followed by the majority of people of India. A Western scholar comments that Hinduism includes "an immense gamut of religiosity from the folkways of simple villagers to highly sophisticated metaphysical systems."[1] (I would say from *Santoshi Ma* to

Nirguṇa Brahman of Śamkara.) But he acknowledges that, despite its diversity, there are some common features. I have tried to restrict my discussion to those common features, but I do not claim that I have touched all the variant views traceable to Hinduism.

In this essay we shall see that Hindu ethics is not religious ethics. It does not require obedience to a set of commandments. Nor is it secular humanistic ethics, in which human beings are said to have free wills, and they are obligated to perform certain duties, independently of interests and desires. It partakes of the nature of both; side by side with scriptural injunctions, many secular virtues have been advocated. The virtues are taught in the intuitive way, through examples in the epics. Perhaps it is best to describe Hindu ethics as virtue ethics. The emphasis is not on the amount of good produced, but rather on what one should be.

"Doing good to others" has not been the supreme value in traditional thought, so Hinduism is not altruistic. Nor is it strictly speaking egoistic, for if self-interest means selfishness, then that has been deplored by almost all Indian thinkers. With the single exception of the Cārvākas, no one else spoke for crude enrichment of the material ego. The Cārvākas are the short-lived polemically important group, who were dissenters from mainstream Hinduism. They are the thinkers who professed the theory of *yāvat jīvet sukham jīvet ṛṇam kṛtvā ghṛtam pivet* or as long as you live, live happily, borrow money to eat ghee. (It is the Indian version of, eat, drink and be merry theory.) Ego is that part of the individual which enables one to say *I*. According to Indian thinkers, attachment to the ego, or *aham*, engrossment with *I* and *mine*, is the root cause of moral degradation, and the moral aspirant is constantly trying to go beyond the *I*. So, Hinduism is not egoistic. Then how shall we categorize it?

The final understanding of the Hindu ethics would depend upon the exact meaning of *self* and *ego*, and the exact meaning of self-interest. We have already noted that the aim of morality here is not to produce more goodness, but to be a better person. So morality here is definitely personalistic, if not egoistic. Perfection of the individual person is considered to be the highest value. Such perfection is achieved through cultivation of moral and religious goodness. "Doing good to others" has been accorded a very high instrumental value, for that is one of the basic ways which leads to moral uplift. Here altruism is an integral part of egoism.

The Hindus have called their values *puruṣārtha*, and *puruṣārtha* literally means the values which the *puruṣa* or the individual desires and which he should desire. These have been described as human value consciously pursued. They have been classified into four groups or *caturvarga*. These are *dharma*, or moral value; *artha*, or wealth; *kāma*, or objects of physical desire; and *mokṣa*, or liberation. This classification is present in the epics and it has been more or less retained through the ages. I find it quite convenient. Of these four, *artha* and *kāma* are obviously ego-centered, especially in their natural form. However, the injunction is that these should be subservient to, and be regulated by, *dharma*. This adds an altruistic dimension at least to *artha*. In one sense even *dharma* and

mokṣa are concerned with the individual or the person. *Dharma* leads to moral betterment of the person. *Mokṣa,* the supreme value, means freedom. It is freedom from sorrow, from endless hankering and desire, from eternal cycle of death and birth. But this is achieved through self-realization. So the emphasis is definitely on the person, the individual agent.

Dharma and *mokṣa* are two spiritual ends and both of them are very much present in Hindu thought. *Dharma* stands for moral rules and virtues, which have been recommended for all and sundry and often have been seen as obligatory. *Mokṣa* is the supra-moral end. It is accepted as the highest value, but it is not obligatory for or meant for everybody. Altruistic trends are present in abundance among the virtues practiced, praised, and eulogized in Hindu thought, but the aim behind them has always been improvement of personality or purification of mind, *ātmaśuddhi* or *cittaśuddhi.* So they are not intrinsically valuable. *Mokṣa* is beyond morality. In *mokṣa* the distinction between *I* and *you* is erased (according to some schools) and correspondingly the egoism/altruism distinction is no longer applicable. Let us look at these two values in more detail.

P. V. Kane opens his *History of Dharmaśāstra* by saying that "Dharma is one of those sanskrit words that defy all attempt at an exact rendering in English or any other tongue."[2] He discusses a number of different alternative meanings of which the one most relevant for our discussion states that *dharma* stands for "some fixed principles or rules of conduct." R. S. Ellwood has the same impression. He says that "Dharma is among the most complex and significant of all concepts in Indian intellectual vocabulary."[3] He starts with the core meaning of *dharma*, which is "to support" or "to bear." In the Ṛgveda *dharma* refers to that which upholds *Ṛta* or the cosmic order. The cosmic order was supposed to be natural as well as moral. In later thought, *dharma* expanded to cover cosmic, social, and moral principles. We are interested in *dharma* in this socio-moral sense. The usually accepted technical definition of *dharma* is that it is the end sanctioned by the injunctions and prohibitions of *śruti.* As a matter of fact, *dharma* as much stands for rituals as for a large body of ethical virtues. We shall peruse briefly some of those virtues.

The epics, the *Upaniṣads*, the philosophical systems, have mentioned a number of moral rules. Some of these are clearly self-regarding in the sense that they aim at improvement of personality and purification of mind. These are truth, cleanliness (*śauca*), celibacy *(brahmacarya)*, austerity (*tapas*), self-control (*damah*), tranquility and calmness (*śamah*), honesty and straightforwardness (*ārjabah*), firmness and patience (*dhṛti*), etc. Again some virtues are distinctly other-regarding, such as charity (*dānah*), compassion (*dayāh*), non-injury *(ahimsā),* protection of one who has taken shelter, etc. The Hindu society has valued these virtues from time immemorial. In all the discussions these virtues have been blended together and, as I suggested before, we shall see that the ultimate motive behind even the other-regarding virtues is self-purification.

Let us turn to the *Upaniṣads* for some concrete examples. In the last poem of *The Waste Land*, What the Thunder said, T. S. Eliot writes:

Ganga was sunken, and the limp leaves
Waited for rain, while the black clouds
Gathered far distant, over Himavant.

Then spoke the thunder Da Datta: What have we given?
and later Da, dayadhvam . . .
and subsequently Da damyata.

He borrowed this from *Bṛhadāraṇyaka*, in which we come across the parable of Prajāpati, who was approached by gods, men, and demons. To all of them, the celestial voice, the thunderbolt, said *da, da, da.*[4] To the gods it meant to be self-controlled (*damyata*), to men, the same sound conveyed to be charitable (*datta*), the demons understood it as saying to be compassionate (*dayadhvam*). So the same precept is understood by different groups differently, depending upon their temperament and moral achievement. To the morally advanced gods, perfection of character, that is, self-control is most important. But for those who are lower in the scale, harmony with others is a necessary virtue to be inculcated. Men should expand themselves through charity. Demons naturally tend to destroy others, so they should practice compassion. Thus the exact implication of the same injunction changes with the moral attainment of the listener. Further, self-improvement is sometimes prescribed through self-control, and at other times through reaching out.

Different *Upaniṣads* have discussed different sets of virtues. *Chāndogya*, for example, gives a list of virtues, such as austerity, charity, straightforwardness, harmlessness, truthfulness, etc.[5] Here we find that the self-regarding and the other-regarding virtues are all blended together.

Taittiriya Upaniṣad has discussed the moral virtues at some length. Some general virtues, which later came to be known as *sāmānya dharma*, such as truth, penance, self-control, hospitality to guests, and offering daily oblations to fire, are enlisted. Later on three sages, severally, emphasize three virtues, namely, truth, penance, and teaching the sacred books. Finally, it discusses charity or *dāna.* Here the emphasis is not on what you give but the mental attitude with which you give. Charity should be practiced with faith and not with un-faith, with magnanimity, with modesty, with awe and sympathy.[6] In the epics the same thought is conveyed through different parables. In the *Bhagavadgītā* Kṛṣṇa speaks of three different types of charity. The best type of charity is one in which something is given because it ought to be given, without expectation of any return. When it is given with expectation of some return it is of comparatively lesser value. The worst one is that in which the giver is full of disdain and a patronizing spirit.[7] This shows that, although men are expected to reach out, to be benevolent, to be good to others, the aim is always to improve oneself by doing this. The quality of the virtue is determined by the mental attitude, which is present with it.

The epics also make this abundantly clear. One may grow hair or shave it; one may wear coarse clothes or skins of animals; one might stay in the forest

and take recourse to different rituals involving hardship and pain to the body; but all these are meaningless if the overall nature is not pure.[8] These point out that morality is not measured by what one does, but rather by the accompanying attitude of the individual.

The philosophical systems have also emphasized the importance of the mental attitude. The *Vaiśeṣika Sūtras* assert that the unrestrained is not elevated even if he observes different external rules of conduct. Vātsyāyana has spoken of virtues of the body, of speech, and of mind. Virtues of the body include charity, protection of the distressed, and service. Virtues of speech include veracity, beneficial speech, and gentle speech. Virtues of mind are comprised of kindness, benevolence, and *śraddhā*.

In Yoga philosophy the basic virtues are classified under *yama* and *niyama*. Praśastapāda comments that *yama* are negative and restrictive, whereas *niyama* are positive and expansive. Virtues can be expressed in a positive form and also in a negative form. When expressed in negative *ahimsā* means cessation from harm or injury to others, when expressed in positive, the corresponding supplement is the definite resolve not to hurt any being. Similarly, *asteya* means not taking other person's things. Here, too, the positive side is the definite resolve to disdain acts of misappropriation. It is to be noted that these virtues in their positive form only emphasize the *resolve* to practice the virtue. These virtues only ensure that *maitri*, or friendship or smoothness in dealings with others, is maintained. *Bhūtahitatva*, or good of all beings, has been mentioned but not focused. This shows that the altruistic virtues are also directed at character building.

The Yogasūtras place *ahimsā* under *yama* with abstention from theft (*asteya*), veracity (*satya*), celibacy (*brahmacarya*), and unworldliness (*aparigraha*).[9] Yoga accords a special position to *ahimsā* saying that, for all moral virtues, this is foundational. It is acknowledged that total and complete *ahimsā* is impossible for we have to harm some living beings in order to maintain our own lives. The Hindus also justify injury to others under special circumstances. The fisherman is justified in killing fish because it is his profession. Or, the warrior is justified in killing the enemy, if it is righteous war. Sometimes they even recommend conditional practice of *ahimsā,* saying that it should be practiced in holy places or on holy days. But the yogi, whose claim is to follow a specifically moral life, must follow *ahimsā* unconditionally, and it is known as *mahāvrata*.

Monier Monier Williams said that *ahimsā* is a "cardinal virtue of most Hindu sects particularly of the Buddhists and Jains."[10] Even if we leave out the latter as non-Hindus, we find that the Hindus have also accepted it as a basic virtue. Even the *Bhagavadgītā*, which is often depicted as a text that aims at justifying war, recognizes the high moral value of *ahimsā* as a virtue. And *ahimsā* is definitely an altruistic virtue.

Another much discussed virtue is *satya*, or veracity. *Satya* has been practiced and eulogized as in *satyameva jayate* or truth is always victorious, or the way of truth is the path of gods. Truth directly means that whatever we see, whatever we hear, we must stick to it in thought, speech, and action. It is also

added that speech should be gentle, and not used to cheat and mislead others. But their treatment of *satya* becomes really interesting, when they add the cautionary clause that, if truth leads to harmful results, then it no longer remains a moral virtue. In the epics many stories have been told to impress upon the hearer this interpretation of truth. If a weak one takes shelter with you, do not tell the strong chaser the whereabouts of the weak. Nārada says that truth is great, but the good of living beings is greater and whatever is good for living beings is truth in my opinion. In Mahābhārata, protection of those who have taken shelter, and pleasing the guest at any cost, were supposed to be great virtues. This shows that altruistic tendencies were greatly valued in Hindu ethics.

We can look at the presence of altruistic tendencies in Hindu thought from another point of view. The religio-metaphysical foundation of Hindu ethics is the belief in a monistic reality that is polytheistic. God is said to be present everywhere. Feeling the presence of God in every human being, Hindus have prayed for the happiness of all. This belief finds expression in their prayers: May everybody be happy. May all be free from ailments. May they see what is auspicious. May no one be subject to misery.[11] But the divine presence is not restricted to human beings only; God is supposed to be immanent in every part of nature. So when they invoke peace they pray not only for all men but also for the good of all the natural world. Thus in one prayer they say: May peace be unto heaven, the sky, the earth, the woods covering different trees, the gods, and everybody, and including even Brahman.[12]

This feeling of oneness with the natural world finds expression in a ritualistic custom, according to which every householder is supposed to perform five great sacrifices every day. Each individual is seen as integrally connected with nature and society and is dependent on them. Nobody has atomic unconnected existence. This dependence of man on nature and society is read as indebtedness and it is obligatory for every householder to pay back. The idea goes back to *Śatapatha Brāhmana*, it has been repeated in *Chāndogya Upaniṣad*, and it has been later codified in the *Dharmaśāstras*. Each individual is indebted to the gods, to his own ancestors for his very existence, to the intellectuals of the past for the vast storehouse of knowledge which he has inherited, and to his fellow men and the animal world for his everyday sustenance. The custom was that the gods should be repaid by offering oblations to fire. The forefathers are repaid by having children, who would carry on the family traditions. The *ṛṣis* are paid back through studying the vedas, men by serving guests, and the animals by giving them food. We need not accept their mode of repayment, but the insight involved is valuable. The very acknowledgment of our inherent dependence on all these factors implies that it is obligatory for us to transcend the limits of the ego-bound life and to work for the good of all. This approach goes against the environmental damages and heartless exploitation of humans or other living beings for one's own self-interests.

Some of the modern thinkers have chosen from these virtues and have practiced them meaningfully and successfully as the supreme value of their life. Mahatma Gandhi, for example, thought of *ahimsā* or nonviolence in this way. In

the Mahābhārata it is said "*ahimsā paramo dharma*" or non-injury is the supreme moral virtue. Gandhiji chose to focus on it, and with his modern approach he has positively worked on it. It became the supreme moral pursuit of his life.

In Swami Vivekananda`s thought these altruistic tendencies receive priority. In this context he says at least three things: First, there are two goals in life; one should try to achieve *mokṣa* for oneself and good of the whole world. Second, he has said, "Doing good to others is one great universal religion." He asked his followers to serve beings with a spirit of worship. In a very famous couplet he has said that to serve the living beings is to serve God. "There are His manifold forms before thee. Rejecting them, where seekest thou for God? Who loves all beings without distinction, He indeed is worshiping best his God." Lastly, he held that one should always remember that by helping others one is helping oneself. It is to be noted that, although he is equating service to living beings with worship of God, he has not totally broken away from the traditional position. For in the end he says that by serving others you improve yourself.

I have very broadly outlined *dharma*, and let us see how it should be characterized in modern terms. Frankena points to two necessary conditions of egoism. First, it is the basic obligation of the agent to promote for himself the greatest possible balance of good over evil. Second, the individual should go by what is his own advantage.[13] Such a theory apparently would be acceptable to many Hindu thinkers, for many of them hold that action, including moral action, issues out of *iṣṭasādhanatājñāna,* or the awareness that the action would lead to my good and there is a balance of good over evil. But Frankena raises a question which is equally relevant here, namely, what does good mean? Some among traditional Hindus held that moral practice might lead to heaven or better life in next birth. Such thoughts are definitely egoistic. But some of them, who practiced the other-regarding virtues, were working for moral uplift, purification of mind, and expansion of the self. An important and influential part of Hindu ethics might be seen as a duty for duty's sake theory as we find in the *Bhagavadgītā.* The *Gītā* decries those who seek rewards for their moral life in heaven. In the *Mahābhārata,* Yudhiṣṭhira states that those who practice morality, seeking rewards in after-life, are traders to morality. Virtues should be practiced for their own sake. Some thinkers hold that our natural propensities are egoistic and *dharma* prescribes altruistic virtues for the maintenance of social stability and harmony. But the Hindus did not look at the altruistic virtues in this way. These are accepted as expression of goodness present in man. So, if because of their preoccupation with the perfection of the individual we like to call Hinduism egoistic, we should add that it is a very refined type of egoism.

Now we come to *mokṣa*, which is self-realization. It is based on the doctrine of two selves, the lower empirical self, or the ego or *aham*, and the higher divine self, or *ātmā*. Broadly speaking *mokṣa* means annihilation of the ego and the realization of the higher self as the essence of being. Philosophers differ among each other as to what exactly is meant by this self-realization. But they all agree that *mokṣa* puts an end to totally ego-bound life. In the *Bhagavadgītā*, there is a

vivid description of a totally ego-centered person. He is arrogant, self-willed, and vain, and he is given to lust and anger. He is the one who says: this, today, has been gained by me, this wealth is mine, and that wealth will also be mine. The enemy has been killed, the others also I will kill. I am powerful and happy and rich, who else is like me? This description is obviously exaggerated. Ordinary men might not be so much engrossed with the *I* and *mine*. Yet, to some, extent they are unduly attached to the ego. Borrowing a term from the *Gītā*, we might say that *Gītā* recommends *anahamvāda*, or no-ego theory. The ideal person is described as *nirmama* and *nirahamkāra*, or as one who is not bound to the *I* and has transcended the limits of the *mine*. This might be called the negative side of *mokṣa*. I would like to draw your attention to this point. We should be aware that many ills of modern life are traceable to this irrational attachment to the ego. The first step towards leading a morally fulfilling life should be transcendence of this attachment.

On the positive side it is a peculiarly self-contradictory situation. *Mokṣa* as a value is qualitatively different from other values. The others are values which are pursued by a natural socially situated individual, but *mokṣa* is transcendence of this naturality. *Mokṣa* is basically freedom from sorrow and the very possibility of sorrow is destroyed here. The root cause of all sorrow is our endless desire and hankering for more goods. Desires are connected with the ego-centered nature of man. According to the traditional thinkers the natural man is not the real self. For some schools, the rectification of this error that the natural man is the self is *mokṣa*. According to others, there is a super personal self, and to realize such a self as true self is *mokṣa*. So in a sense in *mokṣa* there is radical de-individuation and nullification of personality. The individual reaches the highest stage of perfection when he transcends the limits of individuality, when all the properties that constitute his personality are effaced. Here, the difference between the self and others collapse. Following Jacques Vigne we might say that the *I* becomes an impersonal *I*. The question of egoism/altruism no longer arises.

This is theory. In practice we find that the saints who are revered in society as liberated, transcend the limits of the narrow ego. The sense of *I* is retained, but there is no blind attachment to it, it is the center of a reoriented personality. There is transcendence of naturality in the awareness of futility of totally ego-bound life. They attain an expansion of the ego to the extent of destruction of its boundaries and there is boundless love for humanity. I am referring to the Bhakti movement. In the Middle Ages a number of such persons were born in India who propagated the religion of love of humanity and devotion to God. Sri Chaitanya, Meerabai, and Kabir were among those saints.

What can we conclude from this?

Usually egoism and altruism are set as diametrically opposed to each other, and the problem is how to bridge the gulf between the two. As we have already pointed out, some thinkers even feel that egoism is natural and altruism is morally ideal, and the chief problem of life is how to subordinate egoism to altruism. The Hindus have spoken of two different spiritual values: *dharma* and

mokṣa. They belong to two different planes. *Dharma* corresponds to morality. Among the virtues enlisted under *dharma,* we find that altruistic virtues are present in abundance. But they are not valuable in themselves, they are practiced for moral uplift. Here, altruism is a part of egoism.

After attainment of *mokṣa*, the ideal person possesses a transformed personality such that altruism is spontaneous in him. Kṛṣṇa, the superman, says in the *Bhagavadgītā* that I do not have any duty or obligation in the three worlds, yet I work for the good of humanity. Here one does not have to strive to subordinate egoism to altruism. The individual possesses a higher and fuller personality. He does not see any difference between his own self and others and he spontaneously contributes to the happiness of mankind. In fact if we stick to the definition of egoism and altruism strictly, then we have to accept that the concepts are meaningless at this stage.

Postscript

I have not discussed the law of morality, which is supposed to be the foundation of Indian ethics. Here I want to comment on Daya Krishna's view on the law, which I feel is in some way connected with my conclusion. I refer to Daya Krishna's discussion of the nature of morality in Indian thought vis-à-vis the law of *karma.*[15] He says that generally, in the Western tradition the socio-political nature of man is his defining characteristic, whereas in Indian thought the perspective on action is self-centric or *ātman*-centric. The natural world is made intelligible with the help of the notion of causality. But human actions, which are described as good/bad or right/wrong, demand a different type of intelligibility. The law of *karma*, which is an expression of retributive justice, lays down that each individual reap the fruits of his own action. Daya holds that this concept of morality is wedded to a "morally monadic world." I quote from Daya: "if 'moral intellegibility' requires that each human being should reap *only* the fruit of his own actions, then no human being can *really* affect anyone else, however much the appearances may seem to justify the contrary. Nobody can *really* be the cause of my suffering or happiness, nor can I be the cause of suffering or happiness to anybody else."[16] But morality needs some *other*; moral action is not pure willing. This *other* may be a physical situation, a state of being other than myself, my relationship to them, or their relationship to me. He says that, "morality implies an 'other-centric' conscious-ness where one can care for the other because one can affect the well-being of another, however marginal it may be".[17] Real exposedness to, and a genuine concern for, others is the sine-qua-non of moral consciousness. It is difficult to meet the twin demands. On the one hand, each individual is morally monadic, no moral interaction with other individuals is permissible, on the other hand, morality is based on interaction with others. So, Daya's position holds that the law of *karma* implies complete egoism, and altruism is an impossibility. But he says that altruism constitutes the foundation of ethics. Later on he himself solves the problem by differentiating between natural causality and moral causality.

I agree with his analysis in broad outlines but I would differ from him in details. The morally monadic universe demands that each individual suffers the *karmic* consequences of his own action. These consequences are stored up and are supposed to determine the physical and the psychical nature of the agent in his next birth, and some other facts such as birth in a particular family, the pair of parents, natural intelligence, etc., which we have to accept and cannot choose. The law of *karma* involves many clauses, which we can neither verify nor falsify. But be that as it may, morality involved here, would never deny the possibility of interaction with others in the physical plane, or the possibility of doing good to others. One can certainly be the cause of suffering or happiness of others, for these affective states are not *moral* effects. These are natural consequences of an action on which moral property supervenes. Further, morality, as accepted in Indian tradition, does not necessarily require the presence of the *other*. *Dāna* and *tapas* are equally valuable virtues, although *dāna* or charity is not possible without the other, *tapas* or austerity is directed towards self-improvement only. It is held that the moral value of an action is not measured by the natural consequences of the action, not by the amount of good it produces in the world, but by the effect which it has on the character of the agent. Thus if a rich man disdainfully spends a lot of money on improving the condition of the poor, or he does it for fame, his action would be lower in the moral scale when compared to the action of a poor man who gives all that he has with a spirit of service. This emphasis on attitude makes the morality self-centric. This might be described as morally monadic, but this does not bar physical interaction. So, my point is that the law of *karma* focuses on the individual, but it does not rule out the presence of altruistic activities in the moral arena.

Notes

1. R. S. Ellwood, "Hinduism" in *The Dictionary of Bible and Religion*, General Editor, W. H. Gentz (Nashville, Tenn.: Abingdon Press, 1986), 450.

2. P. V. Kane, *History of Dharmaśāstra* (Poona, India: Bhandarkar Research Institute, 1975), 1.

3. Ellwood, *Hinduism*, 450.

4. *Bṛhadāraṇyaka Upaniṣad*, ed. Swami Gambhirananda (Calcutta: Udbodhan Karyalaya, 1944), *Daivi vāganuvadati stanayitnur da da da iti damyata datta dayadhvam iti tadetat trayam siksyet damam dānam dayāmiti* V/2/1-3. Also, R. D. Ranade, *A Constructive Survey of Upanishadic Philosophy* (Bombay: Bharatiya Vidya Bhavan, 1968), 225-226.

5. *Chāndogya Upaniṣad*, ed. Swami Gambhirananda (Calcutta: Udbodhan Karyalaya, 1944), III/17/4. Also Ranade, *Upanishadic Philosophy*, 226.

6. *Taittiriya Upaniṣad* ed. Swami Gambhirananda, (Calcutta: Udbodhan Karyalaya, 1942), *śraddhayā deyam aśraddhayā adeyam, śriyā deyam hriyā deyam, bhiyā deyam, samvidā deyam*, I/11/3. Also Ranade, *Upanishadic Philosophy*, 226-227.

7. *Śrīmadbhagavad Gītā*, XVII/20-23.

8. *Mahābhārata*, III/200/96-97.

9. Patañjali, *Yogasūtra*, ed. Haiharananda Aranya (Calcutta: University of Calcutta, 1949), Sādhanapāda, 30.

10. Monier Williams, *Sanskrit English Dictionary* (Oxford: The Clarendon, 1963), 125.

11. *Sarve bhavantu sukhinah sarve santu nirāmayāah. Sarve bhadrāṇi paśyantu, mā kaścit duhkhabhāg bhavet.*

12. *Dyau śāntiḥ antarikṣam śāntiḥ prthivī śāntiḥ āpaḥ śāntiḥ oṣadhayaḥ śāntiḥ vanaspatayoh śāntiḥ viśve devāḥ śāntiḥ brahmam śāntiḥ sarvam śāntiḥ śāntirevạ śāntiḥ sā mā śāntiredhiḥ.*

13. William K. Frankena, *Ethics* (New Delhi: Prentice-Hall of India Private Limited, 1988), 18.

14. Daya Krishna, "Yajna and the Doctrine of Karma", in *Indian Philosophy, A Counter Perspective* (Delhi: Oxford University Press, 1991), 177-186.

15. Daya, "Yajna," 178.

16. Daya, "Yajna," 179.

Selected Bibliography

Agarwal, M. M. "Arjuna's Moral Predicament," in *Moral Dilemmas in the Mahabharata*. Ed. B. K. Matilal. Shimla, India: Institute of Advanced Study, 1989.

Banerji, N. V. *The Concept of Philosophy*. Calcutta, India: University of Calcutta, 1968.

Basu, Girindra Sekhar. *Bhagavadgītā*. Calcutta, India: privately published by author, 1948.

Bhattacharya, Srimohan, and Dinesh Chandra Bhattacharya Sastri, eds. *Bhāratīya Darśana Koṣa*. Vol. I *(Prācina–Nyāya, Navya Nyāya & Vaiśeṣika Darśana)*. Calcutta, India: Sanskrit College, 1979.

———. *Bhāratīya Darśana Koṣa*. Vol. II *(Sāṃkhya & Pātañjala-Darśana)*. Calcutta, India: Sanskrit College, 1979.

———. *Bhāratīya Darśana Koṣa*. Vol. III *(Vedānta)*. Calcutta, India: Sanskrit College, 1981 & 1984.

Bhattacharyya, Kalidas. *Bharatiya Sanskriti O Anekānta Vedānta*. Burdwan, India: Burdwan University Press, 1982.

———. "Notions of Freedom Compared and Evaluated." In *Communication, Identity and Self-Expression. Essays in Memory of S. N. Ganguly*. Eds. S. P. Banerji and Shefali Maitra. Delhi, India: Oxford University Press, 1984.

Bhattacharyya, K. C. *Studies in Philosophy*. Vol. I. Ed. Gopinath Bhattacharyya. Calcutta, India: Progressive, 1956.

Bhattacharyya, K. C. *Studies in Philosophy*. Vol. II. Ed. Gopinath Bhattacharyya. Calcutta, India: Progressive, 1958.

Bhagavad Gītā. Ed. Nitya Chaitanya Yati. New Delhi, India: D. K. Printworld (P) Limited, 1986.

Bhavanātha Miśra. *Naya Viveka, Tarkapāda*. Ed. S. K. R. Sastri. MUSS 12. Madras, India: Madras University Press, 1937.

Citsukha. *Tattvapradipīkā*. Ed. Swami Yogindrananda. Kasi, India: Udasina Samskrita Vidyalaya, 1956.

Das, Ras Vihary. "Acharya Krishna Chandra's Conception of Philosophy." In *The Journal of Indian Academy of Philosophy*. Vol. II. 1963.

Dasgupta, S. N. *A History of Indian Philosophy*. Vol. I. Cambridge, U.K.: Cambridge University Press, 1922.

Daya Krishna. Ed. *Philosophy of Kalidas Bhattacharyya*. Poona, India: I. P. Q. Publication No. 9, 1985.

———. *Indian Philosophy, A Counter Perspective*. New Delhi, India: Oxford University Press, 1991.

Dharmakīrti. *Nyāyavindu* with *Tīkā* of Dharmottara. Varanasi, India: Chowkhamba Sanskrit Sanstha, 1982.

Dharmakīrti. *Pramāṇavārttika* with *Vṛtti* of Manorathanandin. Varanasi, India: 1968.

Dharmarājādhvarindra. *Vedānta Paribhāṣā*. Ed. Srimohan Bhattacharyya. Calcutta: privately published by author, 1970.

———. *Vedānta Paribhāṣā*. Translated and annotated by Swami Madhavananda. Howrah, India: The Ramakrishna Mission Saradapith, 1942.

Frankena, William K. *Ethics*. New Delhi, India: Prentice-Hall of India Private Limited, 1988.

Gāgābhaṭṭa. *Bhāṭṭacintāmaṇi*. Ed. Suryanarayan Sukla. CSS 25 and 27. Benaras, India: Chowkhamba, 1933.

Gokhale, Pradeep P. "The Logical Structure of Syādvāda." In *the Journal of Indian Council of Philosophical Research*. Vol. VIII, No. 3, 1991.

Gentz, W. H. General Ed. *The Dictionary of Bible and Religion*. Nashville, Tenn.: Abingdon Press, 1986.

Hiriyanna, M. *Outlines of Indian Philosophy*. London, U.K.: George Allen & Unwin, 1932.

Haribhadra Suri. *Anekāntajayapatākā*. Ed. H. R. Kapadia. Baroda, India: Oriental Institute, 1947.

Kane, P. V. *History of Dharmaśāstra*. Poona, India: Bhandarkar Research Institute, 1975.

Kumārila Bhaṭṭa. *Slokavārtika*. Ed. S. K. R. Sastri. Madras, India: Madras University Press, 1940.

Madhusūdana Sarasvati. *Advaitaratnaṛakṣqṇam*. Bombay, India: Nirnaya Sagar Press, 1917.

———. *Advaitasiddhi*. Vols. I and II. Mysore, India: 1937.

———. Commentary on the *Śrimadbhagavadgītā*. Ed. Nalinikanta Brahma. Calcutta, India: Navabharat Publishers, 1986.

Mahābhārata: *Sabhāparva, Banaparva*.

Maitra, S. K. *The Ethics of the Hindus*. Calcutta, India: University of Calcutta, 1956.

Matilal, B. K. *Perception: An Essay on Classical Indian Theories of Knowledge*. Oxford, U.K.: Clarendon Press, 1986.

———. *Logic, Language and Reality*. Delhi, India: Motilal Banarasidass, 1985.

Mohanty, J. N. *Gangeśa's Theory of Truth*. Santiniketan, India: Visva Bharati, Centre of Advanced Study, 1966.

———. *Reason and Tradition in Indian Thought*. Oxford, U.K.: Clarendon Press, 1992.

———. *Essays on Indian Philosophy*. Ed. Purusottama Bilimoria. Oxford, U.K.: Oxford University Press, 1993.

Miśra, Pārthasārathi. *Nyāyaratnākara* Commentary on *Mīmāmsā Slokavārttika*. Ed. M. R. Sastri. Kasi, India: 1896.

———. *Nyāyaratnamālā*. with *Nāyakaratna* by Rāmānujāchāryya. Ed. B. Bhattacharya. GOS LXXV. Baroda, India: 1937.

———. *Śastradīpikā*. Ed. Lakṣmaṇ Sastri Dravida. Benaras, India: Chowkhamba, 1913.

Miśra, Prabhākara. *Bṛhatī Tīkā* on *Śabara Bhāṣya* with *Ṛjuvimalā Pañcikā* by Śālikanātha Miśra. Ed. S. K. R. Śastri. MUSS 3. Madras, India: University of Madras, 1934.

Miśra, Śāliknātha. *Prakaraṇapañcikā*. Ed. M. Sastri. Kasi, India: Chowkhamba, 1904.

Miśra, Sucarita. *Kaśika* on *Mīmāmsā Slokavārttika*. Ed. K. S. Sastri. TSS XC. Trivandrum, India: 1926.

Miśra, Vācaspati. *Nyāyavārttika Tātparyaīkā* in *Nyāyadarśanam*. Ed. Taranath Nyāya Tarkatīrtha. Calcutta, India: Metropolitan Printing and Publishing, 1936.

Nandīśwara. *Prabhākara Vijaya*. Ed. A. K. Sastri & R. N. Sastri. Calcutta, India: Sanskrit Sahitya Parisad, 1926.

Patanjali. *Yogasūtra*. Ed. Hariharānanda Aranya. Calcutta, India: University of Calcutta, 1949.

Prasad, Rajendra. "Theory of Puruṣārtha." In *Karma, Causation and Retributive Morality*. New Delhi, India: Indian Council of Philosophical Research, 1989.

Radhakrishnan, S. *Bhagavadgītā*. 2nd Edition, 5th Impression. London, U.K.: George Allen & Unwin, 1958.

Radhakrishnan, S. *Indian Philosophy*. Vol. II. London, U.K.: George Allen & Unwin, 1940.

Ranade, R. D. *A Constructive Survey of Upanishadic Philosophy*. Bombay, India: Bharatiya Vidya Bhavan, 1968.

Śamkara. *Commentary* on *Śrimadbhagavadgītā* with *Sub-commentary* by Ānandagiri. Ed. MM Pramathanath Tarkabhusana. Calcutta, India: Dev Sahitya Kutir, 1986.

———. *Śārīraka Bhāṣya* on *Brahma-Sūtra* with *Bhāmatī* by Vācaspati Miśra. Ed. Srimohan Bhattacharya. Calcutta, India: Sanskrit Pustak Bhandar, 1973.

Śāntarakṣita. *Tattvasamgraha* with *Pañjikā* by Kamalaśīla. Ed. Swami Dwarikadas Sastri. Varanasi, India: Bauddha Bharati, 1968.

Sri Aurobindo. *Essays on Gītā*. Pondicherry, India: Sri Aurobindo Aśrama, 1959.

Śrīharṣa. *Khandanakhandakhādya*. Ed. Krishnapant Sastri & Govinda Narahari. Vaijapurkar. Varanasi, India: Achyut Granthamala Karyalaya, Samvat 2018.

Stcherbatsky, T. *Buddhist Logic*. New York, U.S.A.: Dover, 1962.

Tilak, Balgangadhar. *Gītārahasya*. Translated by Jyotirindranath Tagore. New edition. Ed. Dhyanesh Narayan Chakrabarti. Calcutta, India: Progressive Book Forum, 1983.

———. *Srimad Bhagavad Gītā Rahasya* or *Karma Yoga Sastra*. Translated by Bhalchandra Sitaram Sukthankar. Poona, India: 1935.

Udayana. *Nyāyavārttika Tātparya Pariśuddhi*. Ed. V. P. Dvivedi. Calcutta, India: 1911.

Upanisad: Bṛhadāraṇyaka, Chāndogya, Taittiriya. Ed. Swami Gambhirananda. Calcutta, India: Udbodhan Karyalaya, 1944.

Vasubandhu. *Vijñaptimātratāsiddhi*. Ed. Sukomol Chaudhuri. Calcutta, India: Sanskrit College, 1975.

Vātsyāyana. *Nyāya Sūtras*. With *Bhāṣya* by Gotama, *Vārttika* by Uddyotkara and *Tātparya Tikā* by Vācaspati Miśra. Ed. Taranath Nyāya Tarkatīrtha and Amarendra Mohan Tarkatīrtha. Calcutta, India: Metropolitan, 1936.

Vidyāraṇya. *Vivaraṇa-Prameya-Saṃgraha*. Part II. Ed. MM Pramathanath Tarkabhusan. Calcutta, India: Basumati Sahitya Mandir, 1927.

Williams, Monier. *Sanskrit English Dictionary*. Oxford, U.K.: Clarendon Press, 1963.

About the Author

Tara Chatterjea stood first in the University of Calcutta's B.A. (Philosophy Honours) Examination, obtained an M.A. in Mental and Moral Philosophy, and did her D.Phil at the same university under the guidance of one of India's finest contemporary philosophers, Dr. J. N. Mohanty. She was a research scholar at Sanskrit College, Calcutta, and taught philosophy at Jadavpur University and Lady Brabourne College. She has long been active at the Friday Seminar Group, a close-knit circle of philosophers interested in different branches of modern and ancient philosophy.

She has presented her work in seminars in India and also in the India Studies Forum at Indiana University, Bloomington.

Knowledge and Freedom in Indian Philosophy